Be My Disciples

Peter M. Esposito
President

Jo Rotunno, MA
Publisher

Anne P. Battes, M.Ed.
Associate Publisher

Program Advisors
Michael P. Horan, PhD
Elizabeth Nagel, SSD

GRADE SIX
SCHOOL EDITION

NIHIL OBSTAT
Rev. Msgr. Robert Coerver
Censor Librorum

IMPRIMATUR
† Most Reverend Kevin J. Farrell, DD
Bishop of Dallas
March 5, 2013

The *Nihil Obstat and Imprimatur* are official declarations that the material reviewed is free of doctrinal or moral error. No implication is contained therein that those granting the *Nihil Obstat* and *Imprimatur* agree with the contents, opinions, or statements expressed.

Acknowledgments

Excerpts are taken and adapted from the *New American Bible with Revised New Testament* and *Revised Psalms*, © 1991, 1986, 1970, Confraternity of Christian Doctrine, Washington, D.C., and are used by permission of the copyright owner. All rights reserved. No part of the *New American Bible* may be reproduced in any form without permission in writing from the copyright owner.

Excerpts are taken and adapted from the English translation of the *Roman Missal*, © 2010, International Commission on English in the Liturgy, Inc. (ICEL); *Rite of Marriage*, © 1969, (ICEL); *Rite of Baptism*, © 1969, (ICEL) All rights reserved. No part of these works may be reproduced in any form without permission in writing from the copyright owner.

Excerpts are taken and adapted from the English translation of the *Catechism of the Catholic Church* for use in the United States of America, second edition, © 1997, United States Catholic Conference, Inc.- Liberia Editrice Vaticana. All rights reserved. No part of the *Catechism of the Catholic Church* may be reproduced in any form without permission in writing from the copyright owner.

Excerpts and adaptations of prayers were taken from the book of *Catholic Household Blessings & Prayers*, © 2007, United States Conference of Catholic Bishops, Washington, D.C. All rights reserved. No part of the book of *Catholic Household Blessings & Prayers* may be reproduced or transmitted in any form or by any means, electronic or mechanical, including photocopying, recording, or by any information storage and retrieval system, without permission in writing from the copyright holder.

Excerpt from Thomas Merton, *Thoughts in Solitude*, © 1986, 1958, Trustees of the Thomas Merton Legacy Trust, Louisville, KY. All rights reserved. No part of *Thoughts in Solitude* may be reproduced in any form without permission in writing from the copyright owner.

Toll Free   877-275-4725
Fax   800-688-8356

Visit us at www.RCLBenziger.com
and BeMyDisciples.com

20766 ISBN 978-0-7829-1639-3 (Student Edition)
20776 ISBN 978-0-7829-1645-4 (Teacher Edition)

2nd Printing.
May 2014.

Contents

Welcome to

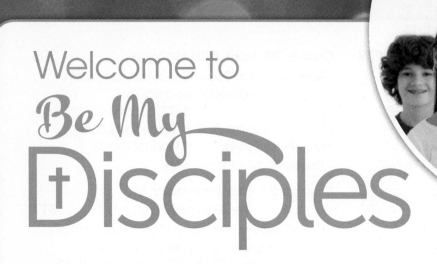

Be My
✝Disciples

God's Plan of Salvation

Just as the story of your life happens over time, so has the story of God's love for his people unfolded in history. This year you will learn many new teachings about God and the story of his people. Complete the activities below and on the next page to see what you already know and to find out what you will learn this year.

1. We Believe, Part One

God revealed himself as a Triune God. Who are the

Three Persons of the Trinity? God the _____,

God the _____, and God the _____

Look on page 40 to check your answer.

2. We Believe, Part Two

This year in Unit 2, you will learn about Jesus' Passion, Death, and Resurrection. What is another name for Jesus'

Passion, Death, and Resurrection? _____

Look on page 80 to check your answer.

3. We Worship, Part One

In this unit, you will learn about the Sacraments of Christian Initiation. What are they?

_____, _____, _____

Look on page 134 to check your answer.

4. We Worship, Part Two

In this unit, you will learn that sin separates us from the love of God.
But God gives us a chance to return to him.
How do we return to God?

_____

Look on page 176 to check your answer.

5. We Live, Part One

Jesus told us to love God and to love our neighbor as ourselves.
What is this Commandment called?

_____

Look on page 256 to check your answer.

6. We Live, Part Two

In this last unit, you will learn that Jesus teaches us that we can call God Father, just as he did. What is the name of the prayer that Jesus taught us to pray?

_____

Look on page 322 to check your answer.

To Bring Glad Tidings

The leader walks at the head of a procession to the prayer space, holding the Bible high for all to see.

All make the Sign of the Cross together.

Leader: Lord, we gather today to honor the gift of your Word. We remember your love for us and that you are always with us.

All: **We praise you, O Lord.**

Leader: The Lord be with you.

All: **And with your spirit.**

Leader: A reading from the holy Gospel according to Luke.

All: **Glory to you, O Lord.**

Leader: (Jesus) unrolled the scroll (of the prophet Isaiah) and found the passage where it was written:

"The spirit of the Lord is upon me, because he has annointed me. to bring glad tidings to the poor.
He has sent me to proclaim liberty to captives and recovery of sight to the blind, to let the oppressed go free, and to proclaim a year acceptable to the Lord."

The Gospel of the Lord.

All: **Praise to you, Lord Jesus Christ**

LUKE 4:17–19

All come forward and reverence the Bible.

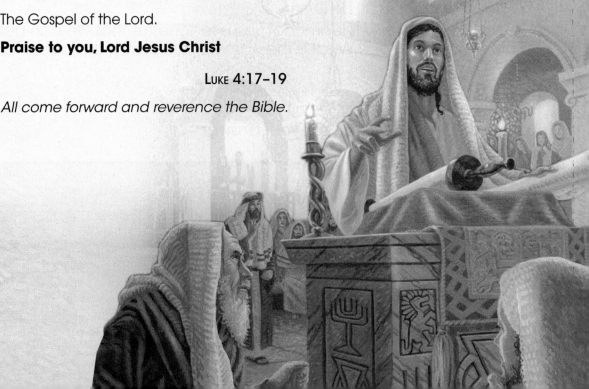

8

We Believe

Part One

God Calls Abraham

The LORD said to [Abraham]: "Go forth from the land of your kinsfolk and from your father's house to a land that I will show you.

"I will make of you a great nation,
   and I will bless you;
I will make your name great,
   so that you will be a blessing. . . .
All the communities of the earth
   shall find blessing in you."

Abraham did as the LORD said. . . . [Abraham] took his wife [Sarah], his brother's son Lot, [and] all the possessions they had accumulated. . . and they set out for the land of Canaan. When they came to the land of Canaan, . . . [t]he LORD appeared to Abram and said, "To your descendants I will give this land."

GENESIS 12:1–3a, 4–5, 7a

What I Know

What is something you already know about these faith concepts?

Divine Revelation

_____

_____

_____

The Covenant

_____

_____

_____

God the Father

_____

_____

_____

Faith Terms

Put an X next to the faith terms you know. Put a ? next to faith terms you need to learn more about.

_____ faith

_____ creed

_____ canon

_____ inspiration

_____ original holiness

_____ Redemption

_____ Original Sin

_____ temptation

Questions I Have

The Bible

What do you know about the two accounts of creation in Genesis?

_____

_____

_____

The Church

What would you like to know about the Creed we say at Mass?

_____

_____

_____

What questions would you like to ask about the mystery of God?

_____

_____

_____

Looking Ahead

In this chapter, the Holy Spirit invites you to ▶

 **EXPLORE** how Catholic youth around the world respond to the gift of faith.

 **DISCOVER** that the gift of faith involves trusting in God's love.

 **DECIDE** how you will profess your faith in word and in action.

CHAPTER **1**

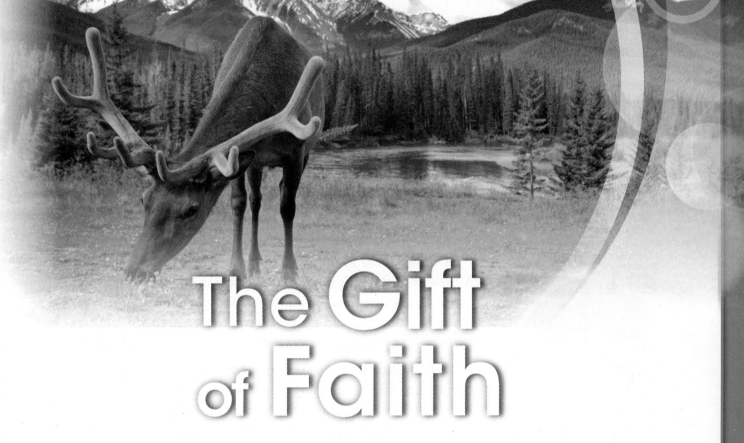

The Gift of Faith

❓ Who is someone you know well? How did you get to know this person?

God has made himself known to us in many ways. Read and think about these words:

"Praise the LORD from the earth,
    you sea monsters and all deep waters . . .
You mountains and all hills,
    fruit trees and all cedars;
You animals wild and tame,
    you creatures that crawl and fly . . .
Young men and women too,
    old and young alike.
Let them all praise the LORD's name,
    for his name alone is exalted,
        majestic above earth and heaven." PSALM 148:7, 9–10, 12–13

❓ How can viewing a scenic landscape help you to know more about God?

Disciple Power

Perseverance in Faith

This gift is the ability to remain steadfast in one's beliefs because of the strength and Gifts of the Holy Spirit working within us. This gift is also helpful when someone is struggling with difficulties and doubts.

World Youth Day

Every two to three years, Catholic youth from all over the world gather in different places for World Youth Day (WYD). They gather at the invitation of the Pope to grow in their faith and friendship with Jesus and to celebrate the faith of the Catholic Church.

In 2013, Catholic youth from around the world gathered with Pope Francis in Rio de Janeiro, Brazil, to celebrate that they are disciples of Jesus. The focus was "Go and Make Disciples of All Nations" (see Matthew 28:19). Some previous World Youth Days were celebrated by over 1,000,000 people in Madrid, Spain (2011) and by 400,000 people in Sydney, Australia (2008).

Celebrating Faith

During World Youth Day, Catholic youth celebrate their faith. Moved by the Holy Spirit, they experience an encounter with Christ. Major events take place, such as the public appearance of the Pope in the "popemobile" and a papal Mass. Teens attending WYD may participate in pilgrimage walks from one church or shrine to another.

Participants in the events display their national flags and chant or sing their favorite national songs. Teens trade shirts, crosses, and icons with one another and carry these on the pilgrimage walks and at festivities. Activities include the re-enactment of Christ's Passion, classes, concerts, a vocations exhibit, the Stations of the Cross, and the opportunity to celebrate the Sacrament of Penance and Reconciliation.

? Why do you think you might enjoy participating in World Youth Day?

Faith Sharing

An important part of World Youth Day is having teens come together to deepen their understanding of the Catholic Church and to discuss ways to live their faith. Bishops and other Church leaders speak to them about the faith. They return to their countries and parishes filled with the commitment to live the Gospel with inspired enthusiasm.

As a result of World Youth Day, many youth return home to perservere, or remain strong, in faith. They are inspired to share the truth about Jesus through acts of faith, hope, and charity with the support of the Church.

? What do you think is inspiring about World Youth Day?

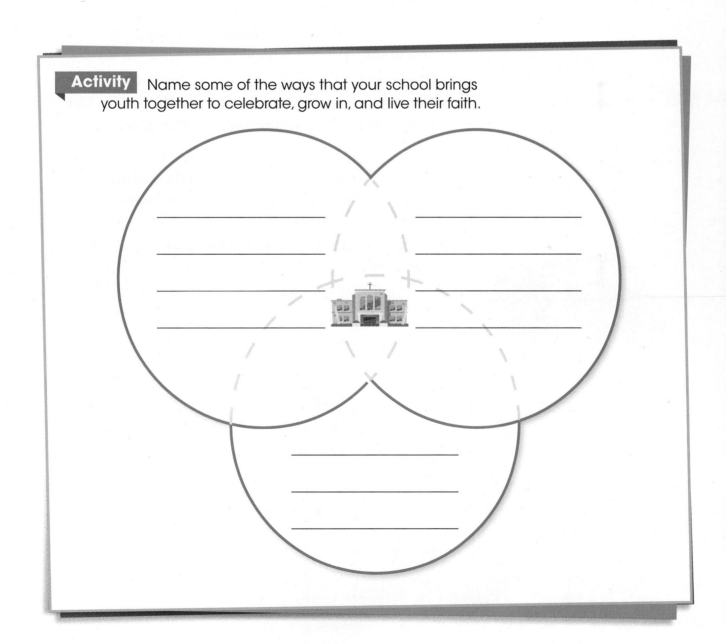

Activity Name some of the ways that your school brings youth together to celebrate, grow in, and live their faith.

Growing in Faith

God placed his Word in our hearts. He planted his love deep in our souls. Jeremiah the Prophet shared this truth about God and us when he wrote:

[God said:] "I will give them a heart with which to understand that I am the LORD."

JEREMIAH 24:7

Whether we are happy or sad, successful or in trouble, God is always with us and speaking to us. His Word within us acts like the sun to light up our days and like the moon to help us see at night. God's Word within us is his grace. The grace of God helps us to recognize and to accept his love. Our challenge is to respond and grow in faith.

Jeremiah also said that God will guide us by helping us to live his covenant of love.

[God said:] "They shall be my people, and I will be their God. One heart and one way I will give them . . . to their own good and that of their children after them."

JEREMIAH 32:38–39

Jeremiah brought them God's message that the Lord wanted more than actions. God wants peoples' hearts to be turned to him. He wants us to truly feel and believe in him. In turn, God will be with us always.

? What do you think it means that God placed his Word in our hearts?

Understanding God's Word

Here are some ways to help us respond and grow in faith:

1. **Pray to the Holy Spirit.** The Holy Spirit is our helper and teacher. He is the One who helps us truly understand all that God makes known to us and has revealed to us in Jesus Christ. The Holy Spirit lives in our hearts and gives us the power to call God "Abba, Father."

2. **Personally know Jesus Christ, the Incarnate Word of God.** Faith in Jesus Christ, the only Son of God and our Lord, is necessary for Salvation. Everything God wants to say to us is revealed through Jesus Christ.

3. **Study the Bible, the inspired Word of God.** We can better understand who God is by reading his Divine Revelation in Sacred Scripture.

4. **Learn the teachings of the Church.** Sacred Tradition and Sacred Scripture are sources of Church teaching. Together they are like a mirror in which the Church looks at and contemplates God.

5. **Listen to the Pope, the bishop in your diocese, and the priests in your parish.** Through their writings, speeches, and homilies, they teach us in the name of Christ how to live our faith. They help us understand God's Revelation more clearly and live it in practical ways.

? In what ways have you responded to God's invitation to grow in faith?

Catholics Believe

Nicene Creed

The Nicene Creed is the creed we usually profess at Mass on Sundays. This creed was written by the Church at the Council of Nicaea in A.D. 325 and the Council of Constantinople in A.D. 381. The Nicene Creed clearly states that the Father, Son, and Holy Spirit are One God in Three Divine Persons. Jesus Christ is true God and true man and is equally God as the Father is God.

Activity Check some of the ways you try to come to know God. Then discuss with a partner what else you can do to know God better.

_____ Pray to the Holy Spirit.

_____ Try to know Jesus better.

_____ Prayerfully read and study Sacred Scripture.

_____ Study the teachings of the Church.

_____ Listen to the preaching and teachings of the Pope and the bishops.

_____ Pray every day.

_____ Be attentive at Mass on Sundays.

The Gift of Faith

Faith is a supernatural gift, meaning a gift from God. It is one of the three Theological Virtues, which are faith, hope, and charity. Faith is not something that we can earn or deserve. We cannot achieve a deep faith through only our own efforts. We need the grace, or help, of the Holy Spirit. We must pray for his grace to truly know God and respond to his love. This kind of faith is not easy or automatic.

God created us with a desire for him in our hearts. God also gave us the freedom to choose or reject him and his love. Accepting the gift of faith often seems difficult; however, God gives us his grace to encourage and strengthen us. God's grace helps us to persevere in our faith. We can grow in faith by learning more about God. We can also choose to accept his love by living a Christian life. Ultimately, God calls us to accept the gift of faith by opening our hearts and minds to live according to his will.

Remaining strong in our faith is not easy to do. There may be times we turn away from God. There may also be times when we face difficulties and we may think that God is no longer with us. But it is important to persevere. We rely on God's grace to live according to his will.

? What are some ways that help you to perservere in your faith?

Praying together at World Youth Day.

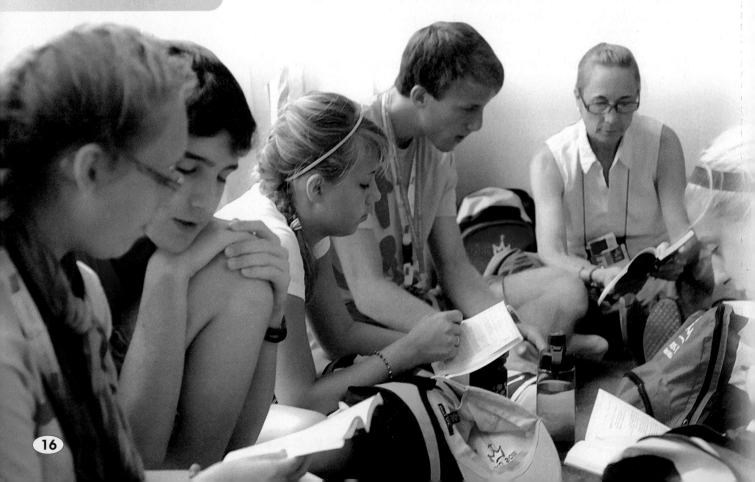

Trust in God

Believing in God relates to trusting God. Jesus revealed that God is our Father who created us out of love, for love, and to be loved. In his love, God reveals himself to us as Father, Son, and Holy Spirit. God knows everything about us and knows our needs before we do. He wants only what is best for us. He shares his life and love for our sanctification.

The Gospel tells us that Jesus' whole life on Earth showed us that God wants our happiness. Our happiness is ultimately found in God. He created us to live in communion with him now on Earth and forever in Heaven. God gave us the Church to help and support us in our journey of faith.

❓ How do you find help and support on your journey of faith?

Faith-Filled People

Miriam

Miriam the Prophet was the sister of Moses and Aaron. After the Israelites crossed the Red Sea during the Exodus, Miriam gathered the women of Israel. With tambourine in hand, she led the women in song and dance as she sang, "Sing to the Lord, for he is gloriously triumphant" (Exodus 15:21).

Activity Describe someone whom you trust who has helped you grow in faith. What did this person do to help you? How did you respond? Design a Web page that honors this person and will help others to grow in faith.

Professing Our Faith

From the beginning, the Church has proudly proclaimed her faith in God in the form of a **creed**. A creed includes the language of the faith as a heartfelt expression of the Church's faith. As members of the Church, we profess our faith together through statements of faith. In a creed, both the individual believer and the entire Church community express the faith. We celebrate and pass on the Word of God alive in our hearts and minds. The Apostles' Creed and the Nicene Creed are the two main creeds of the Church.

The Apostles' Creed

This is one of the earliest creeds of the Church. It is divided into three parts:

- The first part professes our faith in God the Father, who created all that exists, Heaven and Earth.

- The second part professes our faith in God the Son, Jesus Christ, who redeemed humanity from the eternal death of sin.

- The third part professes our faith in God the Holy Spirit and speaks of our sanctification. Our sanctification is the gift of sharing in God's life and love.

The Nicene Creed

This creed is more detailed than the Apostles' Creed, yet both creeds equally express the faith of the Church. When we proclaim the Nicene Creed during Sunday Mass, the grace of the Holy Spirit helps us offer our hearts in faith to God, the Holy Trinity. Because we profess the Nicene Creed together as the Body of Christ, we unite ourselves with believing Christians throughout the world. Each time that we profess our faith, God seals in our hearts the gift of faith.

Activity In the circles, draw a symbol for each part of the Apostles' Creed. Tell a partner how the symbol relates to that part of the creed.

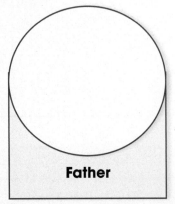

Father

Son

Holy Spirit

I FOLLOW JESUS

Jesus promised the disciples that he and the Father would send the Holy Spirit to be our teacher and helper. You received the gift of the Holy Spirit at Baptism. The Holy Spirit continuously invites you to grow in your faith and friendship with God. The Holy Spirit helps you to persevere and to live the gift of faith with all of your heart, mind, and spirit.

I BELIEVE IN GOD

Read the full text of the Apostles' Creed on page 368. Then write a short reflection about your faith in God the Father, God the Son, and God the Holy Spirit. Describe how your faith helps you make decisions each day.

I Believe in God

1. _____

_____

_____

2. _____

_____

_____

3. _____

_____

_____

MY FAITH CHOICE

I profess my faith in God the Holy Trinity each day both by my words and by my actions. This week, I will profess my faith in God through words and actions. I will

_____

_____.

 Pray, "O Holy Spirit, grant us the grace to persevere in faith. Amen."

1. God placed in our hearts a desire to know, love, and serve him.

2. Jesus' whole life on Earth invited us to have faith in God. Faith is the gift from God to believe in him and the grace to respond freely to that gift.

3. The creeds of the Church are both a profession and a summary of the Church's faith in God.

Chapter Review

Recall

Match each term in Column A with its definition in Column B.

Column A

_____ **1.** faith

_____ **2.** Holy Trinity

_____ **3.** Nicene Creed

_____ **4.** Redemption

_____ **5.** sanctification

Column B

A. our acceptance of God and our willingness to receive his Revelation

B. the gift of sharing in God's life and love

C. the saving activity of God through Christ, delivering humanity from the eternal death of sin

D. a summary of the principal beliefs of the Church that we profess at Mass

E. the mystery of One God in Three Divine Persons

Reflect

What are some ways that you can grow in faith?

_____

_____

_____

_____

_____

_____

_____

_____

Share With a partner describe the three main parts of the Apostles' Creed. Discuss how each Person of the Holy Trinity helps you to live your faith.

We Believe in God

At Baptism, we first profess our faith in God with the Church. Pray this profession of faith, which is taken from the Rite of Baptism.

Leader: Let us profess our faith. Do you reject sin so as to live in the freedom of God's children?

All: I do.

Leader: Do you reject the glamor of evil, and refuse to be mastered by sin?

All: I do.

Leader: Do you reject Satan, father of sin and prince of darkness?

All: I do.

Leader: Do you believe in God the Father almighty, creator of heaven and earth?

All: I do.

Leader: Do you believe in Jesus Christ, his only Son, our Lord, who was born of the Virgin Mary, who was crucified, died, and was buried, rose from the dead, and is now seated at the right hand of the Father?

All: I do.

Leader: Do you believe in the Holy Spirit, the holy catholic Church, the communion of saints, the forgiveness of sins, the resurrection of the body, and the life everlasting?

All: I do.

Leader: This is our faith. This is the faith of the Church. We are proud to profess it, in Christ Jesus our Lord.

All: Amen.

FROM THE "PROFESSION OF FAITH," RITE OF BAPTISM

With My Family

This Week . . .

In Chapter 1, "The Gift of Faith," your child learned:

▶ God invites us to know him and believe in him. God invites us to make him the center of our lives and to discover the experience and meaning of true happiness.

▶ The whole life of Jesus Christ on Earth most clearly and fully reveals that divine invitation. God created us to know, love, and serve him and to be happy with him now on Earth and forever in Heaven.

▶ The Apostles' Creed and the Nicene Creed are the two principal creeds of the Church.

▶ The virtue of perseverance strengthens us to remain strong and steadfast in our faith.

For more about related teachings of the Church, see the *Catechism of the Catholic Church*, 26–49, 142–197, and the *United States Catholic Catechism for Adults*, pages 2–9, 36–47.

■ Sharing God's Word

Read together Jeremiah 24:7. Emphasize that God created us, his Word is alive in our hearts, and his love is deep in our souls.

■ We Live as Disciples

The Christian home and family is a school of discipleship. Choose one of the following activities to do as a family, or design a similar activity of your own:

▶ Make a puzzle to help your child learn the Apostles' Creed by heart. Write the words of the creed on a piece of paper. Then cut the paper into pieces, and together assemble the puzzle pieces.

▶ Share ideas of ways that your family shows that God is at the center of the life of your family. Discuss how family members are signs to others that they are disciples of Christ.

▶ Visit *BeMyDisciples*.com. Look up the profiles of several martyrs of the Church. Discuss how they persevered in their faith, even to freely suffering death for their faith.

■ Our Spiritual Journey

In this chapter, your child prayed a profession of faith based on the "Profession of Faith" in the Rite of Baptism. Read and pray together this prayer on page 21.

For more ideas on ways your family can live as disciples of Jesus, visit **BeMyDisciples.com**

Looking Ahead

In this chapter, the Holy Spirit invites you to ▶

EXPLORE how Baruch called the Israelites to know God's plan.

DISCOVER that God reveals himself and his plan in Scripture.

DECIDE how you can respond to God's Word proclaimed at Mass.

CHAPTER

2

The Word of God

? With the Internet, seeking and finding information today is literally at our fingertips. To what extent do you trust the information available to you?

You can trust God's Word in the Bible. Take a few moments to carefully read these words from the Bible. Listen to what the writer of this psalm is saying about the Word of God:

> "Your word is a lamp for my feet,
>   a light for my path.
> I make a solemn vow
>   to keep your just edicts. . . .
> Your decrees are my heritage forever;
>   they are the joy of my heart. . . .
> Sustain me by your promise that I may live;
>   do not disappoint me in my hope."
>
> PSALM 119:105–106, 111, 116

? How does this passage from Sacred Scripture help you to grow in faith?

Disciple Power

Knowledge

Part of the gift of faith is the desire to know God better. By accepting God's gift of faith, the Holy Spirit perfects our faith with gifts, such as wisdom, knowledge, and understanding. In other words, part of our response in faith is to know God more fully. The light of reason aids us in our journey to love, serve, and know God.

The Prophet Baruch

There was a time when God's people seemed to have very little hope. They were confused about life, and they had difficulty in understanding God's Word. It was a time of great infidelity by the Israelites to the Covenant.

Baruch was a clerk in the king's court and knew how the king and his advisors struggled to save the kingdom because they were under attack from the Babylonian Empire, which was located in modern-day Iraq. Baruch was also the close friend of Jeremiah the Prophet. He acted as Jeremiah's scribe, writing down his prophecies.

Eventually, the Babylonians conquered Israel and took its leaders and many of the people back to the capital city of Babylon. This was a time known as the Exile. During the Exile, the Israelites were forced to live in the country of their conquerors, the Assyrians and the Babylonians. During this time of suffering, God sent Baruch the Prophet and other prophets to speak to his people in Babylonia.

God called Baruch to be his prophet and Baruch wrote down God's message to his people. Baruch called the people to follow God. But the people did not heed the Lord's message.

? What would you advise Baruch to do?

Understanding Suffering

Baruch's message is found in the Book of Baruch. This six-chapter book contains different kinds of writing. This passage is part of a poem:

> "Hear, O Israel, the commandments of life:
> listen, and know prudence! . . .
> You have forsaken the fountain of wisdom!
> Had you walked in the way of God,
> you would have dwelt in enduring peace. . . .
> All who cling to [wisdom] will live,
> but those will die who forsake her.
> Turn, O Jacob, and receive her:
> walk by her light toward splendor."
>
> BARUCH 3:9, 12–13; 4:1–2

In this poem, Baruch tried to help God's People understand both how their suffering had happened and how they could find true happiness in God. So even in difficult times, you can find comfort in knowing that if you cling to God's way, peace will endure. This means that the grace of faith can open your eyes to God's plan of saving love. The gift of knowledge will help you to recognize how what happens in your life can help you understand God's plan of saving love.

? How do you think that God's way might help you through difficult times?

Activity When you pray to God, what image comes to your mind? Draw or write it here.

FAITH FOCUS
In what ways did God reveal himself and his love for all people through the Bible?

FAITH VOCABULARY
Covenant
This is the solemn commitment of fidelity that God and the People of God made with one another, which was renewed in Christ, the new and everlasting Covenant.

Divine Revelation

Through Sacred Scripture, God reveals himself and his plan of Salvation. By the gift of faith, we seek to understand better his Revelation. As we grow in our understanding, we also grow in faith.

In the Book of Exodus, the second book in the Bible and one of the books in the Pentatuech, God reveals his name to Moses and reestablishes the **Covenant**. The Covenant or solemn commitment of fidelity is between God and his Chosen People, the Israelites.

One day while he was tending sheep, Moses saw a bush that was in flames yet was not consumed by the fire. Curious, Moses walked toward this strange sight. As he approached, he heard a voice coming from the bush, saying,

"Moses! Moses! . . . I am . . . the God of Abraham, the God of Isaac, the God of Jacob. . . . Come, now! I will send you to Pharaoh to lead my people, the Israelites, out of Egypt."

EXODUS 3:4, 6, 10

You can just imagine how confused Moses must have been! So he asked,

"[W]hen I go to the Israelites and say to them, 'The God of your fathers has sent me to you,' if they ask me, 'What is his name?' what am I to tell them?" God replied, "I am who am. . . . [T]ell the Israelites: I AM sent me to you."

EXODUS 3:13–14

Look up and read Deuteronomy 6:4-9. What is God asking of you?

The Name of God

Through this Old Testament story, God shares his name with Moses, with the Israelites, and with all people. He says, "I am who am." In Hebrew, that name is YHWH. By naming himself YHWH, God is letting us know that he alone is the Creator and source of all that exists. In revealing his name to Moses, God also established a personal relationship with the Israelites through Moses. Therefore, God reveals to all people that he is always with us. Wherever we are, God is.

God revealing his name to Moses helps us to realize and believe some truths about God with all of our hearts and minds.

- God is a mystery whom the human mind will never fully grasp on its own.

- God says, "I will be with you" and is always faithful to his People.

- God enters history in a loving way and is close to his People.

- God is ready to stand by his People in times of trouble.

? What do you think God revealed about himself through his name?

Activity Using each letter in God's name, write four words that tell something about him.

Y _____

H _____

W _____

H _____

The Inspired Word of God

The Bible, or Sacred Scripture, is the inspired Word of God. This means that God inspired or guided human authors so that they wrote what he intended to reveal. We call this **biblical inspiration**. The various human writers of Sacred Scripture wrote only the truths about God and his plan of love for us that God revealed for our Salvation.

The Bible contains seventy-three books in its **canon**, or official list. These books, or writings, make up the Old Testament and the New Testament.

OLD TESTAMENT The forty-six books of the Old Testament are often grouped this way:

The Pentateuch (Torah): The first five books of the Bible are called the *Pentateuch*, a term that means "five containers." These books, which are also called the written Torah, tell of God revealing himself and establishing the Covenant with the Chosen People, the Hebrews or Israelites.

The Historical Books: The sixteen historical books tell of how God's people sometimes lived the Covenant well and at other times did not.

The Wisdom Books: The seven books of wisdom share advice on how to live the Covenant.

The Prophetic Books: The eighteen prophetic books remind God's people to be faithful to the Covenant and that God will always be faithful to them.

? How would you describe biblical inspiration? What does God reveal to us in the Pentateuch?

NEW TESTAMENT The twenty-seven books of the New Testament are grouped this way:

The Gospels: The four written accounts of the Gospel are the heart of Sacred Scripture because Jesus Christ is their center.

The Acts of the Apostles: The Acts of the Apostles tells the story of the early Church.

The New Testament Letters: The thirteen Epistles, or letters, of Saint Paul help us to understand our faith in Jesus and how to live that faith.

The Catholic Letters: Eight other letters in the New Testament also help us to understand and live our faith.

The Book of Revelation: This final book of the Bible encourages Christians to remain faithful to Jesus when they suffer because of their faith in Jesus Christ.

? What does God reveal to us in the Gospels?

Activity Complete the crossword puzzle below.

ACROSS

1. Sacred Scripture
4. Four accounts of Jesus' life
5. Another word for the Pentateuch
6. _____ of the Apostles

DOWN

2. New Testament letters
3. Books that share advice
7. Books that remind God's people of the Covenant

Write a paragraph about what God reveals to us in the Gospels. Use three of the words from the puzzle in your paragraph.

_____

_____

FAITH FOCUS
How does the story of the
Covenant unfold in the Bible?

The Covenant

The story of the Covenant begins in the Book of Genesis, the first book of the Bible. It continues to unfold with more and more detail even to the last book of the Bible, the Book of Revelation. Some highlights of those details found in Old Testament are:

- God promised that from Eve's descendants would come one who would conquer the tempter, the devil (read Genesis 3:14–16).

- God entered a Covenant with Noah and promised that all living things will continue as long as the world lasts (read Genesis 9:9–17).

- God promised Abraham that he would be the father of a great people (read Genesis 12:1–3).

- At Mount Sinai, God promised Moses and the Israelites that he would be their God. They promised that they would be his people and live the Law he revealed to them (read Exodus 19:4–6).

- The prophets chosen by God reminded his people to live the Covenant and announced a new and everlasting Covenant in the Messiah (read Jeremiah 32:36–43 and Ezekiel 37:26–28).

In the New Testament, Jesus revealed that he is the Christ, the Anointed One or Messiah, the new and everlasting Covenant. In him and through his work, all people can live faithfully according to the will of God. In Jesus Christ, God's final Covenant with the world has been made now and forever.

Even though God reveals himself through Sacred Scripture and through the Sacred Tradition of the Church, he remains a mystery beyond our full comprehension. Because God is the source of all, he is due our worship. We are to praise and thank him for initiating and maintaining the Covenant.

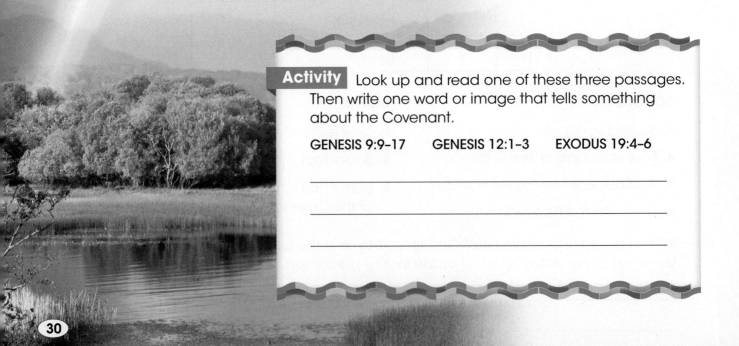

Activity Look up and read one of these three passages. Then write one word or image that tells something about the Covenant.

GENESIS 9:9–17   GENESIS 12:1–3   EXODUS 19:4–6

_____

_____

_____

I FOLLOW JESUS

God wishes for all people to respond to him in faith. We can use the gift of knowledge to assist us in growing in faith. The Scriptures reveal to us God's plan of everlasting love.

THE WORD OF THE LORD

Write three ways your life could be changed by reading, listening to, and studying the Bible.

1. _____

_____

_____

2. _____

_____

_____

3. _____

_____

_____

MY FAITH CHOICE

This week, I will read and listen to the Sunday Gospel and respond to it.

I will _____

_____

_____

 Pray, "Lord, fill my mind and heart so that I may proclaim your Word to others. Amen."

1. The Holy Spirit guided the human writers of Sacred Scripture to faithfully and accurately tell what God intended to reveal.

2. Through the Bible, God reveals himself and his loving plan of Salvation for the world and all people.

3. The Bible tells the story of the Covenant into which God entered with his people. In his only Son, Jesus Christ, God established his Covenant forever.

Chapter Review

Recall

Write a sentence describing each term.

1. Bible _____

2. canon _____

3. Covenant _____

4. inspiration _____

5. Sacred Scripture _____

Write a paragraph describing the Church's teaching about Sacred Scripture. Be sure to include at least three of the terms listed above.

_____

_____

_____

_____

_____

_____

_____

Reflect

What do you think God reveals about himself through the Bible?

_____

_____

_____

_____

_____

Share With a partner, work together to describe how God reveals his Covenant with his people through different men and women in the Bible.

Your Word Is Light

Lectio divina, or "divine reading," is an ancient prayer of meditation. Along with vocal prayer and contemplation, it forms the three main expressions of prayer. Follow these steps to spend quiet time with God, reading and listening to his Word:

1. Open your Bible to a favorite passage or one from this chapter. Sit quietly.

2. Be aware that God is present by the indwelling presence of the Holy Spirit within you. Sign your forehead, lips, and chest over your heart with a small Sign of a Cross.

3. Imagine yourself in a safe place where you can talk and listen to God.

4. Reverently and slowly read the Scripture passage you selected.

5. Speak to God with words, images, or ideas. Take time to talk and listen to God. Say,

> "Your word is a lamp for my feet,
>   a light for my path" (PSALM 119:105).

6. After a few quiet moments, ask the Holy Spirit, "What is your Word saying to me?" Write down any key words or phrases that you remember. Listening with an open heart can help you to be receptive to God speaking to you through his Word.

7. Make a faith decision and put God's Word into action. Realize that the goal of lectio divina is simply being with God by praying the Scriptures.

With My Family

This Week . . .

In Chapter 2, "The Word of God," your child learned:

▶ The Holy Spirit inspired the writers of Scripture to express God's Word faithfully and truthfully as a gift to all people.

▶ The heart of Sacred Scripture is the Gospel, because Jesus Christ, the Incarnate Word of God, is the heart and fullness of God's Revelation.

▶ Sacred Scripture firmly, faithfully, and without error teaches the truth about God's plan for Salvation.

▶ Sacred Scripture reveals God's Covenant, or solemn commitment of fidelity with his Chosen People, the Israelites.

▶ The gift of knowledge, one of the seven Gifts of the Holy Spirit, gives us the grace to deepen our understanding of Sacred Scripture.

For more about related teachings of the Church, see the *Catechism of the Catholic Church*, 50–73, 101–141, and the *United States Catholic Catechism for Adults*, pages 12–27.

■ Sharing God's Word

Read together 1 Thessalonians 2:13 and 2 Timothy 3:16–17. Emphasize that the Bible is the inspired Word of God.

■ We Live as Disciples

The Christian home and family is a school of discipleship. Choose one of the following activities to do as a family, or design a similar activity of your own:

▶ Make a special place in your home to display a Bible. This is called "enthroning" the Bible. Open the Bible each day to a selected passage. This practice can help the family recall the importance of the Word of God in our daily lives.

▶ Include the reading of Scripture to begin your family mealtime prayers. Invite a different family member to select a passage each day. During the meal, have family members share what the passage means to them.

▶ As a family, carefully watch and listen to the news events that are making the headlines. Now imagine that you are a prophet called to remind others about the Covenant. As a family, discuss how you would encourage one another to live as a family according to God's will.

■ Our Spiritual Journey

Praying together is one of the main practices of a disciple of Jesus. In this chapter, your child practiced the *lectio divina* form of prayer. Read about this prayer on page 33. Make this a form of prayer that your family regularly prays together.

For more ideas on ways your family can live as disciples of Jesus, visit **BeMyDisciples.com**

Looking Ahead

In this chapter, the Holy Spirit invites you to: ▶

EXPLORE how sacred art helps us in worshiping God.

DISCOVER that the mystery of the Trinity is at the center of our faith.

DECIDE how you can give honor and praise to God.

CHAPTER

3

The Mystery of God

? What is your favorite mystery story? Which kinds of clues have helped you solve the mystery?

God is mystery. However, he is a mystery totally unlike human mysteries. The mystery of God is not something to be solved but rather accepted. In this reading, God gives us several clues that help us come to know him better.

"In the beginning was the Word,
   and the Word was with God,
   and the Word was God. . . .
What came to be through him was life,
   and this life was the light of the human race;
   the light shines in the darkness,
   and the darkness has not overcome it."

JOHN 1:1, 3–5

? What has God revealed about himself through this Scripture passage?

Disciple Power

Wonder and Awe

Often this Gift of the Holy Spirit is referred to as "fear of the Lord." This gift of awe before God enables us to be aware of God's mystery and majesty. We are humbled by his almighty power, perfect goodness, and unconditional love. Most sacred art reflects this kind of reverence to God and assists us in the worship due to God.

Illuminating Mosaics

Christian artists can help us to know more about the mystery of the loving presence of God within us and among us. Long before we had Bibles for everyone to read, Christians used art to help people "hear" the story of creation and redemption.

Mosaics are one of the earliest forms of art used by Christians. Some of the earliest Christian mosaics date back to A.D. 320, in the Mausoleum of Santa Costanza in Rome, Italy. The creation of mosaics is an art form consisting of pressing colored pieces of material called *tesserae* into soft plaster to form pictures. Often the material used comes from glass or ceramic tiles. Many mosaics illuminate when light reflects off the *tesserae*. This gives the viewer the impression that the image is shimmering or glowing. Mosaics can help people enter into the mystery of God and see him as the source of all that is true, good, and beautiful.

? How do you think art can help people enter into the mystery of God?

Detail from *Jesus Lord* mosaic above the altar in Christ the King Cathedral, Superior, WI

Inspiring Art

Mosaics give drama and life to scenes from the Bible that reveal the story of God's love for us. Often decorating the ceilings and walls of churches, they instruct the faithful about the majesty and mystery of God, and the lives of Jesus, Mary, and other Saints. They illuminate God's plan of creation and Redemption as revealed to us by the Word of God, Jesus Christ.

Christian art, like all the sacramentals of the Church, help us respond in faith to the mystery of the One God, who is Father, Son, and Holy Spirit. Such art invokes in us a sense of wonder and awe for God. It sparks a desire within us to spread the story of God's love by striving to be his living images in the world.

? What art in your church or school helps you to remember God's love for you and all his people?

Activity   Using small pieces of colored paper, glue, and a piece of cardboard, create a mosaic depicting the mystery of God. Sketch your idea for your mosaic here.

The Nature of God

Our minds can never fully understand the holy mystery of God. God is like, and at the same time unlike, anyone or anything we know. God is One, and there is only One God. He is truth and love.

We can come to know something about God through our reason. For example, we can know that God exists. However, we cannot fully understand who God is on our own. We need God to reveal himself to us. We need **Divine Revelation**—God making himself and his divine plan of creation and Salvation known over time. We therefore depend on God revealing himself to us. Through the Word of God, we believe that he has done just that.

Qualities of God

Here are some of the qualities, or attributes, that God has revealed about himself through Sacred Scripture:

Faithful. God is the One who is always faithful to his people.

"The LORD, a merciful and gracious God, [is] slow to anger and rich in kindness and fidelity"

EXODUS 34:6

Truth. God's Word is true, and all his promises come true. God the Son came to bear witness to the truth.

". . . LORD GOD you are God and your words are truth"

2 SAMUEL 7:28

? What examples can you give that show God is faithful and truthful?

Mercy and Love

Here are two more qualities that God has revealed about himself through Sacred Scriptures:

Merciful. God's merciful love endures forever, and in his mercy, all sins are forgiven.

> *God, who is rich in mercy. . . .*
>
> Ephesians 2:4

Love. God is love. God loves us with an everlasting love. Moreover, God so loved the world that he sent his only Son.

> *For God so loved the world that he gave his only Son, so that everyone who believes in him . . . might have eternal life.*
>
> John 3:16

God has revealed these qualities, or attributes, and many others about himself. Each quality helps us to know something more about him. God has revealed himself to be Father, Son, and Holy Spirit.

? What other qualities of God have you learned?

Catholics Believe

Faith in God

Faith leads us to turn to God alone as our origin and our ultimate goal. We are neither to prefer anything to him nor to substitute anything for him (see *Catechism of the Catholic Church* 229). Scripture and Tradition never cease to teach and celebrate this fundamental truth: "The world was made for the glory of God" (*Catechism of the Catholic Church* 293).

Activity Write a cinquain poem celebrating the qualities of God.

Line 1: one-word title for God

_____

Line 2: a two-word phrase that describes the title for God

_____ _____

Line 3: a three-word phrase that describes an action relating to the title for God

_____ _____ _____

Line 4: a four-word phrase that describes a feeling relating to the title for God

_____ _____ _____ _____

Line 5: one-word that refers back to the title for God

_____

FAITH VOCABULARY

▶ **original holiness**
Original holiness is that
first state of grace in which
Adam and Eve shared in
God's divine life. They were
therefore in a perfect state
of grace before the Fall.

▶ **original justice**
Original justice is that first
state of grace before the
Fall, when Adam and Eve
and all of creation were in
harmony.

▶ **sanctify**
To sanctify is to put one in
that state of grace in which
sin is removed and we are
made holy.

The Most Holy Trinity

God has also revealed himself to be the mystery of One God in Three Divine Persons: Father, Son, and Holy Spirit. This is who God is. This is the mystery of the Holy, or Blessed Trinity. The Church has passed on this Divine Revelation in Sacred Scripture and in the Sacred Tradition of the Church. The mystery of the Most Holy Trinity is at the very center of our faith. Believing in God the Holy Trinity is essential to Christian living.

Many other mysteries of faith have their beginning in this mystery of mysteries. For example, the story of the human family begins with God creating us out of love in a state of **original holiness** and **original justice**. In the Fall, humanity lost its original state because of Original Sin. Eventually, God the Father sent God the Son, who became fully human. He became like us in all ways but sin so that we could become sharers in his divinity. The Father and the Son have sent the Holy Spirit to make us holy, or **sanctify** us. He reconciles us with God, who created us to live eternally with him.

We recall this mystery of the Holy Trinity every time we make the Sign of the Cross. We pray in the name of the Father, and of the Son, and of the Holy Spirit to share in the life of the Holy Trinity here on Earth and eternal life.

? How can the Holy Trinity be at the center of your faith every day?

The Trinity, painted by the Russian artist Andrei Rublev around 1410

Made in His Image

In God's plan of creation, human beings have an extraordinary and unique place. The greatness of every person rests on this revealed truth:

God created man in his image;
in the divine image he created him;
male and female he created them.

GENESIS 1:27

God created each person with a soul. The soul bears the imprint of God's image and is the innermost spiritual part of us. The soul is immortal, or never dies. Our soul gives us the ability to share in God's life and love forever.

In the Son and through the Spirit, God the Father reveals the innermost aspect of who God is. The Holy Trinity is a perfect, eternal exchange of love. When we choose to live as images of God, we tell others about his love and give honor and glory to God. In our loving relationships with one another we can reflect the love that exists within the Holy Trinity.

? Which qualities of a holy person do others see in you?

Activity In each blank section of the triangle, write a phrase that describes the work of the Holy Trinity as Creator.

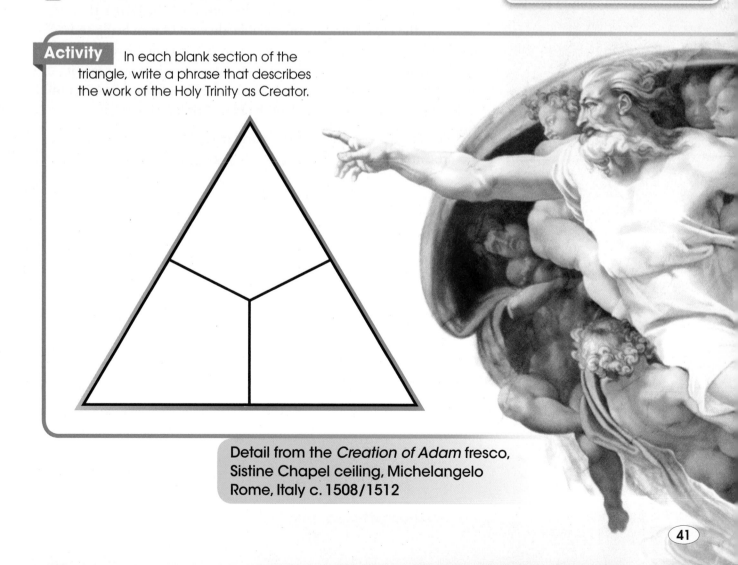

Detail from the *Creation of Adam* fresco, Sistine Chapel ceiling, Michelangelo Rome, Italy c. 1508/1512

41

God the Creator

The very first words of the Bible begin with the story of God's love:

> In the beginning, when God created the heavens and the earth, . . .
>
> GENESIS 1:1

If we listen carefully to the Word of God revealed in the Book of Genesis, we come to know something about God the Creator. We also understand more about the world and ourselves. Here are three things we learn about God the Creator and his creation:

"In the beginning" means that the world had a beginning. The world was not always in existence.

"God created" means that only God can make everyone and everything, out of nothing, without any help.

"Heavens and the earth" is another way of saying "all things visible and invisible" as in the Nicene Creed. Angels, part of God's invisible creation, are spiritual beings who always give glory to God. They serve his saving plan for all creatures.

In creation, God reveals his plan. Because God the Father, the Son, and the Holy Spirit are inseparable, they are One in being and act as one. Each Divine Person of the Trinity has a unique role. God the Father not only created the universe out of love but also keeps it in existence by his Word, the Son, and by the Holy Spirit, the Giver of Life. Thus, creation is the work of the Holy Trinity.

? What clues do you see in the world that gives you a glimpse into the mystery of God?

Activity Find the hidden message by reading across and circling every fourth word in the chart below.

Bible	life	world	Creation	We
Father	Genesis	is	visible	Holy Spirit
Faith	the	invisible	Nicene	angels
work	Earth	God	Creator	of
holiness	plan	love	the	heavens
Son	giver	Holy	creed	glory
soul	Trinity	humans	reveals	Person

I FOLLOW JESUS

God always manifests his love. God never stops giving you signs of his love. If you look closely, there are many clues that give you a glimpse into the mystery of God.

SIGNS OF THE MYSTERY OF GOD

Make a collage of words and pictures of people, places, things, and events that have come to be signs of God and his love for you.

MY FAITH CHOICE

This week, I will reflect God's love for me in the way I treat others. I will

_____

_____

_____

Pray, "O my God, I love you above all things. Send your Spirit to help me love my neighbor as myself for love of you. Amen."

1. God is the mystery of mysteries who has revealed himself and his plan of creation and Redemption.

2. Creation is the work of the Holy Trinity. God is the source of all truth, goodness, and beauty.

3. The mystery of the most Holy Trinity is at the center of our faith.

Chapter Review

Recall

Complete the first four sentences to decipher the hidden message below. Unscramble the circled letters to discover the belief about God that is at the center of our faith.

1. God has revealed himself to be the ___ ___ ___ ⃝ ___ ⃝⃝ of One God in Three Divine Persons.

2. Divine ___ ___ ___ ___ ___ ___ ___ ⃝ ___ ⃝ is God making himself and his plan of creation and redemption known over time.

3. ___ ___ ___ ___ ⃝ ___ ___ ___ is God making everyone and everything, visible and invisible, out of nothing and without any help.

4. ___ ___ ___ ___ ⃝ ___ ___ ___ Sin is the name given to the first sin.

The central belief about God is the mystery of the

___ ___ ___ ___ ___ ___ ___.

Reflect

List some of the qualities of God that reveal who he is to you.

_____

_____

_____

_____

_____

_____

Share   **What do we know about the great mystery of the Holy Trinity? Discuss as a class.**

Give Thanks to God

The Church prays the psalms each day in the Liturgy of the Hours. The Liturgy of the Hours is the official daily prayer of the Church. One way we can pray a psalm is by alternately praying the verses aloud. We call this praying a psalm antiphonally.

All: **Come and see the works of God, awesome in the deeds done for us.**

Group 1: Shout joyfully to God, all you on earth;

Group 2: sing of his glorious name.

All: **Come and see the works of God, awesome in the deeds done for us.**

Group 1: All on earth fall in worship before you;

Group 2: they sing of you, sing of your name!

All: **Come and see the works of God, awesome in the deeds done for us.**

Group 1: Bless our God, you peoples;

Group 2: loudly sound his praise.

All: **Come and see the works of God, awesome in the deeds done for us.**

Group 1: [God] has kept us alive

Group 2: and not allowed our feet to slip.

All: **Come and see the works of God, awesome in the deeds done for us.**

Group 1: Blessed be God, who did not refuse me

Group 2: the kindness I sought in prayer.

All: **Come and see the works of God, awesome in the deeds done for us.**

Psalm 66:1–2, 4, 8–9, 20

With My Family

This Week . . .

In Chapter 3, "The Mystery of God," your child learned:

▶ God is the Mystery of mysteries. We receive the gift and grace of wonder and awe, or fear of the Lord, to help us give praise and thanks to God.

▶ Although we can come to know with certainty that God exists by reason, we depend on his Divine Revelation. Through Sacred Scripture and Sacred Tradition in the Church, God has revealed himself to be the most Holy Trinity—the Mystery of One God in Three Divine Persons: God the Father, God the Son, and God the Holy Spirit.

▶ Jesus Christ, the Incarnate Son of God, has revealed this truth about God to us. This mystery of the Holy Trinity is at the center of our faith.

For more about related teachings of the Church, see the *Catechism of the Catholic Church*, 198–231, 249–267, 355–387, and the *United States Catholic Catechism for Adults*, pages 50–53, 56–69.

■ Sharing God's Word

Read together Exodus 34:6, Deuteronomy 7:9, and 1 John 4:8. Emphasize that through Sacred Scripture, God reveals who he is and his plan of loving goodness for the world. The teachings of the Church help us to understand the true meaning of Sacred Scripture, God's Word.

■ We Live as Disciples

The Christian home and family is a school of discipleship. Choose one of the following activities to do as a family, or design a similar activity of your own.

▶ Invite family members to take turns completing the sentence, "God is . . ." Continue until no one is able to complete the sentence. Distribute art materials and create tablemats displaying words and phrases that your family used to describe God.

▶ Recall that all people are created in the image and likeness of God. Share ideas about how your family is an image of God.

▶ Discuss as a family how religious art in your home can help you keep God and prayer at the center of family life. Start with a family crucifix as a central and important reminder of Catholic family living.

■ Our Spiritual Journey

Daily prayer is vital to the life of a Christian family. In this chapter, your child prayed a prayer based on Psalm 66. Read and pray together this prayer on page 45.

For more ideas on ways your family can live as disciples of Jesus, visit **BeMyDisciples.com**

Looking Ahead

In this chapter, the Holy Spirit invites you to ▶

EXPLORE how the Church works to bring about the Kingdom.

DISCOVER that God reveals himself as both almighty and perfect.

DECIDE how your faith can help you handle temptations in life.

CHAPTER

4

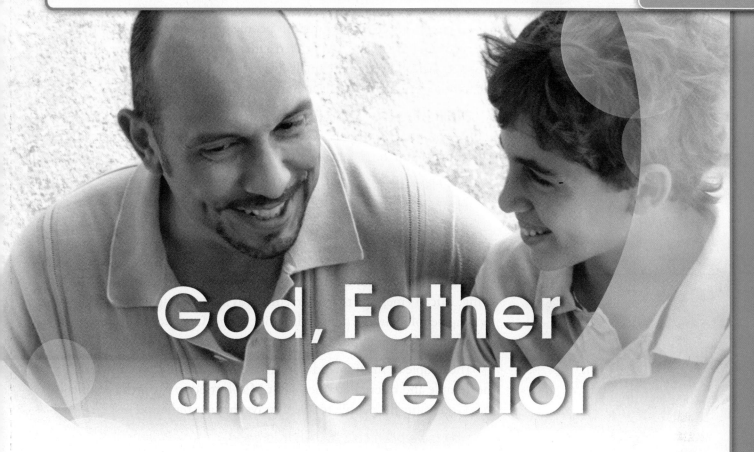

God, Father and Creator

? What are the ideal qualities of a father?

Jesus taught us to call God our Father. You have prayed this prayer for many years. In the Sermon on the Mount, Jesus taught his disciples to pray. This is part of what Jesus said:

> "This is how you are to pray:
> Our Father in heaven,
>   hallowed be your name,
>   your kingdom come,
>   your will be done,
>   on earth as in heaven."
>
> MATTHEW 6:9–10

? What does this prayer tell you about God the Father and your relationship to him? How could you help a friend appreciate God as our Father who loves each of us?

Disciple Power

Justice

Justice is one of the four Cardinal Virtues. Justice is the habit of consistently giving what is due to God and to our neighbor. We give God what is due to him when we worship him alone. Our worship of God includes loving our neighbor and respecting the dignity of every human person. Through Christian justice, we participate in preparing the way for the coming of the Kingdom of God.

The Prophet Micah

God sent prophets to remind his people, the Israelites, on how to live according to his laws. God called a man named Micah as one of his prophets. Micah lived in the small village of Moresheth near Jerusalem. He went to Jerusalem to deliver God's message to the king.

During the time of Micah, many rich people were full of violence and lies. Some storekeepers were dishonest and cheated customers. Micah proclaimed:

> Hear, then, what the LORD says: . . .
> Hear, O mountains, the plea of the LORD,
>   pay attention, O foundations of the earth!
>
> MICAH 6:1, 2

Micah warned that God did not like the way the people were living. Micah's message to the Israelites was about living justly and treating people fairly. If people did not change, God would destroy the city of Jerusalem as a punishment.

The people of his time did not believe Micah. They worshiped in the Temple and offered sacrifices. But Micah tried to show the people that God wants his people to live in ways that are right and just.

> You have been told . . . what is good,
>   and what the LORD requires of you;
> Only to do the right and to love goodness,
>   and to walk humbly with your God.
>
> MICAH 6:8

? How are your words and actions a sign that you are acting justly?

Act Justly

To help the people understand God's message, Micah explained that God was like a man who brought another man to court (see Micah 6:2). God states that while he has kept the Covenant and been faithful to his people, they have not been faithful to him.

God decides that he will punish the people because they do not live justly. They do not deserve to be his people. After Micah died, Jerusalem was destroyed and the people taken into Exile.

Today God still calls us to act justly and to live for his kingdom. We are to take care of the poor, to treat others fairly, and to practice justice.

? Who is someone you know who acts justly or strives to live the Kingdom of God on Earth? How does this person act justly?

Activity What message do you think the world needs to hear today about living justly? Write your own message about the importance of justice.

_____

_____

_____

_____

_____

_____

_____

_____

_____

_____

_____

Almighty Love

The Book of Genesis, the first book of the Bible, contains two accounts of creation. In the first creation account, you learned that God is Creator. He is almighty and omnipotent.

Thus the heavens and the earth and all their array were completed. Since on the seventh day God was finished with the work he had been doing, he rested on the seventh day . . . . So, God blessed the seventh day and made it holy . . .

GENESIS 2:1–3

God is the Father, the Almighty, the Creator of all that is visible and invisible. This means that God created everything and that creation is good. We read, "God looked at everything he had made, and he found it very good" (Genesis 1:31). God is the source of everything that is good, true, and beautiful.

Abba, Father

The second account of creation emphasizes the personal relationship that God has with humanity. After God created Adam, God knew it was not good for him to be alone. So God created Eve as a suitable partner . . . (see Genesis 2:18–19, 21–22).

The events of this account reveal God's presence with humanity and his love for us. When we address God as "Abba, Father," as Jesus did and taught us to do, we acknowledge God's presence with us and his deep personal love for each of us.

? How do you know God is our heavenly Father?

The Love of Our Father

Through Baptism in Jesus Christ, the Son of God, we become adopted sons and daughters of God our Father. God the Father is perfect in his love for us. Jesus constantly taught about the love of the Father. Jesus wants us to know the parental tenderness that God has for us. God desires for all of us to be with him forever. Jesus told his disciples,

"If a man has a hundred sheep and one of them goes astray, will he not leave the ninety-nine in the hills and go in search of the stray?"

MATTHEW 18:12

Again and again in the New Testament we read that we are children of God and that he loves us because he is our Father. His love for us is why he sent his Son to us to make things right again and to bring us back to himself.

? What does being an adopted son or daughter of God mean to you?

Catholics Believe

Salvation

Salvation is the deliverance of humanity from the power of sin and death through Jesus Christ. The Incarnate Son of God, Jesus Christ, died for our sins and revealed God's power over death in the Resurrection. Our faith in Christ is necessary for our Salvation.

Activity Look up and read the following Scripture passages. Think about what God is telling you about himself and your relationship with him. Write your responses here. Share your thoughts with a partner.

John 14:6 _____

_____

_____

Romans 8:15 _____

_____

_____

Galatians 4:5 _____

_____

_____

FAITH VOCABULARY

Original Sin
Original Sin is the sin of Adam and Eve by which they lost the state of original holiness, and by which death, sin, and suffering entered into the world.

sin
Sin is freely choosing to do what we know is against God's will or freely choosing not to do something that we know God wants us to do.

temptation
Temptation is anything that tries to move us to do or say something that we know is wrong or prevents us from doing something that we know is good and that we ought to do.

Separated from God

You have learned that God created humanity in a state of original holiness and justice, or friendship with him. **Sin** and evil, the Bible tells us, made their way into the good world of God's creation when the first humans turned away from God. We give the name **Original Sin** to this turning away from God and his plan of creation.

Original Sin is the **sin** that Adam and Eve committed by freely turning away from God's love and friendship. They freely chose to do what they knew God did not want them to do. They sinned, and by their sin all of humanity lost original holiness and original justice, except Mary, the Mother of God, who was born without Original Sin. Mary remained free from personal sin throughout her entire life. The name given to this unique grace and privilege that God gave to Mary is the Immaculate Conception.

The Scripture story of humanity's fall from grace and loss of original holiness began with the **temptation** of Adam and Eve. Prior to the Fall, God had commanded Adam and Eve:

"You are free to eat from any of the trees of the garden except the tree of knowledge of good and bad. From that tree you shall not eat; the moment you eat from it you are surely doomed to die."

GENESIS 2:16–17

Then the serpent, representing Satan, the Evil One, tempts Adam and Eve by telling them that they will not die. The serpent lies to Eve:

"You certainly will not die! No, God knows well that the moment you eat of it your eyes will be opened and you will be like gods who know what is good and what is bad."

GENESIS 3:4–5

? Why did humanity lose its original holiness and original justice?

Marked by Sin

Adam and Eve gave in to temptation and sinned. They rejected God by rejecting his loving commandment (read Genesis 3:1–7). The loss of original holiness has become part of our fallen human nature. We now share in the effects of Original Sin. The world and all of us in the human family are marked by sin. From the very first moment of our existence, or conception, we need to be reconciled with God.

Through the Sacrament of Baptism, we become adopted sons and daughters of God. We are reborn in Christ with the forgiveness of Original Sin at Baptism. We receive the gift and grace of the Holy Spirit to live as children of God the Father.

? What are some ways we can become reconciled with God?

Faith-Filled People

The New Eve

Christian tradition identifies the Blessed Virgin Mary as the New Eve. Mary always acknowledged God's love for her through her words and deeds. She waited in loving trust for God to fulfill his promise to send the Savior. When the angel announced that God would fulfill his promise through her, Mary responded, "May it be done to me according to your word" (Luke 1:38).

Activity Look at each picture. Under each of the pictures write how that person is being reconciled with God.

_____ _____ _____

_____ _____ _____

Promise of Salvation

God did not reject Adam and Eve after they turned away from him. He approached them as a loving and good father. God promised to send someone to heal the relationship between him and humanity. This is God's plan of Salvation (read Genesis 3:15).

All of God's promises in the Old Testament point to Jesus Christ, the Savior whom God promised to send. In truth, God's promise of eternal life begins with Jesus. In Christ, all of God's promises are fulfilled. Jesus did not abolish the Law and Covenant of Sinai. The Son of God fulfilled and perfected these promises (read Matthew 5:17–18). Jesus Christ is the new and everlasting Covenant (read 1 Corinthians 11:25). Jesus is the Savior of all people. Christ is the center of God's plan of Salvation.

The Son of God, Jesus Christ, became a man, lived on Earth, and was raised from the dead to save us and redeem us from sin and death. In Jesus Christ, we have been healed, or reconciled, with God, with one another, and with all of creation.

What about those who have not heard of Jesus? The answer to that question is very important. God wants everyone to share in his life and love both now and forever. The Church teaches that through the grace of the Holy Spirit, God works quietly and mysteriously to draw all people to himself. All people can be saved who seek to serve and love God with all their hearts. This is both the promise and desire of God (read John 17:1–26).

? How can you live in a way that shows others that Jesus Christ is our Savior?

Christ the Redeemer statue
Rio de Janeiro, Brazil
c. 1922/1931

Activity Describe three acts that Christ has done for us that show the love of the Father for all people. Share your responses with others.

Signs of God's Love

1. _____

_____

2. _____

_____

3. _____

_____

I FOLLOW JESUS

Because of Original Sin, all people lost the state of original holiness that God intended, except for Mary and, of course, Jesus. In every generation since then, people have worked to overcome temptation and to help bring the Kingdom of God in all its fullness.

ACTIVITY

John and Alison want to start a fan page for a famous person. At first they are thinking of a movie star, but they decide to choose a famous person known for humanitarian efforts to build the Kingdom of God. Help them choose a worthy person, and then design a home page for their Web site.

MY FAITH CHOICE

This week, I will do something each day to build the Kingdom of God.
I will

_____

_____

 Pray the Our Father in the silence of your heart. Pause after each petition of the prayer.

1. God reveals himself as Father and Creator, the source of all that is visible and invisible.

2. Original Sin is the sin that Adam and Eve committed by freely turning away from God's love and friendship.

3. In Jesus Christ, the Savior promised by God, we have been healed, or reconciled, with God, with one another, and with all of creation.

Chapter Review

Recall

Complete each sentence using one of the terms provided in the word bank.

Father	presence	justice	Salvation	almighty

1. Jesus Christ, the Son of God, taught us that God is our loving _____.

2. Through the Cardinal Virtue of _____, we participate in the Kingdom of God by following God's Law of Love.

3. In the first account of creation, God reveals that he is _____ and omnipotent.

4. In the second account of creation, God reveals his _____ in a personal way as goodness and love.

5. Our _____ is deliverance from the power of sin and eternal death, made possible by God.

Reflect

Describe the ways that God is a Father to you.

_____

_____

_____

_____

_____

Share Explain how we are still experiencing the results of the first sin today. Share God's plan of Salvation for all people with your class.

Sing to the Lord

The Church prays the psalms each day in the Liturgy of the Hours and at Mass. In the Liturgy of the Word, the Church as a whole assembly prays the psalms in the Responsorial Psalm. In a similar way, this psalm is structured for a leader and the whole class to pray together.

Leader: Sing to the LORD, bless his name;
announce his salvation day after day.

All: **Sing to the LORD, bless his name;**
announce his salvation day after day.

Leader: Tell God's glory among the nations;
among all peoples, God's marvelous deeds.

All: **Sing to the LORD, bless his name;**
announce his salvation day after day.

Leader: For great is the LORD and highly to be praised,
to be feared above all gods . . .
Let the heavens be glad and the earth rejoice.

All: **Sing to the LORD, bless his name;**
announce his salvation day after day.

Leader: Splendor and power go before him;
power and grandeur are in his holy place.

All: **Sing to the LORD, bless his name;**
announce his salvation day after day.

Leader: Give to the LORD, you families of nations,
give to the Lord glory and might;

All: **Sing to the LORD, bless his name;**
announce his salvation day after day.

Leader: Say among the nations: the LORD is king.
The world will surely stand fast, never to be moved.
God rules the peoples with fairness.

All: **Sing to the LORD, bless his name;**
announce his salvation day after day.

PSALM 96:2–4,6, 7,10, 11

With My Family

This Week . . .

In Chapter 4, "God, Father and Creator," your child learned:

▶ The Kingdom of God is the fulfillment of God's plan for all creation in Christ at the end of time when Christ will come again in glory. Each of us is called to help bring the Kingdom of God to its fullness by our words and actions.

▶ The Book of Genesis contains two accounts of creation. In the first, God is revealed as Creator and almighty Father, maker of all that is good, both visible and invisible. The second emphasizes the personal relationship of love that God has with humanity.

▶ God created humanity in a state of original holiness and justice, but our first parents freely sinned. Their Original Sin lost for us the original state of grace.

▶ Through Baptism, we are reborn in Christ and the effects of Original Sin are forgiven. We receive the gift and grace of the Holy Spirit to live as children of God the Father.

▶ God freely entered into a Covenant with humanity, and that Covenant reached its fullness in Jesus Christ, the new and everlasting Covenant. Jesus is the center of God's plan of Salvation.

For more about related teachings of the Church, see the *Catechism of the Catholic Church,* 232–248, 268–354, 388–421, and the *United States Catholic Catechism for Adults,* pages 53–56, 68–75.

◼ Sharing God's Word

Read together John 17:1–26. Emphasize that through Sacred Scripture, God reveals himself as "our Father." In Jesus Christ, the incarnate Son of God, we have Salvation and Redemption. We have been healed, or reconciled, with God, with one another, and with all of creation.

◼ We Live as Disciples

The Christian home and family is a school of discipleship. Choose one of the following activities to do as a family, or design a similar activity of your own.

▶ Choose one of the Scripture passages from this chapter and design a family prayer banner. Display this banner prominently in your home. Use it during family prayer time as a way to focus on God, who loves us and sustains us.

▶ Discuss as a family ways that you experience the fatherly love of God. Choose one way to honor God the Father for all that he provides.

▶ As a family, develop a stewardship plan for how each family member will help take care of the gift of creation that God has given to everyone. Realize that caring for creation involves practicing the virtue of justice.

◼ Our Spiritual Journey

Listening to and praying the Scriptures has a long tradition in the Church. In this chapter, your child prayed a prayer based on Psalm 96. Read and pray together this prayer on page 57.

For more ideas on ways your family can live as disciples of Jesus, visit **BeMyDisciples.com**

Caring for Future Generations

Rodrigo is a farmer in Quichua, Ecuador. He grows food for his family to eat, but now he also grows food to sell at the market. He uses this income to buy meat and other foods for his family. His family also needs the money for clothing, school supplies, and to build an outhouse.

Now timber and cattle companies want to lease his land. They would clear the land completely to use it for lumbering or for cattle grazing. This would mean money for Rodrigo's family. But the land is also important to his culture, and there are sustainable and renewable resources in the rain forest that can bring in money. Also as more and more rainforest is destroyed, weather and temperature around the Earth is changed too. Many believe this will lead to global change and specifically climate change.

Rodrigo is trying to balance his family's need for more money with the need to conserve the rain forest and pass on the land to his children. He wants to act responsibly as a good steward of God's creation and share this value with his family.

WE CARE FOR GOD'S CREATION

God commands us to be good stewards of his creation. We have a responsibility to preserve God's creation for future generations.

MAKING CONNECTIONS

God entrusts us with the responsibility of protecting his creation. This includes making choices that will protect our fragile ecosystem. Rather than destroying the rain forests, using them wisely and responsibly is an example of how people can use renewable and sustainable resources.

with LANGUAGE ARTS

Write different types of letters, such as persuasive, business, and informal, regarding the rain forests. For example, write a letter to the president of a corporation responsible for destructive logging in the Amazon. Persuade him to consider replacing the trees his company cuts down or to use fibers not made from trees in his production of materials. Or write a letter to your government representative asking that he or she support legislation that will help address the issues related to global climate change.

with SOCIAL STUDIES

Decorate your classroom as a rain forest. Consider the many species of animals and plants, the layers of the rain forest—floor, understory, canopy, emergent layer—and the climate. Include posters that tell facts about the rain forests and ways we can protect them.

with MATH AND SCIENCE

Rodrigo owns forty acres of land. If he leases the land to the timber company, he will make approximately $400.00 per acre. Since the land would be worthless after it is cleared, this amount is a one-time payment. If he leases to the cattle company, he will make $60.00 per acre. If Rodrigo harvests the fruits and seeds of the plants in the rain forest each year for medicines, the land will yield $2,400.00 per acre and the rainforest will not be destroyed.

Rodrigo is facing pressure from the representatives of the timber and cattle corporations. He would receive money from them immediately. It would take longer to set up an operation to harvest plants for medicine. Create a chart to show Rodrigo what his options are. Include your own ideas, such as suggesting that Rodrigo clear a little more of his land so that he can grow more crops to sell while he preserves his other acreage to set up the harvesting business. What do you recommend?

Faith Action

Become a conscious steward of God's creation. Name three actions you can take to help preserve the rain forests of the world.

_____

_____

Unit 1 **Review**

A. Choose the Best Word

Fill in the blanks to complete each of the sentences. Use the words from the word bank.

Bible	creation	Father
Redemption	sanctification	Salvation

1. _____ is God creating everyone and everything, seen and unseen, out of nothing and without any help.

2. Jesus Christ, the Son of God, taught us that God is our

loving _____.

3. Through the _____, God reveals himself and his

loving plan of _____ for the world and all people.

4. Through Christ's act of _____, God delivered humanity from the eternal death of sin.

5. The gift of sharing in God's life and love is called _____.

B. Show What You Know

Match the items in Column A with those in Column B.

Column A

A. faith

B. creed

C. Holy Trinity

D. Original Sin

E. justice

Column B

_____ **1.** A supernatural gift from God

_____ **2.** The mystery of One God in Three Divine Persons

_____ **3.** The result of the fall of Adam and Eve

_____ **4.** One of the Cardinal Virtues that is the habit of giving what is due to God and to our neighbor

_____ **5.** Summary of the principal beliefs of the Church

C. Connect with Scripture

*Reread the Scripture passage on the first Unit Opener page.
What connection do you see between this passage and
what you learned in this unit?*

_____

_____

_____

_____

_____

D. Be a Disciple

1. *Review the four pages in this unit titled, The Church Follows Jesus.
What person or ministry of the Church on these pages will inspire
you to be a better disciple of Jesus? Explain your answer.*

_____

_____

_____

_____

_____

2. *Work with a group. Review the four Disciple Power virtues, or gifts,
you have learned about in this unit. After jotting down your own
ideas, share with the group practical ways that you will live these
gifts day by day.*

_____

_____

_____

_____

_____

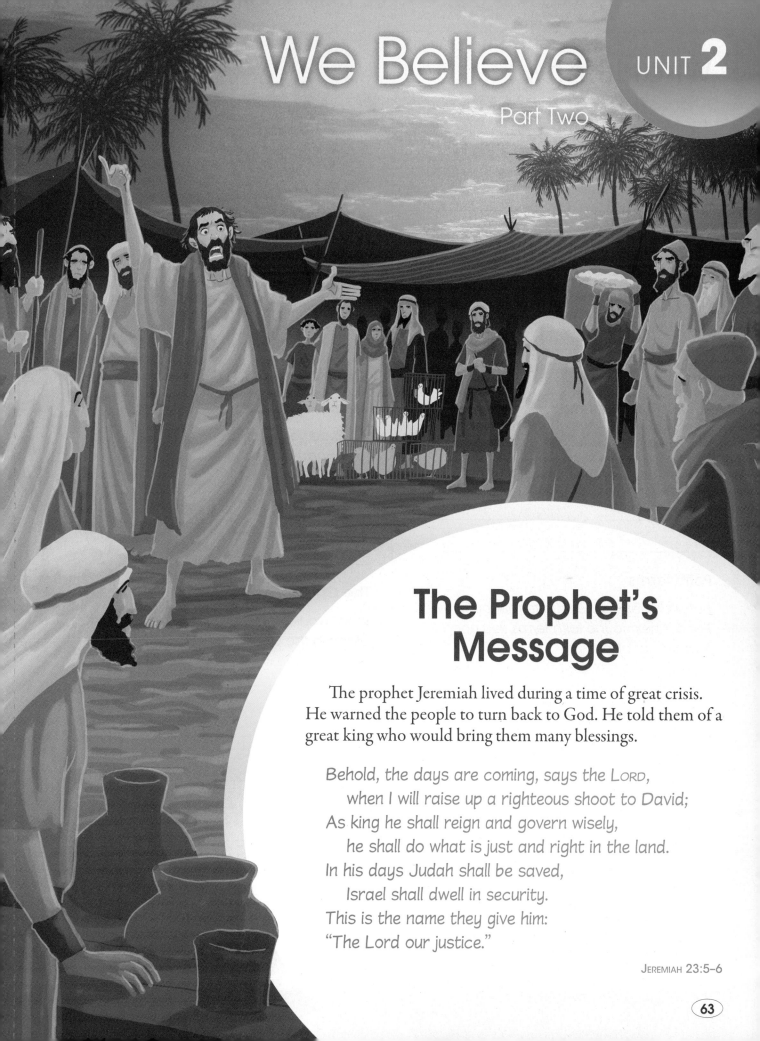

We Believe

Part Two

The Prophet's Message

The prophet Jeremiah lived during a time of great crisis. He warned the people to turn back to God. He told them of a great king who would bring them many blessings.

Behold, the days are coming, says the Lord,
when I will raise up a righteous shoot to David;
As king he shall reign and govern wisely,
he shall do what is just and right in the land.
In his days Judah shall be saved,
Israel shall dwell in security.
This is the name they give him:
"The Lord our justice."

Jeremiah 23:5–6

What I Know

What is something you already know about these faith concepts?

The Paschal Mystery

_____
_____
_____

The Kingdom of God

_____
_____
_____

God the Holy Spirit

_____
_____
_____

Faith Terms

Put an X next to the faith terms you know. Put a ? next to the faith terms you need to learn more about.

_____ Incarnation

_____ Theotokos

_____ Salvation

_____ The Passion

_____ Gospel

_____ Pentecost

_____ Church

_____ Communion of Saints

Questions I Have

The Bible

What do you know about the visit of Mary to her cousin Elizabeth?

_____
_____
_____

The Church

What would you like to know about Mary's place in the Church?

_____
_____
_____

What questions would you like to ask about the Resurrection?

_____
_____
_____

Looking Ahead

In this chapter, the Holy Spirit invites you to ▶

EXPLORE how Mary exemplifies the virtue of humility.

DISCOVER that God the Son became human to reconcile us with God.

DECIDE on how you can commit to living with humility.

CHAPTER

5

Son of God, Son of Mary

? When someone asks you to do something, how do you respond?

Let us listen to what Saint Luke tells us about Mary's response to the angel's message to her:

"The holy Spirit will come upon you, and the power of the Most High will overshadow you. Therefore the child to be born will be called holy, the Son of God. . . ." Mary said, *"Behold, I am the handmaid of the Lord. May it be done to me according to your word."*

LUKE 1:35, 38

? Why do you think Mary responded yes to God? What is the name that the Church gives to this event of the angel Gabriel's announcement to Mary?

Disciple Power

Humility

Humility helps us see and accept the truth about God and ourselves. A humble person acknowledges that God is the source of life and author of all that is good. Humility is often described as "poverty in spirit" when the humble person completely trusts in God.

Mary, the First and Model Disciple

In the Gospel of Luke, the archangel Gabriel, was sent to a place called Nazareth. Gabriel was to give a message to a young woman named Mary. She was not yet married, but she was engaged to a man named Joseph.

The angel appeared to Mary. He said,

"Hail, favored one! The Lord is with you."

LUKE 1:28

Mary was greatly troubled by Gabriel's greeting. She wondered why Gabriel had come and why he said that she was favored by God. Then the angel said to her,

"Do not be afraid, Mary, for you have found favor with God. Behold, you will conceive in your womb and bear a son, and you shall name him Jesus. He will be great and will be called Son of the Most High, and the Lord God will give him the throne of David his father, and he will rule over the house of Jacob forever, and of his kingdom there will be no end."

LUKE 1:30–33

At the announcement of his birth, Mary was the first person to know that God will send his only Son. Mary accepted God's special role for her. Mary said,

"I am the handmaid of the Lord. May it be done to me according to your word." Then the angel departed from her.

LUKE 1:38

? Do you have the courage to accept God's will for you? Why or why not?

The Annunciation
by Margetson William Henry

Mary, a Humble Disciple

Imagine Mary's surprise and confusion when God invited her to be the Mother of his Son. Mary did not understand why God had chosen her yet she was open to what God asked of her (see Luke 1:38).

Full of humility at what God was asking from her, Mary set out to visit her relative Elizabeth, who was also pregnant. It was not an easy journey from Nazareth to the home of Elizabeth. When Mary arrived she was perhaps once again surprised when the much older Elizabeth greeted her.

> "Most blessed are you among women, and blessed is the fruit of your womb. . . . Blessed are you who believed that what was spoken to you by the Lord would be fulfilled."
> LUKE 1:42, 45

Mary responds to Elizabeth with great faith. Mary proclaims,

> "My soul proclaims the greatness of the Lord;
>   my spirit rejoices in God my savior.
> The Mighty One has done great things for me,
>   and holy is his name."
> LUKE 1:46–47, 49

Mary told Elizabeth that all blessings come from God. She realized that her being "blessed" in the eyes of Elizabeth and future believers was not of her own doing. Hers was the response of a true and faithful Israelite, one who knows her part in the Covenant that God made with Abraham and Moses, "God alone is God" (see Psalm 62:2). Mary's humble "yes" models for us what it means to be a true disciple of her Son, Jesus. She is the model for the whole Church of how to follow Jesus.

❓ How would you explain that Mary was a humble person?

Activity   Reflecting on Mary's faith and humility, write a short prayer of praise to God for how he has blessed you this week.

_____

_____

_____

_____

FAITH FOCUS
What is the meaning the Incarnation?

FAITH VOCABULARY
Incarnation
The Incarnation is the belief of the Church that the Son of God became fully man in all ways except sin, while remaining fully divine.

Jesus the Christ

God the Father chose the Blessed Virgin Mary to be the Mother of his Son. She is the handmaid of the Lord, who was a virgin her whole life.

The Incarnation

The Virgin Mary conceived Jesus by the power of the Holy Spirit. He is the Son of God. Jesus is the Second Person of the Trinity, who took on flesh and became fully human in all things except sin. This great event is called the **Incarnation**. Thus the Virgin Mary, Mother of Jesus, is truly the Theotokos, the Mother of God. The Greek word *Theotokos* means "God-bearer."

In the opening passages of the Gospel of John, we read,

> And the Word became flesh and made his dwelling among us, and we saw his glory, the glory as of the Father's only Son, full of grace and truth.
>
> JOHN 1:14

God has revealed to us through Sacred Scripture and Sacred Tradition that his only begotten Son assumed our human nature while remaining fully God. This means that Jesus is both true God and true man.

? What does it mean to know that Jesus is both God and human?

Jesus the Christ – the Incarnation

The New Adam

The early Church called Jesus the New Adam. The Incarnation was the beginning of the new creation, the beginning of restoring God's plan of creation. Jesus, the New Adam brings eternal life.

The Word of God became a man so that we could be redeemed and share in the divine life. In him, God's plan of Salvation and Redemption came true. Because Jesus is fully divine, he brought God's forgiveness and healing to those in need. He taught us how God wants us to live and how to love all people.

Because Jesus was fully human, he experienced joy and sadness, peace and suffering because he was fully human. He thought with a human mind, acted with a human will, worked with human hands, and loved with a human heart. Jesus is a Divine Person with both a human and divine nature. This is a great mystery of faith.

? How does God's plan of Salvation and Redemption affect you?

Activity Read the following Scripture passages. Write how each passage reminds you more of the human or divine nature of Jesus.

John 1:1–5

_____

_____

_____

_____

John 11:32–36

_____

_____

_____

_____

FAITH VOCABULARY

Christ
This title of Jesus identifies him as the Messiah, the Anointed One, whom God sent to save all of humanity.

Lord
This title of Jesus indicates his divine sovereignty, or power.

In His Name

While Jesus lived on Earth and did the work his Father sent him to do, not everyone came to believe he was **Christ**, the Savior and Messiah. Some people were confused and hesitant to believe. Others were hostile.

On one occasion Jesus talked to his disciples about this. He asked them who people said the Son of Man was. They replied,

"Some say John the Baptist, others Elijah, still others Jeremiah or one of the prophets."

MATTHEW 16:14

Then, Jesus asked his disciples, "Who do you say that I am?" Only Peter the Apostle spoke out and confessed his faith in Jesus. Simon Peter said in reply,

"You are the Messiah, the Son of the living God."

MATTHEW 16:16

Like Peter, we too, led by the Holy Spirit, confess our faith in Jesus. We believe in the faith as handed down to us by the Apostles.

? What does it mean to you when you hear that Jesus is the Messiah?

Jesus Is

- **Jesus is Lord.** In Sacred Scripture, the word "Lord" is used for God. Jesus is the Son of the living God. He is the Second Person of the Holy Trinity and is intimately one with the Father in the Holy Spirit (see John 12:44–45; 1 Corinthians 12:3).

- **Jesus is true God and true man.** The Son of God became true man without giving up his divinity. The Son of God became like us in all things but sin. We call this the mystery of the Incarnation (see John 1:14).

- **Jesus is the One whom God promised** to send to deliver his people and to lead them to live the Covenant faithfully. The name of Jesus means "God saves." Jesus is the Messiah and Savior. The title Messiah, or Christ, means "Anointed One."

- **Jesus Christ is the one and only Mediator,** or "go-between," who links God and the human family. He alone reconciles the human family with God (see 1 Timothy 2:5–6; Hebrews 9:15–28).

Being a Christian is not only knowing and believing that Jesus is Lord, the Son of God, the Savior of the World, but also living as his faithful disciples, as Saint Lawrence did.

 Who do you say Jesus is?

Activity In the word search, find and circle names for Jesus.

```
L O R D G C B M T Z Y C
G Z N W O H M E S U M J
I S O N D R D S C A E E
C P S G S I E S H Q D L
G Z B A A S D I R E I I
O Q W G V T I A K T A Z
D B D S E I A H U Y T S
A M A N S S O H C A O A
B C G H A B T R Y B R S
V V T S P Y R S U S E J
C A R L O S Q A N U E L
```

FAITH FOCUS
What was Mary's role in
God's plan of Salvation?

The Mysteries of Salvation

Mary is the first disciple of Jesus. She is the first and greatest Saint of the Church. Mary always points us to Christ. We can look to Mary to teach us and help keep our eyes fixed on Jesus. Mary gazed on the human face of her son, Jesus, and saw God. She kept in her heart the beautiful mystery of her son, Jesus Christ, the Son of God. We are to honor Mary as our mother too, and our hearts are to be like hers.

The Church has given us the Rosary to help us join with Mary and always keep our lives centered on Jesus. There are twenty mysteries of the Rosary. The word *mysteries* points to the mystery of Salvation. There are five Joyful Mysteries, five Sorrowful Mysteries, five Luminous Mysteries, and five Glorious Mysteries. Here is a list of the Joyful Mysteries:

1. The Annunciation (see Luke 1:26–38)

2. The Visitation (see Luke 1:39–49)

3. The Nativity (see Luke 2:1–14)

4. The Presentation in the Temple (see Luke 2:22–38)

5. The Finding of the Child Jesus After Three Days in the Temple (see Luke 2:41–52)

Because of Mary's unique role in God's plan of Salvation, at the end of her earthly life, she was taken up, body and soul, into Heaven. This is called Mary's Assumption. The Church encourages us to pray the Rosary in her honor. It is one way we can bless and honor God with Mary. The Church celebrate October as the Month of the Holy Rosary.

? How would you explain to someone the role Mary plays in God's plan of Salvation?

Activity Design a poster encouraging classmates to participate in the Month of the Holy Rosary. Include events, and reasons that will motivate students to take part.

I FOLLOW JESUS

Mary teaches us how to be humble disciples of Jesus. She is the virgin Mother of Jesus. Because Jesus is the Son of God, Mary is the Mother of God.

THE STORY OF MARY

Review what you learned about Mary in this chapter. Use the Gospel stories and mysteries of the Rosary to assist you. Write your story, give it a title, and illustrate it.

MY FAITH CHOICE

Having reflected on Mary's humility, I will try to be humble this week. I will

_____

_____

_____

Pray, "Heavenly Father, I praise you for giving me this opportunity to act with a humble heart. Amen."

1. God the Father chose the Blessed Virgin Mary to be the Mother of his Son.

2. Jesus is the Second Person of the Trinity who is the Messiah, Christ, or "Anointed One." He is true God and true man.

3. The Rosary is a prayer in which we reflect on the Mysteries of Salvation.

Chapter Review

Recall

Complete the crossword puzzle.

Down

1. The Son of God, the Messiah and Savior

2. The belief that the Son of God became man

3. The Mother of Jesus, the Mother of God

Across

4. The prayerful meditation on events in the life of Jesus and Mary

5. The virtue related to "poverty in spirit"

Reflect

Explain how Jesus is the New Adam for you.

_____

_____

_____

_____

_____

_____

_____

_____

_____

Share Explain how people today are still experiencing the results of the first sin. Share God's plan for Salvation in your own words to your class.

Hail, Holy Queen

We conclude the praying of the Rosary by praying the prayer, Hail, Holy Queen. Catholics have been praying this prayer since the 1100s. Originally written in Latin, it is now prayed around the world.

Here is the Hail, Holy Queen in Polish and English. Pray the Hail, Holy Queen together in the language you know.

Group 1: The angel spoke God's message to Mary,

Group 2: and she conceived of the Holy Spirit.

**All: Hail, holy Queen, Mother of mercy:
Hail, our life, our sweetness,
    and our hope.
To you do we cry, poor banished
    children of Eve.
To you do we send up our sighs,
mourning and weeping
    in this valley of tears.
Turn then, most gracious advocate,
your eyes of mercy toward us;
and after this our exile
show unto us the blessed fruit
    of your womb, Jesus.
O clement, O loving, O sweet
    Virgin Mary.**

Group 1: "I am the lowly servant of the Lord:

Group 2: let it be done to me according to your word."

All: *Witaj Królowo, Matko Miłosierdzia,
życie, słodyczy i nadziejo nasza, witaj!
Do Ciebie wołamy
wygnańcy, synowie Ewy,
do Ciebie wzdychamy jęcząc i płacząc
na tym łez padole.
Przeto, Orędowniczko nasza,
one miłosierne oczy Twoje na nas
    zwróć,
a Jezusa, błogosławiony owoc
    żywota Twojego,
po tym wygnaniu nam okaż.
O łaskawa, o litościwa, o słodka
    Panno Maryjo!*

With My Family

This Week . . .

In Chapter 5, "Son of God, Son of Mary," your child learned:

▶ God the Father chose the Blessed Virgin Mary to be the Mother of Jesus, the Son of God, who became one of us without giving up being God.

▶ In Jesus Christ, the Son of God and the Son of Mary, God's promise and plan of Salvation are fulfilled.

▶ In praying the Rosary, we can honor Mary and meditate on the life of Christ.

▶ Mary is the first and model disciple of her Son. She demonstrates the virtue of humility in her words and deeds, acknowledging that all her blessings are from God.

For more about about related teachings of the Church, see the *Catechism of the Catholic Church,* 422–570, and the *United States Catholic Catechism for Adults,* pages 77–87.

■ Sharing God's Word

Read together Hebrews 2:8–18. Emphasize that Jesus is Lord, yet became human even unto death. In Christ, we are adopted children of God. Christ has reconciled us with God, who promises us eternal life if we live according to the Gospel.

■ We Live as Disciples

The Christian home and family is a school of discipleship. Choose one of the following activities to do as a family, or design a similar activity of your own:

▶ Talk about some of the choices your family has made. How are these choices signs of your faith in Jesus Christ? Reflect on your celebration of the Christmas season. Decide as a family what Christian choices you can make amid the popular consumerism of the season.

▶ Humility can be a difficult virtue for preadolescent sixth graders, who are trying to maintain independence and autonomy. Discuss practical ways your family can live this virtue. Remind your child that humility is not a sign of weakness, but of a strong faith and relationship with God.

▶ Pray the Rosary as a family at home, especially on a feast of Mary, making sure each family member has his or her own rosary. Also participate in a family Rosary at your parish, if and when it is prayed.

■ Our Spiritual Journey

Praying the Rosary helps us see how Mary always points us to Jesus. In this chapter, your child prayed part of the Rosary. Read and pray together the prayer on page 75.

For more ideas on ways your family can live as disciples of Jesus, visit **BeMyDisciples.com**

Looking Ahead

In this chapter, the Holy Spirit invites you to ▶

EXPLORE why Paul of the Cross preached about mercy.

DISCOVER that God's plan of Salvation is found in Jesus Christ.

DECIDE how to witness faith and show mercy to others.

CHAPTER

6

The Suffering Servant

? Why would someone suffer for the sake of another?

Listen to how God describes the Messiah:

> "See, my servant shall prosper,
> he shall be raised high and greatly exalted.
> Even as many were amazed at him—
> so marred was his look beyond that of man,
> and his appearance beyond that of mortals—
> So shall he startle many nations,
> because of him kings shall stand speechless . . .
> Because he surrendered himself to death
> and was counted among the wicked;
> And he shall take away the sins of many,
> and win pardon for their offenses." Isaiah 52:13–15; 53:12

? In what ways do you think this reading describes Jesus?

Saint Paul of the Cross

Disciple Power

Mercy

This fruit of charity is the loving kindness and compassion shown to one who offends us. Even though our sins damage our relationship with God, he still loves us. Throughout his life, Jesus taught how the love of God is one of mercy. Jesus, the Son of God, suffered and died for our sake. Truly, the Paschal Mystery reveals the depths of God's mercy for us.

The Paschal Mystery (the Passion, Death, Resurrection, and Ascension of Jesus Christ) is the heart of the Gospel. For Paolo (Paul) Francesco Daneo, the Passion and Resurrection of Christ was the greatest work of divine love. He understood the depths of God's merciful love revealed in the Paschal Mystery.

Paolo lived in northern Italy during the early 1700s. His father was a wealthy merchant and expected Paolo to continue the business, but Paolo was not sure what he wanted out of life. He volunteered to be in the army for a time, but then had several experiences in prayer that made him realize that God called him to do something else with his life.

Paolo noticed that people were ungrateful for God's love. Paolo believed neglect and ungratefulness were signs that people had forgotten the meaning of God's love for all people, revealed in the Paschal Mystery. He wrote, "The world lives unmindful of the sufferings of Jesus which are the miracle of miracles of the love of God."

Paolo decided to help people become more aware of God's love working in the world, especially the Passion of our Lord Jesus Christ. Dressed in a black robe, he traveled tirelessly for many years throughout Italy, preaching a message of faith and mercy. Wherever he went, he carried a large wooden cross and preached that Jesus' Passion was one of the greatest signs of God's love.

? How is the Cross a sign of God's love for you?

The Passionists

Paolo founded the "Congregation of the Passion," or the Passionists, to help him in his work. The priests that joined his religious order gave parish missions and retreats especially in areas where there were few priests and the people had great spiritual needs. Paolo and the priests in his religious orders also trained other priests to help those who were poor and uneducated. Because of his faith and work, the Church honors Paolo as Saint Paul of the Cross.

Today, there are more than two thousand Passionists who preach the message of the cross in fifty-two nations on five continents. They see Jesus in people who are suffering. They believe that when they help the suffering, they are helping Jesus who said,

"Amen, I say to you, what you did not do for one of these least ones, you did not do for me."

MATTHEW 25:40

? Why does an understanding of the Paschal Mystery help us to reach out to assist those who are suffering?

Activity In each part of the cross, name three ways that people can be led to follow Jesus today.

FAITH VOCABULARY

Paschal Mystery
The Paschal Mystery is Jesus' passing over from life on Earth through his Passion, Death, Resurrection and Ascension to a new and glorified life with the Father.

Salvation
Salvation is the deliverance of humanity from the power of sin and death by God through Jesus Christ, who died for our sins in accordance with the Scriptures.

The Paschal Mystery

Believe it or not, the Gospels were not the first written books of the New Testament. The letters to early Christian communities were the first written parts of the New Testament. Because of the importance of the Gospels, however, the Church placed them at the beginning of that part of the Bible. The authors of the Gospels are Matthew, Mark, Luke, and John. They tell the story of Jesus' life, teaching, and actions.

At the heart of the Gospels is the **Paschal Mystery** of Jesus. The Paschal Mystery is the center of the work that God the Father sent Jesus, his Son, to do on Earth. The word *paschal* comes from a Hebrew word meaning "the passing over." The Paschal Mystery is Jesus' passing over from life on Earth to a new and glorified life with God the Father and God the Holy Spirit.

The Mission of Jesus

The New Testament reveals the fulfillment of God's plan of **Salvation** for all people in Jesus Christ. Jesus shows us how we can respond to God the Father by the way we know, love, and serve him.

While the Old Testament records the events that prepared humankind for the coming of the Messiah, all Scripture is centered on the Person of Jesus Christ. Jesus is the Son of God, the Messiah, the Chosen One, who saved humanity from sin (read Mark 14:61–62; John 19:24).

How would you describe the mission of Jesus?

The Heart of Sacred Scripture

Through the Gospels, there are examples of Jesus being recognized as the Son of God, the Messiah. Two key moments when Jesus is recognized as King and Savior are first. When Jesus rode into Jerusalem on a colt, everyone began to praise God with shouts of joy:

> "Blessed is the king who comes
> in the name of the Lord.
> Peace in heaven
> and glory in the highest."
>
> LUKE 19:38

And second, at the Crucifixion when the centurion and other men watching Jesus die on the cross exclaimed,

> "Truly, this was the Son of God!"
>
> MATTHEW 27:54

The Gospels are the heart of all Sacred Scripture, and the mission of Jesus is the centerpiece of the Gospels.

? What are the ways you show others that you are helping to carry on the mission of Jesus?

Catholics Believe

The Paschal Mystery

The Paschal Mystery has two aspects: by his Death, Christ liberates us from sin; by his Resurrection, he opens for us the way to a new life. Christ's Resurrection is the principle and source of our future resurrection. The Risen Christ lives in the hearts of his faithful while they await that fulfillment.

Activity The ⊂× (fish) is an ancient Christian symbol for Jesus Christ. Reflect on the meaning of the Paschal Mystery. Draw a symbol that expresses your faith in this mystery.

FAITH FOCUS
Why is Jesus the fulfillment
of all of God's promises?

FAITH VOCABULARY
Passion
The Passion is the suffering of
Jesus on his way to the Cross
and his Death on the Cross.

He Freely Suffered Death

Each of the four Gospels includes a Passion narrative. These recountings of Jesus' suffering and Death begin at Matthew 27:32; Mark 15:21; and Luke 23:26–32. In the Gospel of John, the Crucifixion is described:

> So they took Jesus, and carrying the cross himself he went out to what is called the Place of the Skull, in Hebrew, Golgotha. There they crucified him, and with him two others, one on either side, with Jesus in the middle.
>
> JOHN 19:17–18

The Gospel narratives of the Passion tell of the suffering of Jesus as he made his way to the Cross and was crucified on it. Holy Week in the season of Lent we recall Jesus' love for us in his suffering and Death. On Good Friday, we remember Jesus' Death upon the Cross by venerating the Cross.

Jesus sacrificed his life by freely accepting death on a Cross. He was buried and three days later rose from the dead. Christ went down to the dead and opened the gates of Heaven for the just who had gone before him and for those who would come after him.

? Why is the cross an important symbol for you as a follower of Jesus Christ?

The Meaning of Jesus' Sacrifice

The **Passion** and Resurrection of our Lord Jesus Christ took place during the Jewish feast of Passover. Just as a lamb was sacrificed to save the Israelites, Jesus freely sacrificed his life on the Cross to save all people from the power of sin and death. As John the Baptist declared:

> "Behold, the Lamb of God, who takes away the sin of the world."
>
> JOHN 1:29

The Last Supper was a Passover meal, but Jesus gave it new meaning. At the Last Supper, Jesus blessed the bread and wine, and then distributed them as his Body and Blood.

> Then he took the bread, said the blessing, broke it, and gave it to them, saying, "This is my body, which will be given for you; do this in memory of me." And likewise the cup after they had eaten, saying, "This cup is the new covenant in my blood, which will be shed for you."
>
> LUKE 22:19–20

The Eucharist is a memorial of Jesus' Passover—his work of Salvation through his suffering, Death, Resurrection, and Ascension. His Body and Blood enabled his followers to be redeemed from sin and find eternal happiness in the Kingdom of God.

? What does it mean to you that Jesus suffered death for your sake?

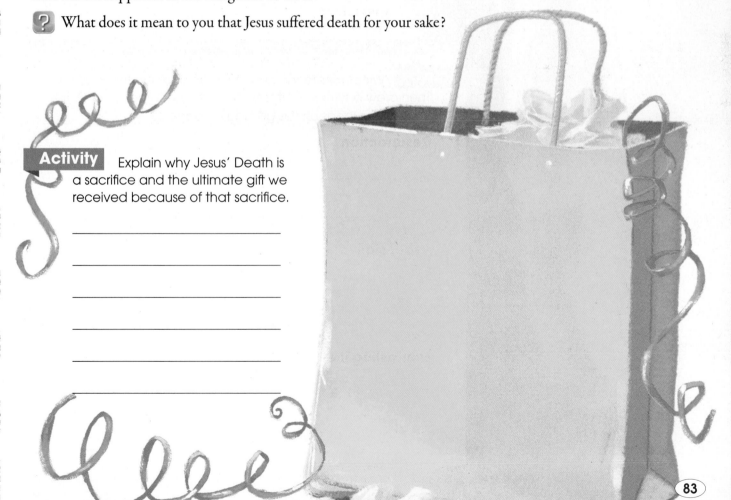

Activity Explain why Jesus' Death is a sacrifice and the ultimate gift we received because of that sacrifice.

_____

_____

_____

_____

_____

_____

The Resurrection by Anton Laurids Johannes Dorph

The Risen Lord

Three days after Jesus died and was buried, Christ rose from the dead with a new and glorified body. All four accounts of the Gospel clearly teach that this event took place. The Resurrection of Jesus is at the heart of our faith in Christ (see 1 Corinthians 15:3–4).

Forty days after the Resurrection, the Risen Christ ascended to the Father in Heaven. God's domain, Heaven, is where Jesus, the Son of God, reigns gloriously at the right hand of God the Father (see Luke 24:50–53). From there, Christ, who is hidden from our eyes, will come again in glory at the end of time to judge the living and the dead (see Matthew 25:31–46). Through Christ's Ascension and exaltation in glory, all humanity has been given an unbreakable promise of everlasting life of happiness with the Trinity, with the angels, and with Mary and all the Saints (see Revelation 22:4–5).

This great mystery of God's love for us is the center of the Gospel, or Good News. Through the Paschal Mystery, all things have been justified, or made right, in Christ with God. Through him, we are saved and will rise to life everlasting.

? When you think of Heaven, what do you picture in your mind?

Activity Write a sentence describing each of the terms below. Then draw a symbol that represents the Resurrection of Christ. Sketch your ideas on the gift bag on page 83.

Resurrection

_____

_____

Ascension

_____

_____

Everlasting life

_____

_____

I FOLLOW JESUS

The Paschal Mystery is at the center of the Gospel. Jesus asks us to share with others our faith in what he has done for all people. Through his actions, we are saved and will rise to eternal life. We, in turn, are to show mercy to others.

LIVING OUR FAITH IN JESUS

You are to be interviewed by a reporter for a Catholic magazine about your faith in Jesus. What example from your life would you like to share? Write your notes for the interview here.

_____

_____

_____

_____

_____

_____

_____

_____

_____

MY FAITH CHOICE

Mercy is one of the virtues of a disciple. I will show mercy to others this week. I will

_____

_____

 Pray, "Lord help me to show mercy to others in my words and actions. Amen."

TO HELP YOU REMEMBER

1. The Paschal Mystery is the Passion, Death, Resurrection, and Ascension of Jesus Christ.

2. Jesus Christ suffered Death for the Redemption and Salvation of humanity.

3. The Resurrection is the principle and source of our future resurrection.

Recall

Write a sentence using all of these words.

Salvation	Passion	Crucifixion	Resurrection	Ascension

_____

_____

_____

_____

Reflect

Why do you think Jesus had to be sacrificed on the Cross so that Salvation could come to the world?

_____

_____

_____

_____

_____

_____

_____

_____

_____

Share Describe the meaning of each of the events of the Paschal Mystery. Share what this means to you in your life.

Stations of the Cross

This Scripture-based version of the Stations has been given to us by Blessed Pope John Paul II. It differs slightly from the traditional Stations which can be found on page 373. Prayerfully journey in silence the Way of the Cross with Jesus.

Leader: Lord Jesus, be with us as we remember your Passion and Death.

1. Jesus in the Garden of Gethsemane.

2. Jesus, betrayed by Judas, is arrested.

3. Jesus is condemned by the Sanhedrin.

4. Jesus is denied by Peter.

5. Jesus is judged by Pilate.

6. Jesus is scourged and crowned with thorns.

7. Jesus takes up his Cross.

8. Jesus is helped by Simon of Cyrene to carry his Cross.

9. Jesus meets the women of Jerusalem.

10. Jesus is crucified.

11. Jesus promises redemption to the good thief.

12. Jesus is on the Cross, with his mother and Saint John at the foot of the Cross.

13. Jesus dies on the Cross.

14. Jesus is placed in the tomb.

Leader: *(after each station)*
We adore you, O Christ, and we bless you.

All: **By your holy Cross, you have saved us and set us free.**

With My Family

This Week . . .

In Chapter 6, "The Suffering Servant," your child learned:

▶ God's plan of Salvation is fulfilled in Jesus Christ, the Son of God.

▶ Through the Paschal Mystery, Christ has saved and redeemed all of humanity, revealing the depths of God's mercy for us.

▶ Three days after he died and was buried, Christ rose from the dead with a new and glorified body.

▶ We have received the promise of eternal life made possible by Jesus Christ, the Son of God.

▶ The virtue of mercy is the loving kindness and compassion shown to one who offends. The Paschal Mystery reveals the depths of God's mercy for us.

For more about related teachings of the Church, see the *Catechism of the Catholic Church*, 571–682, and the *United States Catholic Catechism for Adults*, pages 90–110.

◼ Sharing God's Word

Read together Hebrews 9:15–28. Emphasize that Jesus, the Savior of the world, alone reconciles the human family with God.

◼ We Live as Disciples

The Christian home and family is a school of discipleship. Choose one of the following activities to do as a family, or design a similar activity of your own:

▶ Talk about some of the choices that your family has made recently. How are these decisions signs of your faith in Jesus Christ?

▶ Discuss why standing up for one's faith is sometimes difficult. When would you be willing to stand up for your faith?

▶ When we pray the Sign of the Cross, we profess our faith in Jesus, who freely died on the Cross to save us from sin and death. This week, pray the Sign of the Cross every time you begin to pray.

◼ Our Spiritual Journey

Praying the Stations of the Cross helps us meditate on Jesus' loving sacrifice, both individually and as a community. In this chapter, your child prayed the scriptural Stations of the Cross. Read and pray together the prayer on page 87. Consider taking your children to church to walk the Way of the Cross.

For more ideas on ways your family can live as disciples of Jesus, visit **BeMyDisciples.com**

Looking Ahead

In this chapter, the Holy Spirit invites you to ▶

EXPLORE how the Holy Spirit guided Saint Benedict to use the gift of counsel.

DISCOVER the work of the Holy Spirit within the Church.

DECIDE how you will take part in the work of the Church.

CHAPTER

7

The Holy Spirit

❓ Why is it sometimes difficult to obey rules?

The writer of Psalm 143 may have realized he needed God's help to obey his Laws. Join with him as he prays:

> [LORD,] teach me to do your will,
>   for you are my God.
> May your kind spirit guide me
>   on ground that is level.
>
> PSALM 143:10

❓ How do you know that the Holy Spirit will guide you to do what is right and good?

Disciple Power

Counsel

Counsel, or right judgment, is one of the seven Gifts of the Holy Spirit. This gift, or grace, helps a person sense the moral truth about how to live. The gift of counsel is the ability to judge correctly the daily activity of our lives according to God's will. The source of this gift is the Holy Spirit, who empowers us to form our conscience properly.

St. Benedict (oil on panel), Perugino, Pietro (c. 1445–1523)

Saint Benedict and Saint Scholastica

Christians need one another live the Gospel. Saint Benedict lived in Nursia, Italy, from A.D. 480 to 547. He came from a wealthy family but he left home as a young man to find a way to follow God. Benedict wanted to be alone with God and decided to become a hermit. He lived in a cave for three years, praying and fasting. According to legend, a raven would sometimes bring him food, which is why pictures of Benedict often show him with this bird.

Benedict was not alone for long. Soon men came to learn from this holy man who lived on the mountain. They also wanted to live lives dedicated to God and felt sure that Benedict was holy and could lead them. Soon Benedict found himself in charge of more than a hundred men. He gave them a motto: "Pray and work." He organized them so that they could live together in peace. They cleared the land, planted crops, prayed, and fasted.

Eventually, Benedict and the men with him moved to the top of a mountain and built a home there. It is called Monte Cassino. Nearly fifteen hundred years later, Benedict's Monte Cassino still exists and men still follow the way of life he set forth for them.

? Benedict's motto was "Pray and work." What is your motto of faith?

Saints Benedict and Scholastica

The Rule of Saint Benedict

Benedict wrote a rule of life that spelled out a clear way to live the Gospel in a monastic setting. A monastery is a place where a group of religious people live and work together under a common set of rules. The Rule of Saint Benedict is based on a life of peace as one works and prays in imitation of Christ.

Benedict's rules were so helpful that people came from many places to live together and follow them. Saint Scholastica (A.D. 480 to 543), Benedict's twin sister, was the first woman to choose to follow his rule of life. Soon other women came to live together to follow the same rules.

The followers of Saint Benedict and Saint Scholastica are baptized Christians who consecrate their lives to God. They are known as Benedictines. According to the rules, Benedictines are led by an abbot (for male communities) or a prioress (for female communities). The leader, guided by the Holy Spirit, is responsible for counseling the members on how to live a Christian life.

The Holy Spirit guided Benedict in his own personal life and empowered him to establish his set of rules through the gift of counsel or right judgment. With the aid of the Rule of Saint Benedict, Benedictines today live as disciples of Christ.

 What are ways you can you choose to live a life of peace?

Activity List a good rule by which you can live at home, at school, and in your neighborhood.

Home_____

_____

School_____

_____

Neighborhood_____

_____

FAITH FOCUS
What is the work of the
Holy Spirit in the Church?

FAITH VOCABULARY

Gospels
The Gospels are the first four
books of the New Testament
that pass on the faith of the
Church in Jesus Christ and
in the saving events of the
Paschal Mystery.

Pentecost
Pentecost is the liturgical
feast and holy day when
the Church celebrates the
coming of the Holy Spirit on
the disciples and the birth
of the Church.

The Holy Spirit at Work

In the New Testament, there are four written accounts of the Gospel. They are the **Gospels** according to Matthew, Mark, Luke, and John. Through the guidance of the Holy Spirit, each passes on the faith of the Church in Jesus Christ and in the saving events of the Paschal Mystery. Each announces the Good News of Salvation in Jesus, who is the Lord and Savior of the world.

The four Gospels formed over three different stages. The first stage belongs to the very words and deeds of Jesus. These were directly experienced and remembered by his first followers.

The second stage belongs to the time of the Apostles' preaching about Jesus after the Holy Spirit descended upon them at **Pentecost**. The Apostles told other people about Jesus and what he did.

The third stage belongs to the four Evangelists — Matthew, Mark, Luke, and John. The name *Evangelist* means "announcer of good news." Under the inspiration of the Holy Spirit, each Evangelist wrote his account of the Gospel that the Apostles had passed on about Jesus.

 How can reading a passage from a Gospel be Good News to you?

The Gift of the Gospels

Each of the four accounts of the Gospel passes on the faith of the Church in Jesus from four individual perspectives:

- Matthew pays special attention to the rich Jewish heritage of the Church and to the great teachings of Jesus. For example, one of Jesus' greatest teachings was how to treat people we do not like. Jesus taught:

  "But I say to you, love your enemies, and pray for those who persecute you." MATTHEW 5:44

- Mark emphasizes what it means to be a disciple of Jesus and to walk with him toward the Cross. In this Gospel, Jesus is often shown explaining that it will not be easy to be his follower.

- Luke shows how Salvation in Jesus embraces all people, especially those who are most in need. He healed a Roman centurion's slave (Luke 7:1–10), a crippled woman (Luke 13:10–13), a blind beggar (Luke 18:35–43), ten lepers (Luke 17:11–19), and forgave others their sins, such as the tax collector Zacchaeus (Luke 19:1–10).

- John reflects on the inner meaning of Jesus' words and deeds and writes in a poetic style. His Gospel begins with a beautiful ancient hymn,

  In the beginning was the Word,
  and the Word was with God,
  and the Word was God.

  JOHN 1:1

? Which Gospel do you think you would find most interesting? Why?

Catholics Believe

Social Teachings

The social teachings of the Catholic Church are a set of teachings which provide the basic principles to guide us in how we are to build up the Church and fulfill her work in the world. If we open our hearts and minds to the guidance of the Holy Spirit, living according to these principles will lead us to holiness and a just society. The first and most fundamental principle is the life and dignity of the human person.

Activity Read Matthew 26:6–13, Mark 14:3–9, Luke 7:36–50 and John 12:1–8. Compare how the same event is reported in different ways.

Matthew _____

Mark _____

Luke _____

John _____

FAITH FOCUS
What is the work of the
Holy Spirit in the Church?

The Age of the Spirit

Before Jesus was crucified, he told his disciples that he was going send then an Advocate, or a Helper. After his Resurrection, Jesus appeared to his disciples and told them to wait in the city of Jerusalem,

> ". . . the promise of the Father about which you have heard me speak; for John baptized with water, but in a few days you will be baptized with the holy Spirit."
>
> ACTS 1:4–5

The disciples waited and fifty days after Jesus rose from the dead, the Holy Spirit came to the disciples as promised. This was during the Jewish feast of Pentecost, a time to celebrate God's blessings.

> And suddenly there came from the sky a noise like a strong driving wind, and it filled the entire house in which they were. Then there appeared to them tongues as of fire, which parted and came to rest on each one of them. And they were all filled with the holy Spirit and began to speak in different tongues, as the Spirit enabled them to proclaim.
>
> ACTS 2:2–4

Filled with enthusiasm, Peter the Apostle and the other disciples went into the streets of Jerusalem. There Peter boldly proclaimed the Gospel. People who had come to Jerusalem from many countries to celebrate the Jewish feast of Pentecost listened to Peter and heard him in their own language. Moved by the Holy Spirit, thousands were baptized (read Acts 1:14–41).

? If you had been with the disciples, how do you think the coming of the Holy Spirit would change you?

The Spirit at Work in the World

When Christians think of the Holy Spirit, we might think that the Holy Spirit waited until Pentecost to begin working among the People of God. The truth is that the Holy Spirit has always been at work in the world. We read about the Holy Spirit in the story of creation (see Genesis 2:7; Psalm 104: 30), and with the prophets of the Old Testament (see Zechariah 4:5-6). We also read about the work of the Holy Spirit in the lives of Mary and all of the disciples.

The Holy Spirit was always with Jesus, the Son of God. When he began his public ministry, Jesus announced in the synagogue at Nazareth, *"The Spirit of the Lord is upon me"* (Luke 4:18). The mission of Jesus, the Son of God, and the Holy Spirit always go together. The Holy Trinity always works together. The Father, Son, and the Holy Spirit cannot be separated.

Today on Pentecost, we celebrate the beginning of the work that Jesus commissioned the Church to do (read Matthew 28: 16-20). The Church is a sign and instrument of God's communion with all humanity and a sign in the world of the unity of the whole human race. God's promise made to Abraham came true in Christ. The Holy Spirit inspires the Church to boldly proclaim the Gospel.

? In what ways can the Holy Spirit help you in your daily life?

Activity The qualities that the Holy Spirit brings into our lives are called the Fruits of the Holy Spirit. Give an example of how you might live each of these.

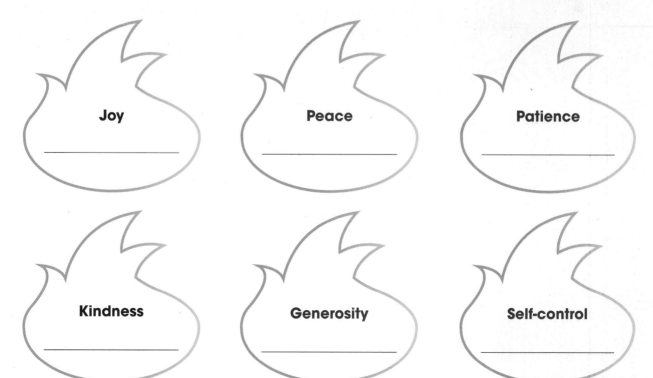

Joy _____

Peace _____

Patience _____

Kindness _____

Generosity _____

Self-control _____

FAITH FOCUS
What does it mean to be
Temples of the Holy Spirit?

FAITH VOCABULARY
charism
A charism is a grace of the
Holy Spirit given to build
up the Church and to help
the Church fulfill her work
in the world.

Temple of the Holy Spirit

The Gospel of John tells us that when the crucified Jesus saw his mother and the disciple he loved standing by the Cross, he said,

> " 'Woman, behold, your son.' Then he said to the disciple, 'Behold, your mother.' "
>
> JOHN 19:26–27

The "beloved disciple" who is at the foot of the Cross stands for all of us who are Jesus' disciples. Mary, the Mother of God, is the mother of all who follow her Son, Jesus. Mary is the Mother of Jesus and the Mother of the Church, the Body of Christ. Mary is the first among all followers of Jesus. We praise her as blessed among all women because of the fruit of her womb, Jesus. The Holy Spirit is always with her (see Luke 1:35).

In his first Letter to the Corinthians, Saint Paul asks the Christian community in Corinth,

> "Do you not know that your body is a temple of the holy Spirit within you, whom you have from God?"
>
> I CORINTHIANS 6:19

The Holy Spirit dwells within each of the baptized and within the whole Church. The Church is the temple of the Holy Spirit.

The Holy Spirit is the source of the Church's life and of her unity as the one People of God. The Holy Spirit is also the one source of the richness of the Church's many gifts and **charisms**.

? What does it mean to say we should be "temples of the Holy Spirit?"

Activity Imagine that you could live in a city or town where the Holy Spirit guides everyone. Describe the look of this city or town. Create a story board showing three things that would happen there.

I FOLLOW JESUS

As a member of the Church, the Holy Spirit dwells within you, giving you the grace to live the Gospel. Among the graces we receive at Baptism are the seven Gifts of the Holy Spirit. These gifts, which are strengthened at Confirmation, help you to take part in the life and work of the Church.

GIFTS OF THE HOLY SPIRIT

Review the seven Gifts of the Holy Spirit found below. Choose three of them and think of people in your family, school, or neighborhood who have these gifts. Name the three people and what gifts they exhibit. Then write a profile (short description) of one of these people.

wisdom   understanding   knowledge
counsel   piety   fortitude
fear of the Lord

Name _____ **Gift** _____

Name _____ **Gift** _____

Name _____ **Gift** _____

Profile of _____

_____

_____

_____

MY FAITH CHOICE

This week, I will use the gift of counsel, or right judgment, to help the Church fulfill her mission of proclaiming the Gospel. I will

_____

_____

_____ .

 Pray, "Come Holy Spirit, fill my heart and enkindle in me the fire of your love. Amen."

TO HELP YOU REMEMBER

1. The Holy Spirit is at work bringing about God's plan of Salvation within the Church.

2. The Holy Spirit strengthens the Church to be a sign of Christ's love for humanity and enables us to proclaim the Gospel.

3. With the Gifts of the Holy Spirit, we can help continue the mission of the Church.

Recall

Use the code to discover this important message about the Gospel.

A	B	C	D	E	F	G	H	I	J	K	L	M
1	2	3	4	5	6	7	8	9	10	11	12	13

N	O	P	Q	R	S	T	U	V	W	X	Y	Z
14	15	16	17	18	19	20	21	22	23	24	25	26

___ ___ ___ ___ ___ ___ ___ ___ ___
4x5 12–4 10÷2   12–5 3x5 24–5 4x4 10÷2 6+6

___ ___ ___ ___ ___ ___ ___ ___ ___
6–5 2x7 12+2 3x5 22–1 9+5 3+0 10÷2 24–5

___ ___ ___
4x5 12–4 10÷2

___ ___ ___ ___ ___ ___ ___
21–10 3x3 28÷2 19–12 2x2 5x3 26÷2

___ ___ ___ ___ ___
3+12 18–12   13–6 8+7 19–15

Reflect

Describe the qualities of a person, like Mary, who is a temple of the Holy Spirit.

_____

_____

_____

_____

_____

_____

_____

Share Work with a partner to write a sentence for each Gospel summarizing what is unique about that Gospel. Tell how you can help share in the mission of Jesus.

Prayer of Intercession

In the prayer of intercession, we pray for others. Jesus constantly prayed for his followers. Let us listen to the prayer of Jesus in the Gospel of John and pray for others to the Father as Jesus did.

Leader: Lord, we gather to listen to your Word. May we always live as the one People of God.

Reader: A reading from the holy Gospel according to John.

All: Glory to you, O Lord.

Reader: *I pray not only for them, but also for those who believe in me through their word, so that they may all be one, as you, Father, are in me and I in you, that they also may be in us, that the world may believe that you sent me.*

JOHN 17:20–21

The Gospel of the Lord.

All: Praise to you, Lord Jesus Christ.

Leader: For those who live in war-torn areas, may they know God's peace.

All: Lord, hear our prayer.

Leader: For those who are ill, may they be given the medical care to ease their pain and suffering.

All: Lord, hear our prayer.
(Pray for others who need God's help.)

Leader: Lord God, Father of all, fill all who call upon you with the love of the Holy Spirit. Make us one in the fullness of faith and fellowship of love. We ask this through Jesus Christ, your Son, who lives and reigns with you and the Holy Spirit, one God, for ever and ever.

All: Amen.

With My Family

This Week . . .

In Chapter 7, "The Holy Spirit," your child learned:

▶ The Gospel is the announcement of the Good News of Salvation in Jesus Christ. The four Evangelists—Matthew, Mark, Luke, and John—wrote their accounts under the inspiration of the Holy Spirit.

▶ The Holy Spirit, the Third Divine Person of the Holy Trinity, is at work within the Church. The Holy Spirit dwells within each of us as members of the one Body of Christ.

▶ As one Church, God calls all the baptized to use the gift of counsel and the other Gifts of the Holy Spirit to take part in the Church's mission, or work, of proclaiming the Gospel.

For more about related teachings of the Church, see the *Catechism of the Catholic Church*, 683–747, 963–975, and the *United States Catholic Catechism for Adults*, pages 102–110, 141-149.

◼ Sharing God's Word

Read together I Corinthians 6:19. Emphasize that the Holy Spirit is the source of the Church's life and her unity as the holy People of God.

◼ We Live as Disciples

The Christian home and family is a school of discipleship. Choose one of the following activities to do as a family, or design a similar activity of your own:

▶ Look at the many things you do as a family. Discuss how each of these helps you take part in the life and work of the Church.

▶ At a family meal, name and talk about the people who help you live the Gospel. Take time to thank God for the gifts they share with your family.

▶ Choose the Gospel of Matthew, Mark, or Luke. As a family, take a short passage and share together your reflection on it.

◼ Our Spiritual Journey

Discernment is a spiritual discipline of the Church that relates to counsel, or right judgment, which is one of the Gifts of the Holy Spirit. Review the steps you take to arrive at a serious decision. Be sure that you are including prayer to the Holy Spirit in your process. Your family decision making as a way of unifying your family's efforts to live the Gospel. In this chapter, your child prayed a prayer of intercession, or praying for others. Read and pray together intercessions for family members and other concerns, based on the prayer found on page 99.

For more ideas on ways your family can live as disciples of Jesus, visit **BeMyDisciples.com**

Looking Ahead

In this chapter, the Holy Spirit invites you to ▶

EXPLORE the life of Saint Marguerite Marie Alacoque.

DISCOVER how the Church is the Sacrament of Salvation.

DECIDE how your life will be an image of the Church for others.

CHAPTER
8

The Mystery of the Church

? If you were describing a member of your family or a friend, what image could you use to help others understand that person's best qualities?

In this prayer, the psalmist used an image to describe God. Quietly read and reflect on this passage:

> The LORD is my strength and my shield,
>   in whom my heart trusted and found help.
> So my heart rejoices;
>   with my song I praise my God.
> LORD, you are the strength of your people. . . .
> Save your people, bless your inheritance;
>   feed and sustain them forever!
>
> PSALM 28:7–9

? What image would you use to describe God?

Peace

Peace is one of the twelve Fruits of the Holy Spirit. Peace on Earth is a reflection of the peace of Christ. Christ has reconciled humanity with God and made the Church the sacrament of unity and peace. Disciples of Jesus are called to be peacemakers.

Saint Marguerite Marie Alacoque

When Marguerite Marie Alacoque was a child in Burgundy, France, more than 360 years ago, she had a strong devotion to the Blessed Sacrament. In fact, she preferred to pray in the peace of silence before the Blessed Sacrament instead of playing with the other children.

At one point, she became seriously ill and was paralyzed. After four years of being confined to her bed, she decided to devote her life to the service of God and the Church. As a result, she was instantly cured and began her life's work.

Marguerite wanted to become a religious sister, but her family hoped she would marry. Eventually, Marguerite's parents agreed, and at the age of twenty-five, she joined the Salesian Sisters.

At a young age, Marguerite had visions of Christ and of Mary. While a Salesian Sister, Marguerite Marie had visions of Christ's heart. In these visions, the Lord showed her a vision of his heart surrounded by flames and circled by a crown of thorns. The flames symbolized his burning love for us, while the crown of thorns symbolized that he sacrificed his life for us.

? What images remind you of Christ's love and peace?

Saint Marguerite Marie Alacoque

Sharing Peace

In these visions, the Lord told Marguerite Marie to set aside a special time for peaceful prayer, a holy hour, in honor of the Sacred Heart of Jesus. Marguerite did what our Lord asked, but the superior of her convent and the local theologians did not think her visions were real. The Lord told her he would send to her a priest who would help her.

This priest was the confessor to the nuns in the convent and he was convinced that Marguerite's visions were genuine. Eventually, he wrote a book about the visions and the Lord's request for a feast day in honor of his Sacred Heart.

When the Catholic Church honors the Sacred Heart of Jesus, the Church is honoring Jesus and his intense love for all of us. The Church honors the Sacred Heart of Jesus with traditional practices of praying before the Blessed Sacrament on the first Friday of the month. It celebrates the Solemnity of the Most Sacred Heart of Jesus on the Friday following the second Sunday after Pentecost.

We can also honor Jesus with acts of charity toward those who suffer. This is a Christan way of bringing a sense of peace to those in need.

? How can we bring a sense of peace to those in need?

Upper Church of Our Lady of the Angels Monastery, Hanceville, AL

Activity Write a prayer in honor of the Sacred Heart of Jesus that will help to bring a sense of peace to others in need.

The Kingdom of God

Jesus Christ established the **Church** with his Apostles and disciples. After the Ascension, the Holy Spirit became the principal guide within the Church. In his writings, Saint Paul teaches that the Church is the Body of Christ, a community of Saints, the Temple of the Holy Spirit, and the Bride of Christ.

Now you are Christ's body, and individually parts of it.

I CORINTHIANS 12:27

These images help us to understand the mystery of the Church as the sacrament of Salvation.

The Communion of Saints

We, as members of the Church, are a communion of "holy people" who participate in God's plan of salvation. The Church is the Communion of Saints. The word *communion* comes from a Latin word meaning "sharing something in common." The Communion of Saints includes all of the faithful members of the Church on Earth and those who have died.

? What does it mean to you that you are part of the Communion of Saints?

The Marks of the Church

The Church has four essential characteristics, or Marks: The Church is one, holy, catholic, and apostolic.

The Church is one. She professes there is "one Lord, one faith, one baptism; one God and Father of all" (Ephesians 4:5–6).

The Church is holy—a "holy nation" living in communion with God the Father, the Son, and the Holy Spirit (see I Peter 2:9). We share in the Seven Sacraments, above all the Eucharist.

The Church is catholic, or universal, inviting all people to become disciples of Jesus, who is the Savior of all people. We share with all people the goods and the blessings that God bestows on us.

The Church is apostolic, that is, rooted in what the Apostles taught in the name of Jesus. The baptized members of the Church share in the charisms of the Holy Spirit. There is an unbroken connection, called apostolic succession, made visible by the Pope, the successor of Saint Peter the Apostle, and the other bishops who are the successors of the other Apostles.

? What are the ways the essential characteristics, or Marks, tell others about the Church and its mission?

Activity Choose one of the Marks of the Church. Decorate the banner with words and images that symbolize that Mark.

God's Reign of Holiness

Like our Old Testament ancestors in faith, who journeyed from slavery in Egypt to freedom in the Promised Land, the Church is a people on a journey of faith. Our destination is the **Kingdom of God.** It will come to completion by God himself at the end of time when Christ will come again in glory.

The Church is both physical and spiritual, both human and divine. Christ is the Head of the Body, and we are the members. All baptized members of the Church—the ordained, the consecrated, and the laity—make up the one Body of Christ. Each member has unique gifts and different responsibilities to build up the Church.

All the baptized, according to their role in the Church, share in the responsibility to evangelize and proclaim the truth of God revealed in Jesus Christ to those who have not heard it or need to hear it again. We are to be Christ to others by living the Commandments and the Beatitudes.

Jesus commanded,

"Go, therefore, and make disciples of all nations, baptizing them in the name of the Father, and of the Son, and of the holy Spirit, teaching them to observe all that I have commanded you. An behold, I am with you always, until the end of the age."

MATTHEW 28: 19–20

We prepare the way for the coming of the kingdom. We bring the truth of God to those who have not heard it. We are forgiving, just, merciful, and compassionate as Jesus taught us. As the People of God, we build up the Church to prepare for the Kingdom of God.

 What are you doing to build the Kingdom of God?

The Pope's Ministry

Jesus gave Saint Peter a unique responsibility in the Church:

"And so I say to you, you are Peter, and upon this rock I will build my church, and the gates of the netherworld shall not prevail against it. I will give you the keys to the kingdom of heaven."

MATTHEW 16:18–19

This unique responsibility is known as the Petrine ministry. Today, the Pope continues this ministry as the successor of Saint Peter and the bishop of Rome. The Pope is the immediate and universal pastor, or shepherd, of the whole Universal Church.

The Pope's ministry includes the responsibility to keep the Church together as one Body of Christ. The Pope also insures that the teachings of the Church are faithful to the truth of Jesus handed down by the Apostles. The Pope supports and encourages all members of the People of God to faithfully proclaim the Gospel.

 What does the Pope do for the People of God?

Activity Name three members of the Catholic Church that you know or have heard about. Write what they do to build up the Church.

Name:

Name:

Name:

Life After Death

The Gospel proclaims that God invites all people to live with him forever. At the moment of death, Christ will judge the way that person has lived his or her life (read Matthew 25:31–32). This is called the particular judgment.

Those who have been faithful to God on Earth will be invited into the Kingdom of God (see Matthew 25:34–40). This is everlasting life in communion with God, the Holy Trinity, and with the Blessed Virgin Mary, the angels, and all the holy men and women who have lived before us. This perfect life with God is called Heaven.

Some people who die are not ready to receive the gift of eternal life in Heaven. After death, they are purified of their weakness and given the opportunity to grow in their love for God. This is called Purgatory.

Sadly, some people choose to turn themselves completely away from God's love. They do this by sinning seriously and not asking God for forgiveness. When people do this and die, they choose to stay separated from God forever (read Matthew 25:41–46). This eternal separation from God is called hell.

? How do you think you need to live in order to spend eternity with God?

Activity Read Matthew 25:31–40. List the actions Jesus names as ways to minister to others in his name. Working with a partner, prepare a skit illustrating a way to serve others.

_____

_____

_____

_____

_____

_____

_____

I FOLLOW JESUS

You are a sign, or image, of the Church. At Baptism, you received the responsibility and the grace to help bring about the Kingdom of God. Peace is one essential characteristic of the kingdom. As Jesus is the Prince of Peace, the Church is to be a people of peace.

SEEING THE CHURCH

Use symbols, images, and words to create a billboard advertisement that tells others about the Church and how she is a sign of peace in the world.

MY FAITH CHOICE

This week, I will be a peacemaker. I will be a clear image of what the Church is. I will

_____

_____

 Think of yourself as an image of the Church. Pray, "Glory be to the Father and to the Son and to the Holy Spirit, as it was in the beginning is now, and ever shall be world without end. Amen."

1. Jesus Christ is the Head of the Church, the Body of Christ. The laity, the ordained, and members of the consecrated life are her members.

2. The Holy Spirit strengthens the Church to be one, holy, catholic, and apostolic.

3. The Kingdom of God begun by God the Father and announced in the Gospels is mysteriously present in the Church and will come about in fullness at the end of time.

Chapter Review

Recall

Use the words below to complete each sentence. Not all words will be used.

blessings	**charisms**	**Communion of Saints**
Kingdom of God	**ordained ministers**	**Petrine ministry**

1. Bishops, priests and deacons are _____.

2. _____ are graces of the Holy Spirit given to help the Church fulfill her work in the world.

3. The _____ is the special ministry of the Pope.

4. The _____ includes all the faithful members of the Church, those on Earth and those in Heaven and in Purgatory.

5. The _____ is all people and creation living in communion with God.

Reflect

How are you a member of the Communion of Saints, working toward the Kingdom of God?

_____

_____

_____

_____

_____

_____

_____

_____

Share Work with a partner to name and describe each of the Marks of the Church. Share it with your class.

Prayer of Vocation

All members of the Church, young people and adults, are called to continue the work of Jesus. We all have the vocation to live our life in Christ.

Leader: God calls each member of the Church to share in the work of Christ. All the baptized have the responsibility to prepare the way for the coming of the Kingdom of God. Let us pray that we hear and respond to God's invitation to spread the Gospel.

Reader: *Jesus went around to all the towns and villages, teaching their synagogues, proclaiming the gospel of the kingdom, and curing every disease and illness. At the sight of the crowds, his heart was moved with pity for them because they were troubled and abandoned, like sheep without a shepherd. Then he said to his disciples, "The harvest is abundant but the laborers are few; so ask the master of the harvest to send out laborers for his harvest."*

MATTHEW 9:35–38.

Reader: The Gospel of the Lord.

All: Praise to you, Lord Jesus Christ.

Leader: Let us take moment so we can respond to Jesus' invitation. *(Pause.)*
Let us pray.

All: Lord God, we pray that all the members of the Church may hear your call to serve your people. We ask this in the name of Christ, our Lord. Amen.

With My Family

This Week . . .

In Chapter 8, "The Mystery of the Church," your child learned:

▶ The Church is the new People of God, the Temple of the Holy Spirit, and the Communion of Saints.

▶ Called by God the Father, all the baptized are joined to Christ through the power of the Holy Spirit.

▶ The whole Church, Christ the Head, and all the members (the laity, the ordained, consecrated religious, and lay ecclesial ministers) are the Body of Christ.

▶ There are four Marks, or characteristics of the Church. The Church is one, holy, catholic, and apostolic.

▶ Peace is a Fruit of the Holy Spirit. Peacemaking is the call of every Christian.

For more about related teachings of the Church, see the *Catechism of the Catholic Church*, 748–962, 988–1060, and the *United States Catholic Catechism for Adults*, pages 111–139, 151–162.

■ Sharing God's Word

Read together Matthew 25:31–40. Emphasize that Jesus clearly teaches that those who faithfully follow his teachings will be invited to join him in the Kingdom of God.

■ We Live as Disciples

The Christian home and family is a school of discipleship. Choose one of the following activities to do as a family, or design a similar activity of your own:

▶ Discuss the four Marks of the Church: one, holy, catholic, and apostolic. Talk about the meaning of each and the ways each of the Marks of the Church is a characteristic of your family.

▶ Read Matthew 25:31–40 at the beginning of a family meal. Decide how your family can join with other members of your parish to follow the teachings of Jesus.

▶ Discuss a way that your family can be an image of the Church in your neighborhood. Put your idea into action.

■ Our Spiritual Journey

Sharing our material and spiritual blessings helps bring about the peace that Christ proclaimed, the peace that comes from all people living in right relationship with God and with one another. What might your family do to bring about this peace within your family and among others? This week pray together that all the members of your family find the strength and perseverance to live the vocation God has intended for them. Pray the ending prayer together on page 111.

For more ideas on ways your family can live as disciples of Jesus, visit **BeMyDisciples.com**

An Uncertain Future

On December 26, 2004, the most powerful earthquake in 40 years erupted under the Indian Ocean near Sumatra. Giant, deadly waves crashed ashore in nearly a dozen countries, killing more than 225,000 people.

Mu is an average eleven-year old Thai boy whose life was turned upside on that December 26. Mu and his family lived on Platong Island in Phang Nga province of Thailand with three hundred others. His father was a fisherman.

The tsunami destroyed the island, and Mu lost his father and his home. Mu is luckier than many. He survived, as did his mother. She is a strong-willed woman who is a part of the women's group at the survivor camp where they live in a tent. She helps prepare food and take care of others.

Mu goes to a makeshift school, but the family has no livelihood and no means of support. Those children who were orphaned by the tsunami receive the most support. As time passes, Mu's mother is afraid that people around the world will forget about the tsunami. She and Mu are scared of what the future might bring.

WE CARE FOR GOD'S CREATION

Every human being is made in the image and likeness of God. God asks us to love our neighbors as ourselves.

Refugee camp for tsunami survivors, Takua Pa, Thailand

MAKING CONNECTIONS

Disasters, as we can see with Mu's family, can strike anywhere at anytime. Christians reach out to people who, for whatever reasons, need the loving assistance of others.

with MATH AND SCIENCE

Write a step-by-step description of what happens to the Earth during an earthquake. Include information on the Earth's surface and plate tectonics. Compare two different earthquakes, for example, the earthquake in the Indian Ocean in 2004 and the earthquake near the East Coast of Honshu, Japan in 2011. Describe where the epicenter was for each of these quakes. Explain how factors, such as the size of the earthquake, its location, the distance of regions from the epicenter, local geography, type of land, construction, and population centers nearby, lessen or make greater the effects of the earthquake.

with SOCIAL STUDIES

Research the religions of the regions affected by the tsunami of 2004. Give a brief history of these religions and how they reach out to help others. Make a recommendation on ways the religious groups can work together to help the tsunami victims into the future. Prepare a written and visual report to share with your class.

with LANGUAGE ARTS

Immediately after a natural disaster, such as the tsunami of 2004, organizations cooperate in rescue and relief efforts. These efforts take care of the immediate needs of survivor. After time passes, the cameras are gone, and the disaster no longer shows up in the headlines. Aid organizations stress the importance of continued assistance during the rehabilitation and reconstruction phase, which can, in some cases, take years.

Write an essay comparing and contrasting rescue and relief efforts with rehabilitation and reconstruction efforts. In your essay remind people of the importance of using their time and resources to continue to help people rebuild their lives in the months and even years after a disaster.

Faith Action

Share with your peers some of the ways your family has worked together to help others. Decide on something you can do together as a class to reach out to people who need your assistance.

_____

_____.

Unit 2 **Review**

A. Choose the Best Word

Read each statement and circle the best answer.

1. Where in the Bible do you find stories about the early Church?

    A. Wisdom Books   B. New Testament

    C. Old Testament   D. Pentateuch

2. The events of Jesus' life that make up the Paschal Mystery are his:

    A. public ministry   B. Arrest and Passion

    C. Passion, Death,   D. birth, baptism, healing
        Resurrection, and Ascension   miracles, and parables

3. Which of the following is not an image of the Church?

    A. Breath of God   B. Body of Christ

    C. Communion of Saints   D. Temple of the Holy Spirit

4. Which of the following is not one of the canonical Gospels?

    A. Matthew   B. Thomas

    C. John   D. Luke

5. The four Marks of the Church are:

    A. one, holy, catholic, and apostolic   B. death, judgment, hell, and Heaven

    C. prudence, justice, fortitude,   D. Matthew, Mark, Luke, and John
        and temperance

B. Show What You Know

Match the words in Column A to the correct definition in Column B.

Column A	Column B
A. Incarnation	____ **1.** The four books of the New Testament
B. Paschal Mystery	____ **2.** The belief that the Son of God became man
C. Kingdom of God	____ **3.** Passion, Death, Resurrection, and Ascension of Jesus
D. Gospels	____ **4.** The fulfillment of God's plan for all creation in Christ
E. Hail, Holy Queen	____ **5.** The prayer at the end of the Rosary

C. Connect with Scripture

*Reread the Scripture passage on the first Unit Opener page.
What connection do you see between this passage and
what you learned in this unit?*

_____

_____

_____

_____

_____

D. Be a Disciple

1. *Review the four pages in this unit titled, The Church Follows Jesus.
What person or ministry of the Church on these pages will inspire
you to be a better disciple of Jesus? Explain your answer.*

_____

_____

_____

_____

_____

2. *Work with a group. Review the four Disciple Power virtues, or gifts,
you have learned about in this unit. After jotting down your own
ideas, share with the group practical ways that you will live these
gifts day by day.*

_____

_____

_____

_____

We Worship
Part One

A Hymn of Celebration

Many of the psalms are songs of praise that the people of the Old Testament sang when they gathered to worship God. We continue that tradition today at Mass.

Blessed is he who comes in the name of the LORD.
We bless you from the Lord's house.
The Lord is God and has given us light.
Join in procession with leafy branches
    up to the horns of the altar.
You are my God, I give you thanks,
    my God, I offer you praise.
Give thanks to the Lord, who is good,
    whose love endures forever.

PSALM 118: 26–29

What I Know

What is something you already know about these faith concepts?

liturgy

_____

_____

_____

The Sacraments of Christian Initiation

_____

_____

_____

sanctifying grace

_____

_____

_____

Faith Terms

Put an X next to the faith terms you know. Put a ? next to faith terms you need to learn more about.

_____ Mass

_____ Sacrament

_____ vocation

_____ Baptism

_____ consecrate

_____ Confirmation

_____ Real Presence

_____ Eucharist

Questions I Have

The Bible

What do you know about the event of Pentecost from the Acts of the Apostles?

_____

_____

_____

The Church

What would you like to know more about the Church's liturgy?

_____

_____

_____

What questions would you like to ask about the liturgical year?

_____

_____

_____

Looking Ahead

In this chapter, the Holy Spirit invites you to ▶

EXPLORE why the Church keeps Sunday as the Lord's Day.

DISCOVER why the Church celebrates the liturgy.

DECIDE on how you can better take part in the Mass.

CHAPTER

Celebrating the Liturgy

? Which routines are part of your life each day? How would you describe these daily routines?

Let us listen to the psalmist describe his daily life:

My heart is steadfast, God,
my heart is steadfast.
I will sing and chant praise.
Awake, my soul;
awake, lyre and harp!
I will wake the dawn.
I will praise you among the peoples, Lord;
I will chant your praise among the nations.
For your love towers to the heavens.

PSALM 57:8–11

? What do these words tell you the psalmist included in his daily life?

Disciple Power

Diligence

Diligence is the persistent ability to combat laziness. Diligence is related to the Cardinal Virtue of fortitude. Saint Peter gives advice to a Christian community to be diligent, or vigilant and steadfast in faith (read I Peter 5:5–11). Full participation at Mass requires diligence.

One Faith, One Lord

No matter where you go throughout the world, the Catholic Church celebrates the Eucharist and the other Sacraments. The look of the churches may be different. Some churches are massive cathedrals filled with statues and stained-glass windows. Others are simple huts. Some are modern, and some are not. But in each church, we gather each Sunday to proclaim the same Gospel and share the same Eucharist.

The language may be different. The music may be different. The people may even dress differently, but what is essential to our liturgy is always the same: Christ is with us as we celebrate and share in his Death and Resurrection.

When the Church gathers to celebrate on Sunday, we proclaim for all to see and hear that Jesus is the Savior of the whole world and of all people. All people are invited to be joined to Christ in Baptism. There is one faith and one Lord, one God who is the Father of all. All people are invited to share in the new life of Christ. All people have the promise of eternal life.

? How is the Eucharist important in your life?

Worship God with Deep Faith

Saint Paschal Baylon shows us how important it is to worship God in the Mass. He lived in Spain between 1540 and 1592. As he was growing up, he worked as a shepherd. Paschal loved being a shepherd because during the long hours in the fields, he could pray. People began calling him the Holy Shepherd.

When he was twenty-four, the Franciscan friars recognized Paschal's holiness and he joined them. He became known for his devotion to the Eucharist and spent many hours in prayer. He grew closer to God. Paschal lived by example and showed how to grow in diligence and love for God and others.

Saint Paschal Baylon reminds us today to put God first in our lives and to worship God at Mass. The Church celebrates his feast on May 17.

? Why do you think the Eucharist was so important to Saint Paschal Baylon?

Activity Write an article for your school's Web site inviting others to join your Catholic school to learn about worshiping God. In the article, how would you explain the importance of the Mass to someone who did not know anything about the Catholic Church? What does the Mass tell people about our faith?

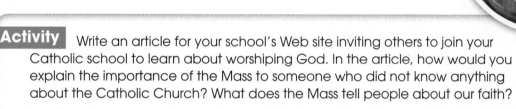

FAITH FOCUS
Why does the Church
celebrate the liturgy?

FAITH VOCABULARY
liturgy
Liturgy is the work of the
Church of worshiping God.
Liturgy includes words,
signs, symbols, and actions
used to give praise and
thanks, honor and glory to
God the Father.

▶ **Sacraments**
Sacraments are the seven
sacred signs and causes of
grace given to the Church
by Christ to continue his
saving action among us
through the power of the
Holy Spirit.

The Work of God's People

The **liturgy** is the work of the Church, the People of God. In the liturgy, the Church worships God the Father through the ritual actions. A ritual is similar to a routine, something that we repeat over and over again. The rituals of the Church include words, objects, and actions in the celebration of the liturgy.

The Church worships God because he alone is God. He is the source of all the blessings of creation and Salvation. We praise and thank God. We worship him as the one Body of Christ. With Christ, as the Head of the Church and with the Holy Spirit animating our hearts and minds, we give honor and glory to God. We give praise and thanksgiving to God our Father, together with Christ through the Holy Spirit.

In every liturgical celebration, the story of God's loving plan of creation and Salvation is proclaimed in our midst. That is why the Liturgy of the Word is part of every liturgical celebration. In the Liturgy of the Word, the Holy Spirit prepares the worshiping assembly to encounter Christ, the Word of God. God speaks and we listen attentively and respond diligently with open hearts.

❓ What are some of the prayers and ritual actions of our liturgy that have special meaning to you. Why?

The Sacraments

The Seven **Sacraments** are at the heart of the liturgy of the Church. When the Sacraments are celebrated, we are joined with the whole Church on Earth and in Heaven. The Sacraments are the seven main liturgical signs of the Church given to us by Jesus Christ. They are signs of God's grace through which we share in his life.

The Sacraments allow us to share in Christ's saving work and make us sharers in the life of God, the Holy Trinity. The Sacraments anticipate the Kingdom of God and give us the grace to choose eternal life with God.

In the Sacraments, our prayers and ritual actions reveal what is beyond what we see. Christ's saving work is being made present by the Holy Spirit. We are sharing in the life of the Holy Trinity. Christ touches our lives and we are changed.

? How do you think the Sacraments you have received helped to change your life?

Catholics Believe

Rites of the Catholic Church

There are different approved rites celebrated within the Catholic Church. These rites witness the diverse liturgical traditions of the Church around the world. Most Catholics in the United States celebrate the Latin Rite. Other rites include the Byzantine, Alexandrian (or Coptic), Syriac, Armenian, Maronite, Ukrainian, Syrian, Romanian, Russian, Malabar, and Chaldean rites. Such diversity points the unity of the Church, and her universality in celebrating the mystery of Christ for all people.

Activity Think of some words, objects, and actions within the Mass. Discuss why each of your choices is important to the celebration of the liturgy.

	Ritual	Importance
Words:	_____	_____
	_____	_____
	_____	_____
Object:	_____	_____
	_____	_____
	_____	_____
Action:	_____	_____
	_____	_____
	_____	_____

The Book of Leviticus

Ritual has always been part of the worship of God's people. Some of the rituals of the Catholic Church have developed from the traditions and laws of God's people in Old Testament times. That is why reading the Old Testament, for example, can help us to learn about the liturgy.

The Book of Leviticus, the third book of the Pentateuch, served as a liturgical handbook for the Levites, the priests of the Israelites. Leviticus contains a section called the Holiness Code. In this section, we find the rituals and rules for celebrating the Sabbath. The Holiness Code begins with the Sabbath:

> The LORD said to Moses, ". . . For six days work may be done; but the seventh day is the sabbath rest, a day for sacred assembly, on which you shall do no work. The sabbath shall belong to the LORD wherever you dwell."
>
> LEVITICUS 23:1, 3

The Book of Leviticus then details the rituals for the observance of the feasts of Passover and unleavened bread. Celebrating the Sabbath and Passover rituals helped the Israelites to share in the love of God. It helped them remember all that God had done for them, and to live their Covenant with God.

Many of our prayers and ritual actions are from the Bible too. Jesus used Old Testament words and ideas to explain his mission for our salvation. The Old Testament is part of our worship heritage. For example, we understand that the Mass is a sacrifice because of our heritage from the Old Testament.

? What is one ritual at Mass that helps you show your love to God?

Sacramental Signs

The Sacraments of the Catholic Church also include rituals. They include prayerful words with signs and symbolic actions. Some of these words, signs, and symbolic actions are essential to the celebration of a Sacrament. They cannot be eliminated or changed in its celebration. For example, the words the priest says at the consecration of the bread and wine at Mass should not be eliminated or changed. However, other parts of the rite, or celebration of, a Sacrament, such as the music we sing, can change.

? Why do think that Christ and his Body, the Church, use signs and symbolic actions to celebrate the Sacraments?

Faith-Filled People

Abraham

At Mass during Eucharistic Prayer I, the Church proclaims Abraham to be "our father in faith." God and Abraham entered into the Covenant. Abraham believed that God was always present with him. Abraham trusted God and lived a life of hope in the future God promised to him and his family. You can find out more about Abraham in Genesis 12:1–7; 22:2–18.

Activity Look at the stained-glass images of the Sacraments on pages 124 and 125. Write the name of the Sacrament and what each of the images tell us about that Sacrament.

_____

_____

_____

_____

_____

_____

_____

_____

_____

_____

_____

FAITH FOCUS
How can the seasons of
the liturgical year bring us
closer to Christ's life?

The Liturgical Year

The Church celebrates her liturgy throughout the year. She celebrates it every day throughout the day somewhere in the world. The Church celebrates the liturgy in the languages spoken by people all over the world.

Just as the calendar year has different seasons and is filled with many holidays, so too the Church liturgical year is composed of different seasons and feasts. The liturgical feasts are mements for us to commemorate those events and people who help us to encounter Christ. For Catholics, the liturgical year is a time of receiving grace — a yearlong celebration of our life in Christ.

Advent. Advent is a liturgical season to prepare for Christ's coming among us. This is the beginning of the liturgical year marked by the color purple.

Christmas. This season celebrates that the Son of God became one of us without giving up his divinity and is the Savior of the world. This season, the colors white or gold are used.

Lent. Lent is a liturgical season that calls us to change our hearts, seek God's forgiveness, prepare candidates for Baptism, and renew our commitment to live our Baptism. The color purple is used and it represents penance and reconciliation.

Easter Triduum. The Easter Triduum, or "the three days," is the center of the entire liturgical year. It begins on Holy Thursday evening, continues on Good Friday, and concludes with the celebrations of the Easter Vigil and Easter Sunday.

Easter. The fifty days of the Easter season, which culminates on Pentecost, are a time of proclaiming the mystery of the new life that we have in the Risen Christ. The colors white or gold are used.

Ordinary Time. During this period, we hear the story of Jesus from one of the four accounts of the Gospels—Matthew, Mark, Luke, or John. We learn the meaning of being a disciple of Jesus in the daily activity of life. Green is used to indicate the growth of discipleship during this time.

Feasts. The solemnities and feasts of the Lord and of Mary, the Apostles, martyrs, and other holy men and women deepen our sharing in God's work in our world.

? Which are your favorite parts of the liturgical year?

I FOLLOW JESUS

The Holy Spirit prepares you to celebrate the Sacraments. Jesus is always there, leading the Church in her celebration of the Seven Sacraments. The words, objects, and actions used in these celebrations help us to participate and express our faith more fully.

A RITUAL CELEBRATION

Plan a ritual prayer celebration for your class. Choose words, objects, and actions that will involve your classmates in the celebration. Tell how these help us participate.

Theme: _____

Words (Including Scripture): _____

_____

Objects: _____

_____

Actions: _____

_____

What the Church Does	How these Help Us Participate
_____	_____
_____	_____
_____	_____

MY FAITH CHOICE

Before participating in Mass this week, I will remember that we encounter Christ during Mass. At Mass, I will:

_____

_____

 Pray, "O Eternal Father, grant that I may remain steadfast in faith and diligent in giving you honor and praise. Amen."

1. The celebration of the liturgy is the Church's work of worshiping God.

2. The Seven Sacraments are the center of the Church's liturgy. They make us sharers in the life of God through the power of the Holy Spirit.

3. Throughout the year, the Church praises God the Father for what he has done and continues to do for us.

Recall

Match the terms in Column A with their meanings in Column B.

Column A

1. _____ liturgy

2. _____ Advent

3. _____ Sacraments

4. _____ liturgical year

5. _____ Easter Triduum

Column B

A. The Church's yearly cycle of seasons and feasts that make up the Church year of worship.

B. Beginning of the liturgical year

C. The three-day celebration that is at the center of the liturgical year of the Church

D. The seven main celebrations of the Church's liturgy, given to us by Christ, that make us sharers in the life of God

E. The Church's work of worshiping God

Reflect

What are three ways the Sacraments impact your life?

_____

_____

_____

_____

_____

_____

_____

_____

_____

Share Work with a partner to explain some of the key words and actions we use to celebrate the Sacraments. Share why these actions are important to us.

Give Glory to God!

A doxology is a prayer of praise to God the Father in the name of Jesus through the power of the Holy Spirit. Conclude with this ritual prayer from the conclusion of the Eucharistic Prayer.

Leader: Lord God, Father of all, send us the Holy Spirit to open our hearts to give you praise and thanksgiving.

Reader 1: For the gift of Jesus Christ who suffered, died, and was raised from the dead so we might enjoy the promise of eternal life,

All: We praise you and give you thanks.

Reader 2: For Mary, the Mother of God and the Mother of the Church, whose yes to you gave us Jesus,

All: We praise you and give you thanks.

Reader 3: For all the Saints whose faith, hope, and love model for us ways to say yes to your invitation to know, love and serve you,

All: We praise you and give you thanks.

Reader 4: For the Church, the Body of Christ, who guides us on our earthly journey to our heavenly home,

All: We praise you and give you thanks.

Leader: Let us acknowledge that all of our blessings come from God our Father. *(Pause.)* Let us join with Christ and give glory to God the Father.

**All: Through him, and with him, and in him,
O God, almighty Father,
in the unity of the Holy Spirit,
all glory and honor is yours,
for ever and ever.
Amen.**

Doxology, Eucharistic Prayer,
Roman Missal

With My Family

This Week . . .

In Chapter 9, "Celebrating the Liturgy," your child learned:

▶ The liturgy is the Church's work of worshiping God. It centers on the Eucharist and the other Sacraments.

▶ The whole Church gathers with Christ to share in the life of the Holy Trinity. We bless and give praise, thanks, honor, and glory to the Father.

▶ Through the power of the Holy Spirit, we, as members of the Church, remember and are made sharers in the Paschal Mystery.

▶ Throughout the liturgical year, we join with Christ to share in his work of Salvation.

▶ Each of us is called by God to be diligent and steadfast in faith.

For more about related teachings of the Church, see the *Catechism of the Catholic Church*, 1076–1109, 1136–1186, 1206, and the *United States Catholic Catechism for Adults*, pages 165–179.

■ Sharing God's Word

Read together Psalm 95:1–7. Emphasize that the Seven Sacraments are signs and sources of God's grace through which we are made sharers of the life and work of Jesus Christ, the Son of God. Talk about your family's diligent participation in the celebration of the Eucharist and the Sacrament of Penance and Reconciliation.

■ We Live as Disciples

The Christian family and home is a school of discipleship. Choose one of the following activities to do as a family, or design a similar activity of your own:

▶ When you take part in the Mass this week, notice the liturgical decorations and the priest's vestments. Talk about what they tell you about which liturgical season is being celebrated.

▶ Create a doorknob hanger or wreath for the front door of your home. Decorate it so that it is a reminder of the current liturgical season.

■ Our Spiritual Journey

The Church has always prayed doxologies, short formulaic prayers praising God, within the rites. Memorize the doxology on page 129. Pray it as a mantra or a simple spontaneous prayer throughout the day. This will help focus your living the dismissal at Mass. "Go in peace, glorifying the Lord by your life" (*Roman Missal*).

For more ideas on ways your family can live as disciples of Jesus, visit **BeMyDisciples.com**

Looking Ahead

In this chapter, the Holy Spirit invites you to ▶

EXPLORE how Charles Lwanga helped people live their faith in Christ.

DISCOVER the meaning of Baptism.

DECIDE on how to serve others as Jesus did.

CHAPTER

10

The Sacraments of Christian Initiation: Baptism

[?] Think of a time that you joined with friends to become members of a group. What actions did you take to demonstrate that you belonged with the group?

John the Baptist was standing in the Jordan River. He was inviting people to turn their lives back toward God. The Gospel tells us that Jesus came down to the Jordan when John was there. Listen to what the Gospel of Mark tells us:

> It happened in those days that Jesus came from Nazareth of Galilee and was baptized in the Jordan by John. On coming up out of the water he saw the heavens being torn open and the Spirit, like a dove, descending upon him. And a voice came from the heavens, "You are my beloved Son; with you I am well pleased."   MARK 1:9–11

[?] What do these words from Mark's Gospel tell you about Jesus? What does the Church do to help you have a sense of belonging to God?

Disciple Power

Modesty

Modesty is one of the Fruits of the Holy Spirit. These are signs that a person is cooperating with the grace of the Holy Spirit. A modest person protects his or her inner self. Modesty encourages a person to respect the dignity of every human person, including oneself.

Saint Charles Lwanga

Charles Lwanga, like Saint John the Baptist, called people to conversion. He called people to change their lives. He called them to turn back to God. He called them to be steadfast in their living as God wants them to live.

In the late 1800s, Catholic missionaries were successfully spreading the Gospel in central Africa, including modern-day Uganda. One of these Catholic missionary groups was the Society of Missionaries of Africa. These missionaries were so successful that many people converted and were baptized. One such convert was Charles Lwanga.

Charles lived in a kingdom violently ruled by a ruthless man, King Mwanga. He was cruel to children, especially teenage boys, who were his servants. Charles was in charge of these servants and lived in the king's compound with them. In secret, Charles taught the Catholic faith to many of these young boys. He taught them that they belonged to God and that Jesus Christ is the Son of God and our Savior. Charles taught them to protect themselves from Mwanga's violent and sinful ways. With his help, they found the strength to respect their God-given dignity.

? What is one way you can live the way Jesus wants you to live?

Banner of 22 African Martyrs who were Canonized by the Roman Catholic Church.

Choosing Christ

King Mwanga became furious with Charles. In great anger, the king ordered the gates of his compound closed so that no one could leave. Fear spread. Charles gathered those who were Christians for prayer. Others joined them and were baptized that night.

King Mwanga summoned all of his servants and demanded that they choose to side with him or Christ. Charles stood and chose Christ. Others followed. This enraged Mwanga even more. So he had them put to death.

Saint Charles Lwanga and his companions suffered because of their faith. They protected the dignity of their bodies with their lives. They were the first canonized Saints from modern Africa.

? What are some ways that you have heard about where someone stands up for others?

Activity Who are three people you know or have heard about, who have stood up to protect the dignity of people? How do their actions show their love for Christ?

Name _____

Actions _____

_____

_____

Name _____

Actions _____

_____

_____

Name _____

Actions _____

_____

_____

FAITH VOCABULARY

Christian Initiation
Christian Initiation is the liturgical process by which a person becomes a full member of the Church.

Baptism
Baptism is the Sacrament of Christian Initiation in which we are joined to Jesus Christ, become members of his Church, are reborn as God's adopted children. We receive the gift of the Holy Spirit, and Original Sin and personal sins are forgiven.

The Sacrament of Baptism

Baptism, Confirmation, and the Eucharist are the three Sacraments of **Christian Initiation.** Through the celebration of these three Sacraments, beginning with **Baptism,** a person is joined to Christ and his Body, the Church. The unity of all three Sacraments of Christian Initiation is required for the complete initiation of a person into the Body of Christ, the Church.

The first Sacrament of Christian Initiation is Baptism. In the Rite of Baptism, the Church uses baptismal water. Jesus told Nicodemus:

> "Amen, amen, I say to you, no one can enter the kingdom of God without being born of water and Spirit."   JOHN 3:5

Water can be both a sign of life (as in a flowing stream) and of destruction (as in a raging flood). Throughout the history of God's people, water has been a sign of cleansing from sin and being reborn into new life. The Church has understood the events of Noah's ark (read Genesis 7:6–23), the Crossing of the Red Sea (read Exodus 14:26–31), and the Jordan River as moments when God provided a new beginning for his Chosen People. In Baptism, water is a sign of our new life in Jesus.

? How would you describe to someone why water is used in Baptism?

New Life in Christ

Christ instituted, or gave, the Church, the Sacrament of Baptism and the six other Sacraments. Jesus showed us the beginning of new life in him when he allowed John to baptize him in the Jordan River. You read this account from the Gospel of Mark on page 131, now read the account from Luke.

> After all the people had been baptized and Jesus also had been baptized and was praying, heaven was opened and the holy Spirit descended upon him in bodily form like a dove. And a voice came from heaven, "You are my beloved Son; with you I am well pleased."
>
> LUKE 3:21–22

On the Cross, the crucified Jesus is a sign of new life with his pierced side flowing with blood and water (read John 19:31–37). Christ makes possible our entrance into the Kingdom of God by giving the Church this Sacrament. In Baptism, we die to sin and are reborn into a new life with God the Holy Trinity. Since the early days of the Church, both adults and children have been baptized. Baptism is the gateway, or doorway, to new life in the Holy Spirit and to Salvation in Christ.

[?] Why is Baptism important to the Church and in your life?

Catholics Believe

Chrism

Sacred Chrism is one of the three oils that the Church uses in her rituals. Chrism is primarily used to consecrate (to set aside for a holy purpose) people, places, and things for the service of God and his people. Chrism is used in the Sacraments of Baptism, Confirmation, and Holy Orders. It is also used to consecrate churches and altars.

Activity Write or draw some of your ideas for a mural about Baptism.

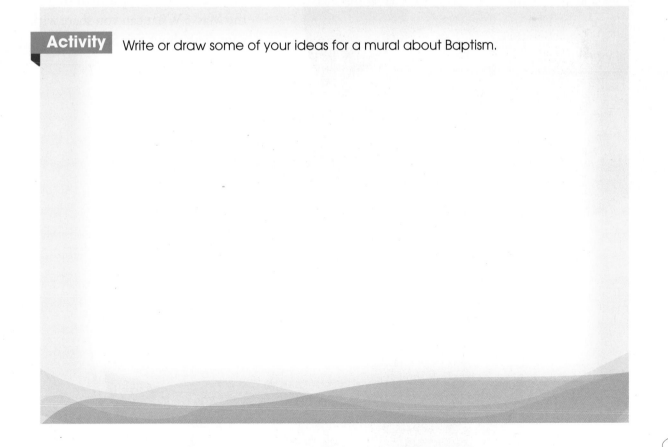

The Rite of Baptism

In different ways, the sign of water in the Old Testament prepared for its use in the Sacrament of Baptism. In the prayers for the blessing of the water used in Baptism, we hear why water is a symbol of the story of Salvation. For example, in the Book of Exodus, we read that God led his people through the water of the Red Sea, saving them from slavery.

Just as the people of Israel were saved from Egypt by being able to cross the Red Sea, so too, God saves us from sin in the water of Baptism. By hearing the words and following the actions the Church uses in the celebration of Baptism, we can come to know the meaning of this Sacrament.

The Rite of Baptism in the Latin Church always includes the minister of the Sacrament immersing a person three times into the baptismal water or pouring the water three times over the person's head. The minister of Baptism does this action saying, "I baptize you in the name of the Father, and of the Son, and of the Holy Spirit." These are the essential elements of the celebration. Without these words and actions, there is no Baptism.

? Have you ever attended a Baptism or experienced a Baptism during the Mass? What can you share with your class about this Sacrament?

Ritual Actions

The celebration of Baptism also has these parts, or ritual actions:

Anointing with Chrism: The minister anoints the baptized person with Sacred Chrism. This signifies the person shares in the work of Christ the Priest, Prophet, and King.

Clothing with a white garment: The baptized person is given a white garment to wear. The newly baptized person has a new dignity of some one who has been joined to the Risen Christ.

Presentation of a lighted candle: A baptismal candle that has been lighted from the Easter candle is presented to the newly baptized or to the parents and godparents of a newly baptized infant. This symbolizes that the baptized person is to walk always with Christ and always keep the flame of faith alive in his or her heart.

[?] Which of the ritual actions of Baptism is most meaningful to you and why?

Activity Imagine you will be interviewing a young person or an adult who was recently Baptized and became a member of the Catholic Church. Prepare for the interview by writing three questions you would ask this person.

Question 1

_____

_____

_____

Question 2

_____

_____

_____

Question 3

_____

_____

_____

FAITH FOCUS
What are the sacramental
graces of Baptism?

FAITH VOCABULARY
sanctifying grace
Sanctifying grace is the
grace that heals our human
nature, wounded by sin,
by giving us a share in the
divine life of the Holy Trinity.

The Graces of Baptism

What happens when we are baptized? The term *sacramental graces* is used to tell us what happens. It tells us what effects that Baptism has on a person who is baptized. These are the sacramental graces a person who is baptized receives:

- We are joined to Christ in his dying and rising. We receive new birth in Christ and become adopted sons or daughters of God the Father.

- We receive the gift of the Holy Spirit.

- We become members of the Church, the Body of Christ, and are made sharers in the priesthood of Christ.

- We receive the gift of **sanctifying grace.** We are freed from all sin—Original Sin and personal sins.

- We are spiritually marked as belonging to Christ forever. This mark, which no sin can erase, is called a sacramental character. This mark means that Baptism can be received only one time and can never be repeated.

Baptism, as with all Sacraments, is the work of the Church. It is the work of Christ and the members of the Church.

? What does belonging to Christ forever mean for the way you should live?

Activity Create an image for Baptism that includes one or more of its ritual elements.

I FOLLOW JESUS

In Baptism, the minister (priest or deacon) anointed the crown of your head with Chrism. He said that God was now anointing you to serve others as Jesus did. Remembering that Jesus served others with humility and modesty, complete the activity below.

ANOINTED TO SERVE

In the circle, write one thing you can do to serve others as Jesus did. On each of the four lines coming out from the circle, write how that action helps protect the dignity of the person you are serving.

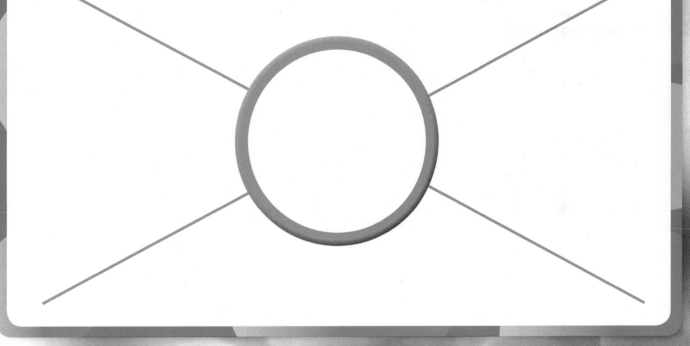

MY FAITH CHOICE

This week, I will remember how I was chosen by God and anointed with Chrism in Baptism to serve him and others as Christ did. I will put on Christ and will act modestly by

_____

 Pray, "Jesus you are the Son of God, the One who shows us how to love and serve God. Help me to be humble and modest like you. Amen."

1. A person becomes fully initiated into the Church through the celebration of the Sacraments of Christian Initiation: Baptism, Confirmation, and Eucharist

2. Baptism is the first Sacrament we receive; it is the doorway to new life in the Holy Spirit and Salvation in Christ.

3. Through Baptism, we receive the gift of the Holy Spirit. God makes us sharers in his divine life. We are called to serve others as Christ did.

Chapter Review

Recall

*Write **T** if the statement is true. Write **F** if the statement is false. Correct the false statements.*

1. _____ The Sacrament of Baptism is our gateway to life in the Holy Spirit.

2. _____ Through Baptism, we are spiritually marked as belonging to Christ.

3. _____ Baptism frees us from all future sins.

4. _____ In the Rite of Baptism, both water and oil are used.

5. _____ Baptism is a Sacrament that can be repeated.

Reflect

What are the ways sanctifying grace can help you in your life?

_____

_____

_____

_____

_____

_____

_____

_____

_____

_____

_____

Share

Describe three of the sacramental graces a person receives in the Sacrament of Baptism. Share what this can mean in your life with a classmate.

Bless Us Today, Lord

In the Old Testament, kings and priests were anointed with oil. This was a sign that they were chosen by God for a special service to God's people. Anointing with oil was also a sign that God would be with them to help them in their work. Use this prayer to recall God's presence with us.

Leader: In Baptism, we were anointed with Chrism as members of the Body of Christ, the Church. Let us recall our anointing at Baptism. (Pause).

Lord, you freed us from sin in the water of Baptism. (Raise a clear bowl of water).

All: **Bless us today, O Lord.**

Leader: Lord, you anointed us as members of Christ's Body.
(Raise a container of oil).

All: **Bless us today, O Lord.**

Leader: Lord, you are the Light of the world.
(Lift up a candle).

All: **Bless us today, O Lord.**

With My Family

This Week . . .

In Chapter 10, "The Sacraments of Christian Initiation: Baptism," your child learned:

▶ Through Baptism, we first receive new life and Salvation in Christ and become members of the Church, the Body of Christ.

▶ Through the baptismal water and the grace of the Holy Spirit, Original Sin, and everything that separates us from God is washed away.

▶ In Baptism, we are sealed with the gift of faith helping us to participate in the life and work of the Church.

▶ As disciples of Jesus, we are to be modest in all aspects of life.

For more about related teachings of the Church, see the *Catechism of the Catholic Church*, 1210–1284, and the *United States Catholic Catechism for Adults*, pages 181–199.

■ Sharing God's Word

Read together John 3:3–6. Emphasize that through the Sacrament of Baptism, we are reborn of water and the Holy Spirit.

■ We Live as Disciples

The Christian home and family is a school of discipleship. Choose one of the following activities to do as a family, or design a similar activity of your own:

▶ Water can symbolize many things. Talk about what water symbolizes for you. Share ideas about how water helps you understand what happens in Baptism.

▶ Place a dish of holy water in a convenient location in your home. Bless each other and yourselves as you come and go during the day and before bedtime. Remember that in Baptism, we are made sharers in the life of God.

■ Our Spiritual Journey

Daily rituals that involve the use of water fill our lives each day. These can be sacred moments. Stop and pause as you wash your hands or take a drink of water. Remember the gift of living water that you received and that is vital to your life as a follower of Jesus. This week as a family, pray together, "Bless us today, O Lord."

For more ideas on ways your family can live as disciples of Jesus, visit **BeMyDisciples.com**

Looking Ahead

In this chapter, the Holy Spirit invites you to ▶

 **EXPLORE** how the Chinese martyrs witnessed their faith in Christ.

 **DISCOVER** that in Confirmation, the Holy Spirit strengthens us.

 **DECIDE** on ways to live as a witness for Christ.

CHAPTER

11

The Sacraments of Christian Initiation: Confirmation

? To whom do you look for guidance and help when you are confused or afraid? Why?

During the time of the Jewish festival of Pentecost, the Holy Spirit came upon the disciples of Jesus when they were fearful, and they were given the strength and courage to proclaim the Gospel. Listen to how Luke describes that event.

> And suddenly there came from the sky a noise like a strong driving wind, and it filled the entire house in which they were. Then there appeared to them tongues as of fire, which parted and came to rest on each one of them. And they were all filled with the holy Spirit and began to speak in different tongues, as the Spirit enabled them to proclaim.
> ACTS OF THE APOSTLES 2:2–4

? What promise of Jesus came true in this reading?

Fortitude

Fortitude is one of the four Cardinal Virtues. It is the strength of mind and will to do what is good in the face of adversity or difficulty. It enables a person to be a steadfast witness for Christ.

Land of Martyr Saints

For centuries, Catholics in China have responded to the call of the Holy Spirit to be witnesses for Christ. In the 500s, the Gospel was preached in China, and the first church was built there around the year A.D. 600. The Jesuit missionary Saint Francis Xavier arrived in China and preached the Gospel there in the 1600s. But the Chinese emperors did not accept Christianity. They considered it to be a foreign religion and did not want foreign ways changing their society. When they discovered Christians in their midst, the rulers of China often had them killed. Through the centuries, the Catholics in China have lived and died for their faith with great courage.

From the mid-1600s to 1930, 120 Chinese martyrs have been named Saints by the Church. The first of these martyrs was the Dominican priest and missionary Father Francisco Fernández de Capillas. He was killed in 1648 by the invading Manchu Tartars, who were trying to conquer China and overthrow the emperor. They imprisoned him and then tortured and beheaded him while he was praying the Sorrowful Mysteries of the Rosary.

The courage of Catholics in China only grew stronger and, from 1796 to 1856, twelve more Chinese Catholics died for their faith in Christ. Among these were Agnes Cao Guiying, Peter Liu, Jerome Lu Tingmei, Lawrence Wang Bing, and Agatha Lin Zao, who were all catechists. These catechists were committed to their faith and chose to share the love of Jesus Christ with others.

？ How do you show others that you are a Christian?

The Gift of Courage

The courageous acts of faith continued into modern times. In the 1900s, beginning with the Boxer Rebellion, the courage of more than ninety Catholics in China cost them their lives. Among these *martyrs* were: Paulus Lang Fu and Andreas Wang Tianqing, age 9; Maria Zeng Xu, age 11; and Anna Wang and Simon Qin Chunfu, age 14.

The English word *martyr* comes from the Greek word meaning "witness." The Church in China is a courageous living witness to the power of the Holy Spirit at work, leading the Church to fulfill Jesus' command to preach the Gospel to all nations.

? Do you know, among your friends or family, any person who is a witness to the faith of the Church? How are they a living witness to the faith?

The icon of the Holy Orthodox Martyrs of China, c. 1900

Activity Reflect on the meaning of the word "martyr." Use the letters of the word to write words or phrases (such as courageous) describing the qualities or works of a martyr.

M
A
R
T
Y
COURAGEOUS

Using some of the words or phrases, write a prayer of thanksgiving for martyrs giving witness to their faith in God.

FAITH FOCUS
Why does the Church celebrate the Sacrament of Confirmation?

FAITH VOCABULARY
Confirmation
Confirmation is the Sacrament of Christian Initiation that strengthens the grace of Baptism and in which our life in Christ is sealed by the gift of the Holy Spirit.

Confirmed in Christ

Most Roman Catholics today are baptized as infants and are confirmed many years later. In the Eastern Catholic Churches, **Confirmation** is administered immediately after Baptism and is followed by participation in the Eucharist.

The Sacrament of Confirmation perfects and strengthens the graces of Baptism. The baptized receive and accept important Christian responsibilities and the graces to fulfill those responsibilities. They accept the grace and commit to join Christ in his mission to prepare for the coming of the Kingdom of God. They cooperate with the grace of the Holy Spirit and, as members of the Church, bring healing and reconciliation to the world.

Requirements for Confirmation

In the Roman Catholic Church, there are unique requirements for a baptized person preparing to receive the Sacrament of Confirmation. These requirements are:

- **Faith:** The person must be baptized. Candidates for Confirmation must profess their faith with the Church.

- **Age:** Today, young people who are Roman Catholic are confirmed at various ages, usually when they are young teens.

- **Grace:** Candidates must also be in a state of grace. They must be free of mortal sin. Their relationship with God must be close.

- **Will, or Choice:** Candidates must have a clear and deliberate intention to receive the Sacrament. In other words, they are to accept the responsibilities of being a witness for Christ.

? How can you be a living witness for Christ?

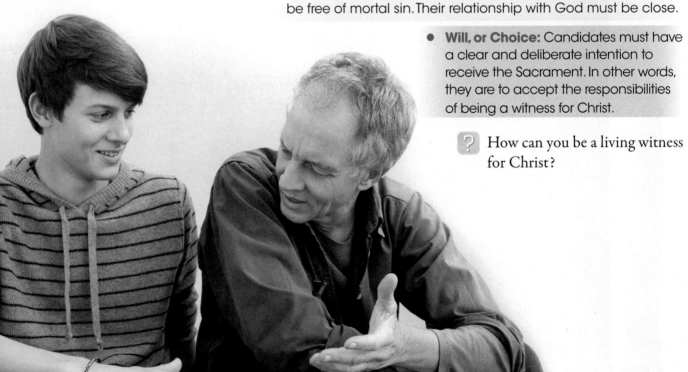

Preparing for Confirmation

Confirmation marks our lifelong commitment to be witnesses for Christ. With the help of the Holy Spirit, we prepare ourselves for Confirmation. This preparation includes prayer, service, and reception of the Sacrament of Penance and Reconciliation.

Preparing for Confirmation also includes choosing a sponsor. A sponsor is someone who gives spiritual help and encouragement to a person preparing to receive Confirmation. Because Confirmation continues and deepens the grace of Baptism, it is fitting that a Confirmation sponsor be one of the baptismal godparents.

? What spiritual qualities would you want to have if you were a Confirmation sponsor for someone?

Activity Write your full name on the line below. Using the letters in your name, create words that describe you and your faith in Christ.

_____ _____ _____
     First   **Middle**   **Last**

_____

_____

_____

_____

FAITH FOCUS
What are the parts
of the Sacrament of
Confirmation?

FAITH VOCABULARY
consecrate
To consecrate is to set
aside and dedicate for a
holy purpose.

Anointing in the Old Testament

Anointing with oil is essential to the Rite of Confirmation. Oil is used as a sign to **consecrate** a person, or set that person aside for a holy purpose. In different ways, the ritual of anointing with oil in the Old Testament prepared us for its use in the Sacraments of the Church. In the First Book of Samuel, for example, we read about the anointing of David, the shepherd boy whom God had chosen to be king of Israel.

The Lord told the prophet Samuel to go to Jesse of Bethlehem, who had many sons. One of these sons would be the next king of Israel. God told Samuel he would tell him who to anoint. So Samuel did as the Lord told him and went to Bethlehem to see Jesse and his sons. As the sons came to visit with Samuel, it was not until David (the youngest one) came that God told Samuel to anoint him (read 1 Samuel 16:1–13).

This anointing was a sign that the Spirit of God lived within David and would help him to do the work that God had chosen him to do. In the Sacrament of Confirmation we are anointed with oil to be consecrated to the Lord too.

? If anointing with oil sets someone aside for a holy purpose, what changes in your life would you make if you were anointed?

The Rite of Confirmation

The Rite of Confirmation is usually celebrated during the Eucharist. This helps point to the unity of the three Sacraments of Christian Initiation. When Confirmation is celebrated during Mass, it begins after the reading of the Gospel. The parts of the Rite of Confirmation when celebrated during Mass and separated from Baptism are:

Presentation of the Candidates: The pastor or a representative of the parish presents the candidates, if possible, by name to the bishop.

Homily: The homily is to help the candidates understand the mystery of Confirmation.

Renewal of Baptismal Promises: The *confirmandi* (those to be confirmed) renew the profession of faith that they made at Baptism or that their parents and godparents made in union with the whole Church at that time.

The Laying on of Hands: In the Roman Rite, the bishop or the priest delegated by him extends his hands over the confirmandi. Since the time of the Apostles, this gesture has signified the gift of the Holy Spirit. The minister of the Sacrament prays, invoking the Gifts of the Holy Spirit.

Anointing with Chrism: The candidates come forward with their sponsors. The sponsor places his or her right hand on the candidate's shoulder. The bishop places, or lays, his hand on the head of the one being confirmed and says, "Be sealed with the Gift of the Holy Spirit," as he anoints the forehead of the baptized person being confirmed. At the same time, the bishop anoints the person's forehad with the Sacred Chrism.

The Sacraments of Christian Initiation celebrate our becoming members of the Church and our sharing in the life of God. Confirmation, like Baptism, imprints a spiritual mark on our souls. For this reason, it can be received only one time.

? How does the symbol of oil in the Old Testament help us understand Confirmation?

Faith-Filled People

United States Conference of Catholic Bishops (USCCB)

The bishops are anointed to lead the Church in worshiping God, proclaiming the Gospel to all people, and living as disciples of Christ. The U.S. bishops work together as a conference to fulfill their responsibilities. Together they work to unify, coordinate, encourage, promote, and carry out Catholic activities in the United States of America.

Activity Write a prayer asking God to help you prepare to live as someone who has been anointed and received the Holy Spirit.

_____

_____

_____

The Effects of Confirmation

At Confirmation, we receive and accept some important responsibilities and graces to fulfill those responsibilities. The graces and responsibilities, or the effects, of Confirmation are:

- We receive the grace of the outpouring of the Holy Spirit in our lives.

- We accept grace and commit to join Christ in his mission to prepare for the coming of the Kingdom of God.

- We cooperate with the grace of the Holy Spirit and bring healing and reconciliation into the world.

- The grace of the Holy Spirit strengthens our bond with the Church and her mission to defend the faith.

- The grace of the Holy Spirit guides us to live as signs of the Covenant as the prophets did.

We receive the seven-fold Gifts of the Holy Spirit to remain witnesses for Christ, even in the face of misunderstanding, ridicule, and suffering. The confirmed person receives the strength and power to confidently profess his or her faith in Jesus, the Lord and Savior of the world, and to live as a witness for him.

? What are some of the strengths that you might need to profess your faith in Jesus?

Activity Write a brief description of a person (real or fictional) who is living the call to be a witness for Christ. What kind of person is he or she?

_____

_____

_____

_____

_____

_____

_____

I FOLLOW JESUS

You are called to be a living witness for Christ. Strengthened with the Gifts of the Holy Spirit, you continue the work of Christ as a member of the Church, in your home, school, neighborhood—or wherever you are.

SEALED BY THE HOLY SPIRIT

Create a motto or brief statement describing yourself and what you can do right now to be a witness for Christ.

MY FAITH CHOICE

With the gift of courage, or fortitude, I can be strong in my stance as a witness for Christ. I will put my witness motto into action this week. I will

_____

_____

 Pray, "Lord and Giver of life, continue to strengthen me with your gifts so that I may be a witness for Christ. Amen."

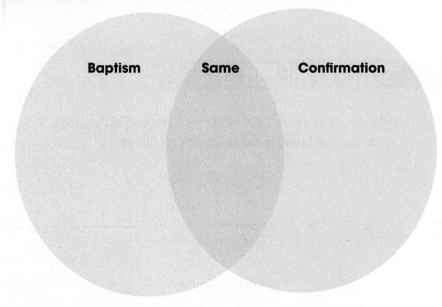

TO HELP YOU REMEMBER

1. The Sacrament of Confirmation perfects the grace of Baptism.

2. Like Baptism, the Holy Spirit marks us with his seal in Confirmation. This sacramental character leaves an indelible spiritual mark imprinted on our souls.

3. In the Latin Rite of Confirmation, the bishop or priest-delegate rests his hands on the top of each candidate's head as he anoints each candidate's forehead with Chrism.

Chapter Review

Recall

Compare and contrast the Sacraments of Baptism and Confirmation. Write the unique features of each Sacrament in the large circles. In the center, space tell how they are the same.

Baptism   **Same**   **Confirmation**

Describe what the anointing with Chrism in Confirmation tells us about Confirmation.

_____

_____

_____

Reflect

Choose one of the symbols and actions used during the Rite of Confirmation and explain how it helps you to better understand the Sacrament.

_____

_____

_____

_____

Share Describe how the Sacrament of Confirmation might help someone to become more responsible about their faith. Discuss and share as a class.

Come, Holy Spirit

We first receive the gift of the Holy Spirit at Baptism and are sealed with the gift of the Holy Spirit at Confirmation. Pray together for the strength of the Holy Spirit.

Leader: On the day of Pentecost, tongues of fire parted and came to rest on the disciples. They were all filled with the Holy Spirit.

Reader: A reading from the letter of Paul to the Galatians,

The fruit of the Spirit is love, joy, peace, patience, kindness, generosity, faithfulness, gentleness, self-control. Against such there is no law. Now those who belong to Christ [Jesus] have crucified their flesh with its passions and desires. If we live in the Spirit, let us also follow the Spirit. Let us not be conceited, provoking one another, envious of one another.

GALATIANS 5:22–26

The word of the Lord.

All: **Thanks be to God.**

Leader: Remember that the Holy Spirit dwells within us. Let us ask the Holy Spirit to give us the grace to be living witnesses for Christ.

All: **Come, Holy Spirit,**
fill the hearts of your faithful.
And kindle in them the fire
of your love.
Send forth your Spirit
and they shall be created.
And you will renew the
face of the earth.
Amen.

With My Family

This Week . . .

In Chapter 11, "The Sacraments of Christian Initiation: Confirmation," your child learned:

▶ In the Sacrament of Confirmation, the graces of Baptism are strengthened by the Gifts of the Holy Spirit.

▶ The Holy Spirit marks, or seals, the confirmed with an indelible spiritual mark. Confirmation, therefore, may be received only one time.

▶ The confirmed person receives the fortitude and courage to profess and confidently give witness to his or her faith in Jesus Christ.

For more about related teachings of the Church, see the *Catechism of the Catholic Church*, 1285–1321, and the *United States Catholic Catechism for Adults*, pages 201–211.

■ Sharing God's Word

Read together I Samuel 16:1–13. Emphasize that the Spirit came upon David, who was chosen by God, to serve his people as king. Recall the anointing of your family members in Confirmation and relate that anointing to the story of David.

■ We Live as Disciples

The Christian family and home is a school of discipleship. Choose one of the following activities to do as a family, or design a similar activity of your own:

▶ Invite family members to name someone they know who is confirmed and is living as a witness for Christ. Describe what this person does that reflects Christian living.

▶ When you participate in Mass this week, find the ambry in your parish. The ambry is where the blessed oils are kept. These oils are used in the Sacraments. Talk about how you are living out your baptismal anointing.

■ Our Spiritual Journey

Jesus proclaimed in the synagogue in Nazareth that the Spirit of God was upon him. That same Spirit came upon the disciples in the upper room in Jerusalem. The Spirit came upon you when you were baptized, continues with you wherever you are, and will be with you wherever you go. We can look to the Holy Spirit in prayer to give us the gifts we need to follow Christ. This week as a family, pray the prayer to the Holy Spirit found on page 153.

For more ideas on ways your family can live as disciples of Jesus, visit **BeMyDisciples.com**

Looking Ahead

In this chapter, the Holy Spirit invites you to ▶

 **EXPLORE** how Óscar Romero gave praise and thanks to God.

 **DISCOVER** how the Eucharist is a memorial.

 **DECIDE** on how Jesus' presence helps you to glorify God.

CHAPTER
12

The Sacraments of Christian Initiation: The Eucharist

? Symbols and signs point to something beyond themselves. For example, smoke may be a sign of a fire. What symbols and signs have you seen or heard, and what are their meanings?

In this psalm, God is praised for remaining faithful to his Chosen People by keeping his promises:

> He spread a cloud as a cover,
>   and made a fire to light up the night.
> They asked and he brought them quail;
>   with bread from heaven he filled them.
> He split the rock and water gushed forth;
>   it flowed through the desert like a river.
>
> PSALM 105:39–41

? What signs are used in this psalm to remember God's love for his people?

Disciple Power

Archbishop Óscar Romero

Christians since the early days of the Church have given their lives out of love for God and others. Óscar Romero, the archbishop of San Salvador, gave up his life serving Christ and the people of San Salvador.

Óscar Arnulfo Romero y Galdámez was born in 1917 in San Salvador. He had 5 brothers and 2 sisters. His father was a carpenter and he was taught to be a carpenter as well, but he wanted to become a priest. When he grew up he was ordained a priest in 1942. He was known as a good, hardworking priest.

In 1977, when Óscar was appointed archbishop of San Salvador, the government was unjust and corrupt. The people were disappointed because they thought he would not fight for them and felt that he would not stand up for what was right. One day when a close priest friend was killed by government soldiers for working with the poor, Archbishop Romero realized that he had to fight for justice and try to put an end to the injustices in his country. He spoke openly about it and wrote about what was happening in his country. He asked other countries to put pressure on the Salvadorian government to change.

? What are some ways you and your classmates can bring about justice for others?

A Faithful Archbishop

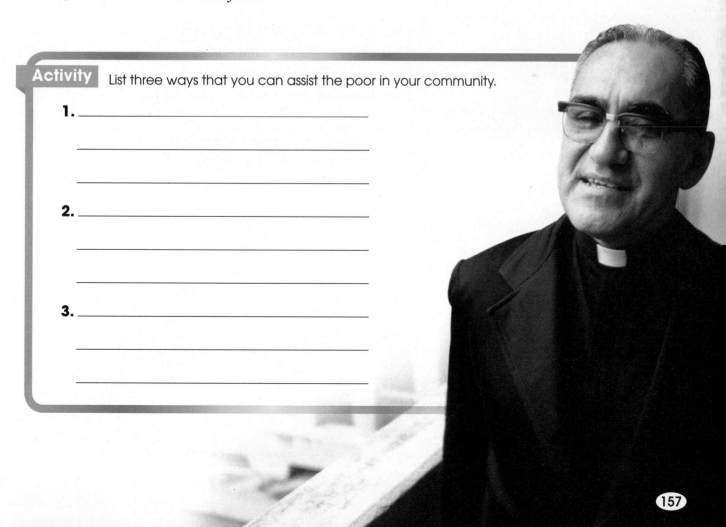

On March 24, 1980, as Archbishop Romero began to raise the consecrated bread in his hands, he was shot through his heart and killed. He was assassinated because he truly lived the command we all receive during the Concluding Rites of the Mass, "Go in peace, glorifying the Lord by your life."

During his homily at that Mass, Archbishop Romero said, "Those who give their lives to the service of the poor through love will live like the grain of wheat that dies. The harvest comes from the grains that die. We know that every effort to improve society, when society is so full of injustice, is an effort that God blesses, God wants, and God demands of us. I am bound by God's command to give my life for all the people of El Salvador, even those who want to kill me."

Archbishop Romero was faithful to Jesus Christ and his message. He believed that the Gospel demanded that he serve the poor and be their voice. He was truly bread of life for the poor. Like the grain of wheat, he died to bring a harvest of justice to the people of his country.

 What changes did Archbishop Romero go through in his life that show his faithfulness to Jesus?

Activity List three ways that you can assist the poor in your community.

1. _____

_____

_____

2. _____

_____

_____

3. _____

_____

_____

The Sacrament of the Eucharist

Many of the Old Testament events point to, or prefigure, the mystery of the Eucharist, which we celebrate at Mass. Three accounts in the Old Testament, in particular, provide excellent examples of how God provided nourishment for his Chosen People, who in return offered thanksgiving to God. These are the stories of Melchizedek, the Passover, and the story of manna from Heaven.

The Gift of Nourishment

Melchizedek

Upon settling in Canaan, Abram (Abraham) celebrated victory over an enemy ruler with Melchizedek, king of Salem. This story has a deep meaning for Christians. Three elements in this Old Testament story prefigure Christ's giving of himself to us in the Eucharist.

When Abram returned from his victory . . . Melchizedek, king of Salem, brought out bread and wine, and being a priest of God Most High, he blessed Abram with these words:

"Blessed be Abram by God Most High,
    the creator of heaven and earth;
And blessed be God Most High,
    who delievered your foes into your hand."

GENESIS 14:17–20

These elements are the inclusion of bread and wine, the offering of bread and wine as gifts to God, and the grateful remembrance of what God has done for his people.

? In what ways is the story of Melchizedek similar to how we celebrate Mass?

Nourish Us, O Lord

Two other key events in the Old Testament point to the Eucharist.

Passover

During the events of the Exodus, God protected and saved his people from slavery and plagues. In remembrance of God's saving power, the Israelites celebrated Passover each year with unleavened bread, the Passover lamb, bitter herbs, and wine (read Exodus 12:1–20). Jesus Christ, the Lamb of God, gave us a new Passover meal in the Eucharist.

Manna

While the Israelites wandered in the desert searching for the Promised Land, God gave them manna to eat (read Exodus 16:1–18). Manna is a bread-like substance produced on a shrub. This account reveals how God continually provided nourishment to his people. The Church teaches that manna prefigured the Eucharist, the Bread of Life God gives us.

? How does knowing about manna deepen your understanding of the Eucharist?

Activity Write news headlines describing how the three events in the Old Testament point to the Eucharist.

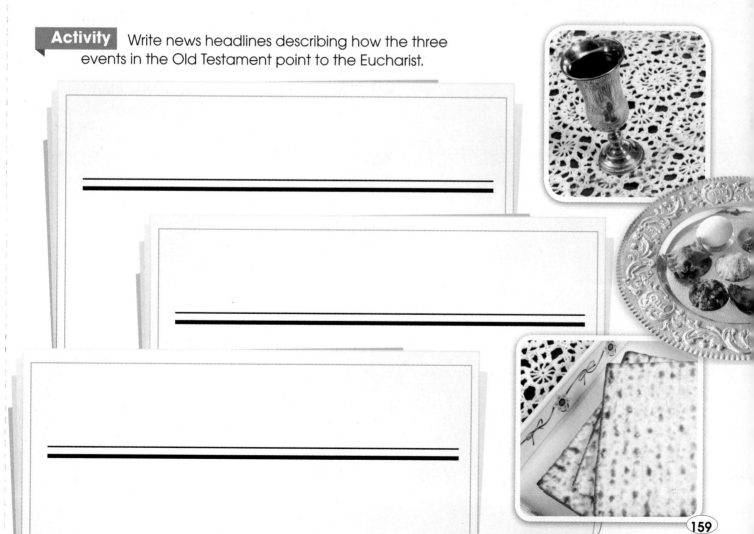

FAITH FOCUS
What does the Church
celebrate at Mass?

FAITH VOCABULARY
Eucharist
The Eucharist is the
Sacrament of the Body
and Blood of Christ; the
Sacrament of Christian
Initiation in which we
receive the Real Presence
of Christ and are most fully
joined to Christ and to
the Church.

Mass
Mass is the main
sacramental celebration
of the Church at which we
gather to listen to God's
Word and through which
we share in the saving
Death of Christ and give
praise and glory to God
the Father.

The Mass

The **Eucharist,** prefigured by the manna, the offering of Melchizedek, and the Passover meal, is the great Sacrament of God's love. Celebrating the Eucharist at **Mass** recalls and makes present the one sacrifice of Christ. This is why we talk about the Sacrifice of the Mass.

The two parts of the Mass are the Liturgy of the Word and the Liturgy of the Eucharist. These two parts make up one single act of worship that we call the Mass.

Nourishing Minds and Hearts

The proclamation of God's very own word in the Scriptures is the center of the Liturgy of the Word. The Word of God feeds us, nourishing our minds and hearts. It also inspires us to praise and thank God for showing us a path for living.

At Mass on Sundays and major feast days, we usually listen to three readings. The first reading is usually taken from the Old Testament. The Responsorial Psalm helps us reflect on the message of the first reading. The second reading is usually taken from the New Testament.

The Gospel reading is the last of the three readings. We hear about the actions and teachings of Jesus from one of the four Gospels in the New Testament: Matthew, Mark, Luke, or John.

? What is one of your favorite Gospel stories? What do you think God is saying to you?

Blessing and Thanksgiving

In the Liturgy of the Eucharist, the Church celebrates the great prayer of blessing and thanksgiving to God the Father. God calls each of us to participate through our prayers of praise and thanksgiving. We all have the essential role of participating in the Mass. Together we celebrate the memorial - we remember what God makes present through our actions in the liturgy.

The presiding priest has a unique role. He is the only one who can consecrate the bread and wine, which become the Body and Blood of our Lord. This is because Christ, the High Priest, acts through the presiding priest and offers the Sacrifice of the Mass.

During the Eucharistic Prayer, the priest pronounces the words of consecration. Through his words, and by the Holy Spirit, the bread and wine are truly changed into the Body and Blood of Christ. Christ is truly present in the Eucharist. Then the consecrated bread is broken for us to share. The people are invited to process forward and receive Holy Communion. In this way, we receive Christ himself. This is what we mean by the Real Presence of Christ.

[?] What aspect of the Mass do you enjoy most?

Activity In your own words, describe what happens during the two main parts of the Mass.

Liturgy of the Word

_____

_____

_____

_____

_____

Liturgy of the Eucharist

_____

_____

_____

_____

_____

Holy Communion

In and through the Mass, Christ is present. We encounter Christ in the faithful assembled, in the Word of God proclaimed, in the priest who is minister of the Mass, and most importantly in the Eucharist. In Holy Communion, we are united to Christ and to one another. The Eucharist preserves the life of grace received at Baptism. In this state of grace, we are separated from sin. We are strengthened to live our faith and be witnesses for Christ.

Therefore, the Church calls us to obligate ourselves to receive the Eucharist at least once a year. Strengthened and united as the Body of Christ, the Church professes the Eucharist as the source and summit of her life. This is truly a celebration to give thanks and praise to God. The amazing effect of the Eucharistic liturgy is that the Eucharist makes us the Body of Christ. We receive Holy Communion and become a holy communion, a people united in Christ.

? How do you encounter Christ in the Mass?

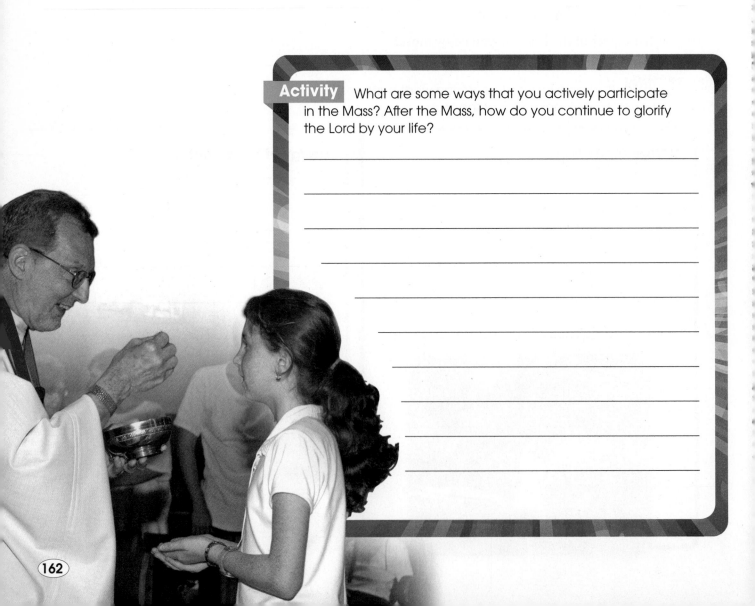

Activity What are some ways that you actively participate in the Mass? After the Mass, how do you continue to glorify the Lord by your life?

_____

_____

_____

_____

_____

_____

_____

_____

_____

I FOLLOW JESUS

Receiving the Eucharist in Holy Communion strengthens your union with Jesus and the Church. Each time you participate in the Mass, you receive the call and the grace of the Holy Spirit to faithfully love and serve the Lord.

THE BREAD OF LIFE

Quietly read these words of Jesus. Reflect on what they tell you about being a disciple of Jesus:

> Jesus said to them,
> "I am the bread of life;
> whoever comes to me
> will never hunger, and whoever
> believes in me will never thirst"
>
> JOHN 6:35

Describe how the Bread of Life helps you to be a disciple of Christ.

_____

_____

_____

_____

_____

_____

MY FAITH CHOICE

Through the week, I will live the Mass and glorify God. I will stay faithful to Jesus. I will

_____

_____

 Pray, "Father, you have given us your Son, the Bread of Life. Nourish me with your Word so that I may remain faithful. Amen."

1. Many events in the Old Testament prefigure, or point to, the mystery of the Eucharist.

2. We encounter Christ in and through the Mass. The two parts of the Mass are the Liturgy of the Word and the Liturgy of the Eucharist. These two parts make up one single act of worship that we call the Mass.

3. The Eucharist is a memorial of the Paschal Mystery.

Chapter Review

Recall

Read each sentence and unscramble the words to complete it.

1. The Sacrament of the _____ is the Sacrament
   shaucErit
   of the Body and Blood of Christ.

2. The _____ meal prefigures the Last Supper
   sPaersov
   and the Eucharist.

3. During the Eucharistic Prayer, the priest pronounces the words of

   _____. These are the words Jesus spoke at the
   crcontionsea
   Last Supper.

4. The _____ is the main sacramental celebration of
   saMs
   the Church.

5. _____ is a breadlike substance that prefigured
   naMan
   the Eucharist.

Reflect

Explain what it means to you that the Eucharist is a memorial of the Pashal Mystery.

_____

_____

_____

_____

_____

_____

_____

Share   Work with a partner to share how you will live the Mass. Share your responses with the class.

Praise to You, Lord!

The Eucharist nourishes us to live the Gospel. Celebrate the following Liturgy of the Word. Then go forth and be bread for the world.

Leader: Heavenly Father, giver of all blessings, thank you for the gift of your Son, Jesus, the Bread of Life. Send the Holy Spirit to help us serve others as your Son did.

Reader: A reading from the holy Gospel according to John.

All: **Glory to you, O Lord.**

Reader: So Jesus said to them, "Amen, amen, I say to you, it was not Moses who gave the bread from heaven; my Father gives you the true bread from heaven. For the bread of God is that which comes down from heaven and gives life to the world."

So they said to him, "Sir, give us this bread always." Jesus said to them, "I am the bread of life; whoever comes to me will never hunger, and whoever believes in me will never thirst."

John 6:32–35

The Gospel of the Lord.

All: **Praise to you, Lord Jesus Christ.**

Leader: Let us now pray to God the Father as Jesus taught.

All: **Our Father . . .**

Leader: Let us offer one another a sign of peace. *(Pause.)*

All: **Thanks be to God.**

With My Family

This Week . . .

In Chapter 12, "The Sacraments of Christian Initiation: The Eucharist," your child learned:

▶ The Old Testament stories of Melchizedek, Passover, and the manna prefigure the Eucharist.

▶ The Eucharist is the Sacrament of the Body and Blood of our Lord, Jesus Christ.

▶ In the Mass, the bread and wine truly become the Body and Blood of Christ through the power of the Holy Spirit and the words of the priest.

▶ At the end of Mass, we are sent forth to go glorify God by our lives.

▶ Faithfulness is a Fruit of the Holy Spirit that is the steadfast commitment to Jesus Christ.

For more about related teachings of the Church, see the *Catechism of the Catholic Church*, 1322–1419, and the *United States Catholic Catechism for Adults*, pages 215–232.

■ Sharing God's Word

Read together I Corinthians 11:17–34. Emphasize that the Eucharist is the Sacrament of the Body and Blood of Christ. Sharing in the Eucharist nourishes us and strengthens us to love and serve God and one another.

■ We Live as Disciples

The Christian home and family is a school of discipleship. Choose one of the following activities to do as a family, or design a similar activity of your own:

▶ Find a favorite bread recipe and make homemade bread as a family. Talk about the unique ingredients needed to make bread rise. Use the bread for a special meal.

▶ When you take part in the Mass this week, listen and think carefully about the readings and prayers. After Mass, discuss what you heard and thought about during Mass.

▶ Talk about some ways you can participate in Mass more actively. Invite each family member to share how the family can help encourage conscious, active participation in Mass.

■ Our Spiritual Journey

Fasting helps us deepen our awareness of our dependence on God. The Eucharistic fast deepens our desire for receiving the Body and Blood of Christ. It helps strengthen our union with him and the Church. A faithful Catholic receives Holy Communion frequently. It acknowledges that we are not alone. This week pray together as a family, "Thank you, God, for the gift of Jesus, your Son, the Bread of Life. Send the Holy Spirit to help us serve others as your Son did. Amen."

For more ideas on ways your family can live as disciples of Jesus, visit **BeMyDisciples.com**

Sister Rose's Passion

One day, in the early 1930s when she was eleven years old, Rose Thering and her father were driving through the farming town where they lived. "There's a new pharmacist in town," her father told her. Then he whispered, "He's Jewish." Rose was confused. When they arrived home, Rose asked her mother, "Why did Daddy whisper that?" Rose's mother would not answer.

As Rose grew older, she heard more and more comments about Jews. She discovered that there was a deep "anti-Jewishness," as she called it, in her country. Some people, and even some religion books, called Jews "children of the devil" and "Christ-killers."

"Jesus was a Jew," Rose thought to herself. "Mary was a Jew. I can't imagine God not loving people who are Jewish."

Rose became a Dominican sister. She wanted to teach and help others love God. Sister Rose has worked hard her whole life to change people's attitudes about the Jewish people. Her work even helped change the Catholic Church's views toward Jewish people. Everywhere she goes, Sister Rose reminds people of what intolerance, prejudice, and bigotry can do. She tells about how these things led to the extermination of millions of people in the Holocaust.

In a documentary about her life, Sister Rose's Passion, which was nominated for an Academy Award, Sister Rose is meeting with a group of schoolchildren. She tells the students that they can make a difference by standing up for what is right. "When you see a bully on the playground you say, 'Enough. No more.'"

Sister Rose is an example of a person who has spent her life defending basic human dignity and human rights of people. How will you stand up for human rights for everyone, everywhere?

WE ARE FROM GOD

Our dignity comes from being made in the image and likeness of God. We are called to see God in other people, especially those we may not like.

Sister Rose Thering, OP; photographs of people who died in the Holocaust from the Hall of Names in Yad Vashem, Israel's Holocaust memorial museum.

MAKING CONNECTIONS

There are many situations in which people's human dignity is not shown the respect it deserves. There are also many situations where the basic human rights of people need to be defended. All people deserve dignity and respect.

with SOCIAL STUDIES

Develop a research project on the history of the Jewish people during the first and second centuries. Pay particular attention to how they were treated by the Roman Empire and by the early Church. Include in your research project, how the treatment of the Jewish people may have impacted them. Did it change the ways they lived, where they lived, the foods they ate, religious traditions, or relationships? Share what you learned and ways you can show respect for the Jewish people.

with MATH AND SCIENCE

During the Holocaust, close to six million Jewish people out of a Jewish population of more than nine-and-a-half million people in thirteen countries were put to death. Use your math skills to develop a "Statistics of the Holocaust" chart. Include in your report, the number of Jewish people in the world today. How has the Jewish faith grown or not grown since the end of the Holocaust? Report your findings to the class. Then as a class, determine what you can learn from the statistics about the Jewish people.

with LANGUAGE ARTS

Read *Number the Stars* by Lois Lowry. This book emphasizes the qualities of courage, caring, and standing up for what is right. The story, based on fact, is set in Denmark during World War II and tells of that country's efforts to save their Jewish citizens. Choose one part of the story and write a skit based on that part of the story to share with your class. At the end of the skit, deliver an epilogue to share the conclusion of what happened in this true story.

Faith Action

Write a journal entry this week based on this question: How can I make a difference for good in my world by respecting the dignity of every person?

_____

_____

Unit 3 **Review**

Name _____

A. Choose the Best Word

Fill in the blanks within the paragraph by using the terms in the word bank.

Last Supper	Salvation	Holy Communion
Word	Sacraments	Paschal Mystery

The story of God's loving plan of creation and **(1)** _____ in Jesus Christ is proclaimed and celebrated by the Church in

the **(2)**_____. Through rituals, the Church celebrates

the liturgy, and we are made sharers in the **(3)** _____ of Jesus Christ. The Sacrament of the Eucharist is celebrated

at Mass. During the Liturgy of the **(4)** _____, we listen to readings from Scripture. During the Liturgy of the Eucharist,

we do what Jesus did at the **(5)** _____.

B. Show What You Know

Read each statement and circle the best answer.

1. Which season of the Church year celebrates the Resurrection of Jesus?

   A. Lent   B. Easter

2. What is a Sacrament?

   A. Words and actions used in   B. A sacred sign and cause of
      the liturgy   grace in the Church

3. Which Sacrament is not a Sacrament of Christian Initiation?

   A. Ordination   B. Confirmation

4. What are the two main parts of the Mass?

   A. Liturgy of the Word and   B. Consecration and Concluding Rites
      Liturgy of the Eucharist

5. What gift do we receive through the Sacrament of Baptism?

   A. Original Sin   B. Holy Spirit

C. Connect with Scripture

*Reread the Scripture passage on the first Unit Opener page.
What connection do you see between this passage and
what you learned in this unit?*

_____

_____

_____

_____

_____

D. Be a Disciple

1. *Review the four pages in this unit titled, The Church Follows Jesus.
What person or ministry of the Church on these pages will inspire
you to be a better disciple of Jesus? Explain your answer.*

_____

_____

_____

_____

_____

2. *Work with a group. Review the four Disciple Power virtues, or gifts,
you have learned about in this unit. After jotting down your own
ideas, share with the group practical ways that you will live these
gifts day by day.*

_____

_____

_____

_____

_____

We Worship
Part Two

Your Sins Are Forgiven

A Pharisee invited Jesus to attend a banquet at his house. A sinful woman came in behind Jesus. Weeping, she bathed his feet with her tears and dried them with her long hair. She kissed his feet and anointed them with a special ointment.

When the Pharisee who had invited him saw this he said to himself, "If this man were a prophet, he would know who and what sort of woman this is . . . she is a sinner. [Jesus said,] "You did not anoint my head with oil, but she anointed my feet with ointment. So I tell you, her many sins have been forgiven; hence, she has shown great love. But the one to whom little is forgiven, loves little." He said to her, "Your sins are forgiven. . . . Your faith has saved you; go in peace."

Luke 7:39, 46–48, 50

What I Know

What is something you already know about these faith concepts?

Examination of Conscience

_____

_____

_____

The Sacraments of Healing

_____

_____

_____

The Sacraments at the Service of Communion

_____

_____

_____

Faith Terms

Put an X next to the faith terms you know. Put a ? next to the faith terms you need to learn more about.

_____ mortal sin

_____ venial sin

_____ penance

_____ hospice care

_____ ordination

_____ bishop

_____ spousal love

_____ complementarity

Questions I Have

The Bible

What do you know about the healing miracles of Jesus?

_____

_____

_____

The Church

What more would you like to learn about the Church's authority?

_____

_____

_____

What questions would you like to ask about the vocation to the priesthood, religious life, or lay ecclesial ministry?

_____

_____

_____

Looking Ahead

In this chapter, the Holy Spirit invites you to ▶

EXPLORE the life of a mother whose strength helped her son.

DISCOVER the graces of Penance and Reconciliation.

DECIDE how you will demonstrate self-control and sacrifice.

Penance and Reconciliation

? How easy is it for you to accept forgiveness?
How difficult is it for you to forgive someone?
How do you seek forgiveness?

In Luke's account of Jesus pardoning the woman who had sinned, Jesus explains to his disciples that love is a sign that her sins are forgiven:

"So I tell you, her many sins have been forgiven; hence, she has shown great love. But the one to whom little is forgiven, loves little." . . . [Jesus] said to the woman, "Your faith has saved you; go in peace."

LUKE 7:47, 50

? How did the woman show her love and faith in Jesus?
What can you do to show love to God and others?

Disciple Power

Self-control

Self-control is a Fruit of the Holy Spirit that comes from a steadfast commitment to God. A person with self-control demonstrates that God's will comes first in life. Self-control helps us do what is good and just. When others see self-control in us, we become witnesses for Christ by placing the needs of others before our own and following the will of God the Father, in whom we place our trust.

A Woman of Strength

Faith and love are at the center of the life of Saint Monica. As a young girl, Monica was strong-willed and devoted to her Christian faith. Born in Tagaste, North Africa (modern-day Algeria) in 332, her determination carried over into her adult life. As was customary then, Monica had an arranged marriage with a man named Patricius, who was not a Christian. Together they had three children, one who was named Augustine.

As a wife and a mother, Monica had a difficult time. Patricius led a sinful and violent lifestyle, and Augustine was a reckless teenager. Despite this, Monica prayed patiently for their conversion.

Under the guidance of Saint Ambrose, a holy bishop who gave her advice, Monica remained strong in her faith and devoted to her family. Patricius witnessed his wife's commitment. He eventually changed his sinful ways and was baptized in the Church.

As for Augustine, he was not interested in God or religion as a young man. His mother never gave up on him, however, and prayed for him every day. Augustine saw her discipline and grace-filled ability to allow God to lead her in life. Her daily example of self-control gradually influenced Augustine, and he too changed his life and was baptized. Augustine eventually became a priest and then a bishop. He was one of the foremost religious people of his time. His writings have inspired millions of Catholics.

? What can you learn from Saint Monica's example?

Augustine and Monica
Charles Holl, c. 1810–1882, engraving painting by Ary Scheffer

Faithful to God

Today many see Saint Monica as an example of a strong African Christian woman. No matter how frustrating life seemed, she was true to her understanding of God's plan for her. She did not despair and give up her beliefs nor did she become bitter and unhappy. She remained faithful to God.

Had it not been for Monica's faith and commitment to her family, the world may not have ever known her or her son. The Church celebrates the life of Saint Monica on her feast day, August 27.

? What are some examples of times when self-control is needed at home, school, and in the world?

Activity In the chart, under each heading, name a situation when you could demonstrate self-control during each part of the day. Then write what you can do to demonstrate self-control. In the last column write a brief prayer to the Holy Spirit to help you.

	Situation	Action	Prayer
Morning			
Day			
Evening			

FAITH VOCABULARY

Sacrament of Penance and Reconciliation
Penance and Reconciliation is a Sacrament of Healing through which we receive God's mercy and forgiveness, through the ministry of a priest, for sins that we have committed after Baptism.

venial sin
A venial sin is less serious than a mortal sin; it is a sin that does not have all three conditions necessary for a sin to be mortal.

mortal sin
A mortal sin is a serious failure in our love and respect for God, our neighbor, and ourselves. For a sin to be mortal, it must be gravely wrong, we must know it to be gravely wrong, and we must freely choose it.

God's Forgiveness

The self-control of Saint Monica shows how understanding God's plan for you can keep you true to the faith and love of God. Some people, however, do not stay true to this love.

God did not create suffering, violence, and death. God did not plan for people to hurt, oppress, or abuse one another, or for one group of human beings to hate another. God did not create the beauty and order of creation to be tarnished by neglect, pollution, or greed. All these evils came into the world not from God's hands but through human choice. Sin disrupts the goodness of creation.

When we sin, we turn away from the love of God and of other people. We hurt ourselves, and we need spiritual healing. In the Sacraments of Healing, our relationship with God and with the Church is renewed. Both the **Sacrament of Penance and Reconciliation** and the Sacrament of the Anointing of the Sick are Sacraments of Healing. We need the healing given by God, who alone can forgive sins. In his mercy and goodness, God shares his power to forgive sins with the Church, the Body of Christ. He shares this forgiveness through the celebration of the Sacraments.

❓ When do students your age need God's healing most?

Sacraments of Forgiveness

Baptism is the first Sacrament of forgiveness. In Baptism, Original Sin and all personal sins are forgiven. Jesus also gave the Church the Sacrament of Penance and Reconciliation for the forgiveness of sins committed after Baptism. He said to his disciples,

"Receive the holy Spirit. Whose sins you forgive are forgiven them, and whose sins you retain are retained."

JOHN 20:22–23

This Sacrament helps us to accept responsibility for all the choices we make. This work of forgiveness is continued through the ministry of bishops and priests.

The Eucharist is also a Sacrament of foregiveness. Sharing in the Eucharist joins us more closely to Christ and to others. **Venial sins** are forgiven. **Mortal sins**, however, must be confessed in the Sacrament of Penance and Reconciliation. Celebrating Reconciliation and receiving the Eucharist regularly helps us deepen our relationship with God and others.

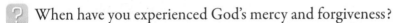 When have you experienced God's mercy and forgiveness?

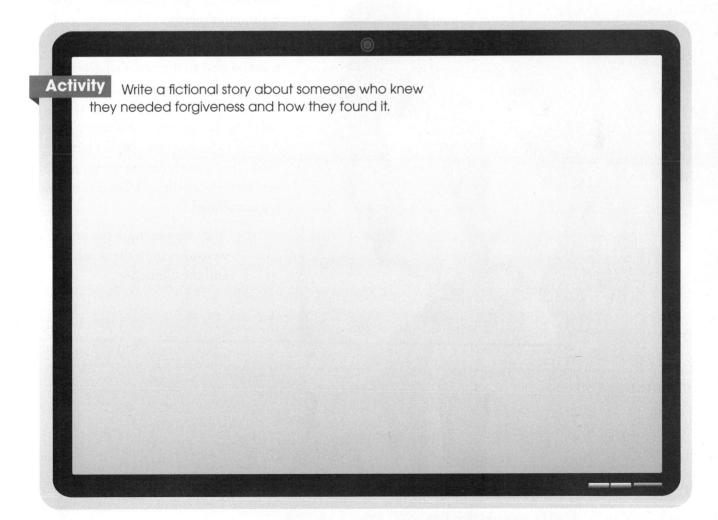

Activity Write a fictional story about someone who knew they needed forgiveness and how they found it.

Reconciling Our Relationships

We can celebrate reconciliation whenever we express our need for God's mercy and are sorry for our sins. The Sacrament of Penance and Reconciliation is the way we celebrate reconciliation for sins that we have committed after Baptism. It includes both the priest, who is the minister of the Sacrament, and the penitent, who is seeking reconciliation with God and the Church.

Before confessing our sins to the priest, we first prepare for the Sacrament through an examination of conscience. This is a reflection on our lives in light of the Gospel. It expresses our desire to enter into a deeper relationship with God. When we examine our conscience in this way, we are opening ourselves to God's grace. Reconciliation heals and transforms us into a new life with Christ.

The Rite of Penance

Another name for the Sacrament of Penance and Reconciliation is Confession. When we meet the priest, he welcomes us in the name of Jesus and the Church, inviting us to repentance. He may read a story or passage from the Bible, and then we confess, or tell the priest our sins, and express our sorrow.

The Church teaches that the penitent must confess to the priest all grave sins committed and not yet confessed. The Church forbids a priest ever to tell anything he hears in Confession. This frees us to be open and honest with God. The Church does not require that venial sins be confessed, but it is strongly recommended.

? Why do you think the priest welcomes us in the name of Jesus and the Church?

Go In Peace

After we confess our sins, the priest may suggest ways to grow closer to God. He then asks us to perform an act of penance. This way we can take responsibility for what we have done and atone for the wrong we have committed. This penance might include a prayer, acts of charity, or works of mercy. The priest then asks us to tell God that we are sorry for our sins by praying the Act of Contrition.

On behalf of the Church, the priest then extends his hands over us and says a prayer of absolution. Through absolution by the priest, God heals us and grants pardon for our sins. Having confessed with a contrite heart and with the willingness to change, the Holy Spirit re-sanctifies us as temples of God. Finally, with the priest, we praise God for his mercy, and the priest encourages us to go in peace as a living sign of God's redeeming love.

? What does it mean to have a contrite heart and the willingness to change? Why do you think this is important for forgiveness?

Activity Write ways that someone might turn their backs on God and sin. Then write a proverb, or wise saying, that could remind that person how to avoid this kind of sin. Use the Book of Proverbs in the Bible to help you.

Turning away from God	Wise Saying
1. _____	_____
_____	_____
2. _____	_____
_____	_____
3. _____	_____
_____	_____

FAITH FOCUS
What are the effects of the
Sacrament of Penance and
Reconciliation?

The Graces of Reconciliation

Celebrating the Sacrament of Penance and Reconciliation heals you spiritually. The Sacrament of Penance and Reconciliation:

- restores and strengthens the life of graces with God, which sin has caused us to lose or weaken.

- renews our relationship with the Body of Christ, the Church.

- frees us from eternal separation from God.

- gives us the gift of peace and forgiveness, and the grace to follow Jesus Christ faithfully—even in the face of difficulties.

Jesus teaches that there is punishment connected with sin. In the Gospel, he tells his disciples that when he comes again, he will separate the good from the wicked. To the evil ones he will say,

"Depart from me, you accursed, into the eternal fire prepared for the devil and his angels. . . . I was thirsty and you gave me no drink, a stranger and you gave me no welcome, naked and you gave me no clothing, ill and in prison, and you did not care for me."

MATTHEW 25:41-43

Punishment for sin is one of the consequences of our sinful acts. Through prayers, good works, and indulgences the faithful can obtain remission, or release, from this temporary punishment caused by sin. The baptized members of the Church can do this for us and for the souls in Purgatory. When we stray from God through sin, he calls us back with his mercy into his loving embrace within the Church.

? How does the Sacrament of Penance and Reconciliation affect you?

Activity   Inventory the unnecessary material things in your life—those things you could really live without. Compare your list with others and discuss how having too much can distract us from what is most important in life and lead us far from God.

_____

_____

_____

_____

I FOLLOW JESUS

Jesus gave the Church the Sacrament of Penance and Reconciliation so that we could have a way to seek and celebrate God's forgiveness for our sins. You can prepare to celebrate this Sacrament by examining your conscience. Ask the Holy Spirit to help you take an honest look at your words and actions so that you can have better control of them and ask for God's forgiveness.

EXAMINATION OF CONSCIENCE

Work with a partner. Refer to the lists of Ten Commandments, Beatitudes, and Works of Mercy in the back of your textbook. From these references and from your knowledge of what God asks you to do, make a list of five questions that Christians should ask themselves in order to evaluate their daily words and actions. Record your questions below.

1.

2.

3.

4.

5.

MY FAITH CHOICE

This coming week, I will show my commitment to God through works of mercy and love. I will

_____

_____

 Pray, "Lord, let me be a witness for Christ through self-control and sacrifice. I ask this in Jesus' name. Amen."

Chapter Review

Recall

Fill in the missing word to complete the sentences.

1. The first Sacrament of forgiveness is _____.

2. _____ sins must be confessed in the Sacrament of Penance and Reconciliation.

3. Through the _____ received in the Sacrament of Penance and Reconciliation, our relationship with God and the Church is restored and renewed.

4. In the Sacrament of Penance and Reconciliation, we receive the _____ needed from God, who alone can forgive sins.

5. Through _____ by a priest, God heals us and grants pardon for our sins.

Reflect

Why would someone need the healing and forgiveness found in the Sacrament of Penance and Reconciliation?

_____

_____

_____

_____

_____

_____

_____

_____

_____

Share   Work with a partner to explain why this Sacrament is best called Penance and Reconciliation. Share with your class.

The Act of Contrition

In the Rite of Penance before we receive absolution, the priest asks us to express our sorrow for our sins with the Act of Contrition. Take a moment of silence to examine your conscience using the questions you wrote for today's activity. Then pray this prayer together.

Leader: Father Almighty, we trust in your great compassion and mercy. Help us to seek your forgiveness always.

All: **Make known to me your ways, LORD; teach me your paths.**

Reader 1: *Remember your compassion and love, O LORD; for they are ages old. Remember no more the sins of my youth; remember me only in light of your love.*

All: **Make known to me your ways, Lord; teach me your paths.**

Reader 2: *Good and upright is the Lord, who shows sinners the way, Guides the humble rightly, and teaches the humble the way.*

PSALM 25:6–9

All: **My God,
I am sorry for my sins with all my heart.
In choosing to do wrong
and failing to do good,
I have sinned against you,
whom I should love above all things.
I firmly intend, with your help,
to do penance,
to sin no more,
and to avoid whatever leads me to sin.
Our Savior Jesus Christ
suffered and died for us.
In his name, my God, have mercy.
Amen.**

With My Family

This Week . . .

In Chapter 13, "Penance and Reconciliation," your child learned:

▶ God shares his power to forgive sins with the Church through the Sacrament of Penance and Reconciliation.

▶ Through Penance and Reconciliation, we receive forgiveness for the sins committed after Baptism.

▶ Confession of sins, contrition (or sorrow), penance, and absolution are always part of the Rite of Penance.

▶ Discipline and self-control demonstrate our commitment to God.

For more about related teachings of the Church, see the *Catechism of the Catholic Church*, 1420–1498, and the *United States Catholic Catechism for Adults*, pages 233–247.

■ Sharing God's Word

Read together John 20:21–23. Emphasize that Jesus gave the Church the power to forgive sins.

■ We Live as Disciples

The Christian home and family form a school of discipleship. Choose one of the following activities to do as a family, or design a similar activity of your own:

▶ When your family has strife in your relationships, practice the movement of conversion: seek repentance, identify the harm done, express contrition and forgiveness, and pray for God's grace to renew the relationship.

▶ During mealtime or bedtime prayers, occasionally include the prayer of the penitent: Lord Jesus, Son of God, have mercy on me a sinner.

■ Our Spiritual Journey

Living a life more pleasing to God includes seeking his forgiveness and mercy. Conditioning our hearts to accept God's mercy often involves sacrifice and putting the needs of others before our own. This is possible by practicing self-control. How can you, as a family, practice self-control so that sacrifice is a priority? This week as a family, pray together, "Father Almighty, we trust in your great compassion and mercy. Amen."

For more ideas on ways your family can live as disciples of Jesus, visit **BeMyDisciples.com**

Looking Ahead

In this chapter, the Holy Spirit invites you to ▶

EXPLORE the gentleness that people experience from hospice care.

DISCOVER the healing ministry of Jesus in the Anointing of the Sick.

DECIDE on a moral way of caring for one who is suffering.

CHAPTER
14

Anointing of the Sick

? What helped you feel better the last time you were sick? What do you think is needed for someone to feel healed spiritually?

In this psalm of lament, the person is severely afflicted and pours out his anguish and pain before the Lord.

> LORD, hear my prayer;
>   let my cry come to you.
> Do not hide your face from me
>   now that I am in distress. . . .
> For my days vanish like smoke;
>   my bones burn away as in a furnace . . .
> From my loud groaning
>   I become just skin and bones.   PSALM 102:2–3A, 4–6

? How do you think the Lord, who is love and mercy, responds to those who are suffering?

Disciple Power

Gentleness

When we exercise the virtue of temperance, the Holy Spirit provides us with this fruit, which is related to self-control. A gentle person is one who pardons injury and is free from harshness, even in the face of injury or illness. A sense of gentleness is a sense of calming peace and care in the way we treat others and ourselves.

The Caring Warmth of Family

Everyone, at some point in his or her life, experiences sorrow and pain. With the support of family and faith in God, we can find comfort during such times of difficulty. Here is what one teen named Edgardo recently experienced.

"This past weekend was a really hard time," he told his friend, Tom, at school. "My family and I visited my grandfather, who was receiving **hospice care**."

Edgardo told Tom that Lolo, his grandfather, had been living at Sunrise Community for the past two years. His family visited Lolo almost every Sunday after Mass. "This time was different," he said, "I knew it as soon as we walked into his room."

Tom asked what was so different this time. "I know you love your grandfather," he said, "but you've said it can be hard visiting him sometimes because he is so sick." "This time was different," Edgardo replied. "This time there was a strange sense of peace and calm even though Lolo was feeling weak and was still in bed."

"Lolo asked me over to his bed to tell me something," Edgardo went on to say. Tom interrupted, "What did he tell you?"

"Edgardo," he said, "remember that there is no bread too hard for warm coffee." Tom asked, "What did he mean by that?"

? What do you think Edgardo's grandfather meant when he said, "Remember that there is no bread too hard for warm coffee"?

Family Love

Edgardo began to explain to Tom what his grandfather was trying to tell him. Edgardo told Tom, "Lolo would say that often to me. Years ago, I asked my father what Lolo meant. My father said it is a wise Filipino saying and that I will learn what it means as I grow older."

"What else happened?" Tom asked. "That was it." Edgardo smiled. "The priest came and anointed him with oil, and we prayed together. Lolo then closed his eyes. My father held Lolo's strong hands, and then Lolo passed away. It felt so peaceful and calm, even though I was crying."

[?] What are some things you can do when a family member is ill?

Activity   Write a prayer to the Holy Spirit to help someone in your family or a friend who is ill.

_____

_____

_____

_____

_____

_____

_____

_____

_____

_____

_____

_____

_____

_____

FAITH VOCABULARY

Anointing of the Sick
The Anointing of the Sick is the Sacrament of Healing that strengthens our faith, hope, and love for God when we are seriously ill, weakened by old age, or dying.

hospice care
Hospice care is a ministry of caring for the terminally ill by offering them gentle end-of-life care that respects the dignity of the human person according to Church teachings.

Healing the Sick

In the Old Testament, we read the story of how the people of Israel became ill in the desert (see Numbers 21:4–9). At God's direction, Moses lifted up a bronze serpent, and all who looked on it were healed. The Church has understood that lifting up the bronze serpent prefigured the lifting up of Jesus on the Cross. By his suffering, Death, and Resurrection, Jesus heals the whole human family. Each of us is called to embrace Jesus' healing by receiving grace in the Sacraments.

Throughout his life on Earth, Jesus healed those who were sick physically and spiritually. Matthew tells us:

Jesus went around to all the towns and villages, teaching in their synagogues, proclaiming the gospel of the kingdom, and curing every disease and illness.

MATTHEW 9:35

In the Gospel of Luke, people flocked to Jesus in the hope that he would cure them of their various diseases.

At sunset, all who had people sick with various diseases brought them to him. He laid his hands on each of them and cured them.

LUKE 4:40

This work of Jesus invited people both to see how much God loves them and to place their trust and faith in him.

? What stories about Jesus' healing can you recall and share with your class?

Healing in Jesus' Name

Jesus also sent his disciples to carry out his ministry of healing in his name.

> So [the Twelve] went off and preached repentance. They drove out many demons, and they anointed with oil many who were sick and cured them.
>
> MARK 6:12–13

Today, the Church continues Jesus' ministry of healing through the Sacraments of Healing, including the **Anointing of the Sick.** Anyone who is seriously ill can receive the Sacrament of the Anointing of the Sick. For those who are in danger of death because of illness or old age, the Sacrament is especially important.

? What do you think are the healing effects of the Sacrament of the Anointing of the Sick?

Respect for Those Who Suffer

Those who suffer illness or physical limitations deserve special respect. Even if death is imminent, the normal care of a sick person should not be interrupted, nor is it morally permissible to intentionally end someone's life if they are suffering greatly or are terminally ill. We are not to prolong a person's natural death through the over-zealous use of medical treatment.

Activity Choose one of the following Gospel accounts of Jesus' healing ministry. Write a short play based on the Gospel account. Act it out with a group of your classmates.

Healing a blind man:	John 9:1–7, 35–38
Healing a sick man:	John 5:1–8
Healing an official's son:	John 4:43–53 or Luke 7:1–10
Healing a crippled man:	Luke 5:17–25

Healing a dying girl and a sick woman:
Luke 8:40–55; Matthew 9:18–26; or Mark 5:21–43

Healing two blind men: Matthew 20:29–34

Title:

_____

Biblical Figures:

_____

_____

Identify the Healing:

_____

_____

_____

Jesus' Message:

_____

_____

_____

Ministering to the Sick

From her very beginning, the Church has ministered to the sick in a special way. The New Testament Letter of James states:

> Is anyone among you sick? He should summon the presbyters of the church, and they should pray over him and anoint [him] with oil in the name of the Lord, and the prayer of faith will save the sick person, and the Lord will raise him up. If he has committed any sins, he will be forgiven.
>
> JAMES 5:14–15

The Church understands that illness is upsetting and can be very frightening, especially when a person is in danger of death. Illness reminds us that our lives are in God's hands.

We remember that Jesus himself suffered and is with us in our suffering, as is the entire community of the Church. We comfort and support one another when we are well, and depend on others when we are ill. The Sacrament of the Anointing of the Sick is one way that we seek God's healing and mercy.

The Anointing of the Sick may be received each time we become seriously ill. We also may receive this Sacrament more than once during the same illness if our sickness becomes worse. Those who are to undergo surgery are also encouraged to receive this Sacrament.

? How do you think someone who is ill might understand their illness through the eyes of faith?

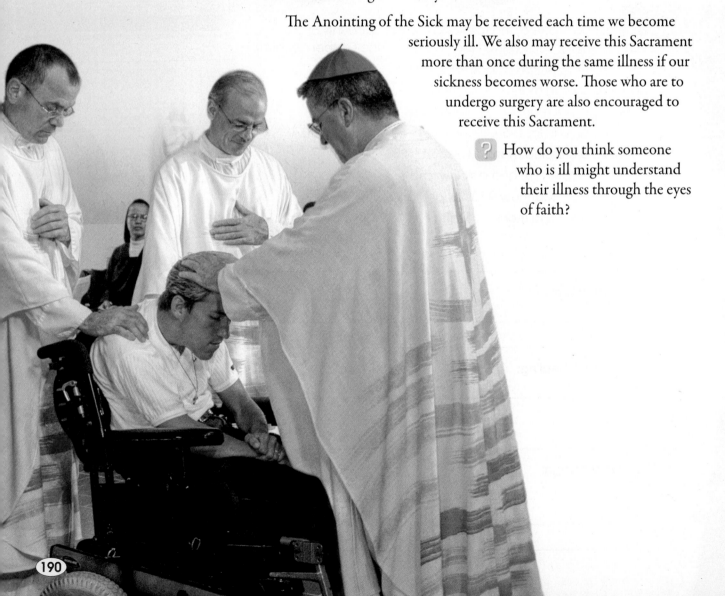

Rite of Anointing

In the Rite of Anointing, there are three essential aspects to the celebration of the Sacrament: the prayer of faith, the laying on of hands, and the anointing with oil. Only the priest is the minister of the Sacrament.

The oil used to anoint is blessed by the bishop, or if necessary, blessed by a delegated priest. The priest usually anoints the forehead and hands of the sick, but other parts of the body may also be anointed, if deemed necessary.

The Church uses oil because of its natural healing powers and because anointing oil is soothing and comforting. The oil is a sign of healing and signifies the comforting presence of God for the sick person. When the priest is generous in its use, the sick person can better experience the sign of the Holy Spirit's healing and strengthening presence.

Through the celebration of the Sacrament of the Anointing of the Sick, Christ's work of healing continues in the world today. His healing presence helps the sick and dying find courage, strength, and hope.

? What do you think a person may experience when receiving the Sacrament of the Anointing of the Sick?

Activity Work with a group. Create a poster to publicize a service of healing that your parish is having. Include a slogan that will encourage the whole parish community to attend. Write your ideas for a slogan here.

_____

_____

_____

_____

_____

_____

_____

FAITH FOCUS
What are the graces of the
Sacrament of the Anointing
of the Sick?

The Graces of Holy Anointing

In the Sacrament of the Anointing of the Sick, we receive many graces. Some of the important graces of this Sacrament are:

Our sufferings are united with those of Jesus, and in this union, we find strength and consolation, knowing that the Lord is with us.

We receive peace and courage to face our sufferings as a gift from the Holy Spirit.

We can receive the forgiveness of our sins if we are unable to celebrate the Sacrament of Penance and Reconciliation.

Our health may be restored; however, equally important, we receive a spiritual healing by the intercession of the Church.

We are prepared for our final journey to eternal life when we are very ill and near death.

Through the celebration of the Sacrament of the Anointing of the Sick, Christ continues his work of healing among us. Having our close family and friends by our side when we receive this Sacrament is beneficial in experiencing the support and love of the whole Church. With faith and trust in God, we can face our suffering by offering it up as our sacrifice, in imitation of Christ's suffering on the Cross.

? What are some of the ways your parish or school works with people who are sick? Talk with your friends about things you and they can do to help.

Activity Brainstorm a list of activities that your school does to support and care for those who are ill. Identify areas where you and your class can help.

Activities Your School Does	How you can help

I FOLLOW JESUS

One of the important characteristics of Jesus' healing was his gentle touch. The Church sees his gentle touch as a sign of respecting the dignity of the human person, especially in times of pain and suffering.

GENTLE OFFER OF HOPE

Think of people in your family, your neighborhood, school, or parish who may be physically or spiritually suffering. Choose a way you could help to ease their pain —a card, a poem, or a drawing that would offer them hope and encouragement in the name of Jesus. Use this space to outline or sketch your idea.

MY FAITH CHOICE

This week, I will be more aware of people and situations that need healing. I will offer a gentle hand when I can. I will

_____

_____

 Pray, "Lord Jesus, may your gentle touch restore those who are suffering and lead them to your glory. Amen."

1. The Church continues Jesus' ministry of healing in the Sacraments of Healing, including the Sacrament of the Anointing of the Sick.

2. The Anointing of the Sick is the Sacrament that strengthens our faith and trust in God when we are seriously ill or dying.

3. The Rite of Anointing consists of the prayer of faith, the laying on of hands, and the anointing with oil.

Chapter Review

Recall

Read each sentence, and choose the best answer to complete it. Circle the corresponding letter to the correct answer.

1. The Sacrament of the Anointing of the Sick is especially for those who
   a. are in danger of death because of illness or old age.
   b. have already died.
   c. are not feeling well.

2. In the Rite of Anointing, who anoints the body of the sick person?
   a. the doctor
   b. the priest
   c. the closest family member

3. Which of the following is an essential element used in the celebration of the Sacrament of the Anointing of the Sick?
   a. holy water
   b. bread
   c. blessed oil

4. The Sacrament of the Anointing of the Sick can be celebrated
   a. once in a person's life.
   b. more than once in a person's life.
   c. weekly.

5. One of the graces of the Sacrament of the Anointing of the Sick is
   a. receiving the Body and Blood Christ.
   b. being baptized.
   c. finding strength and consolation that the Lord is with us.

Reflect

Why do we celebrate the Sacrament of the Anointing of the Sick?

_____

_____

_____

Share Describe to a member of your class the Rite of Anointing.

Prayer for the Sick

Saint James tells us to pray for the sick. During its care for the sick and dying, the Church prays a brief form of the Litany of the Saints. Think of people you know or have heard about who are sick, and write in their names to include in this prayer.

Leader: **All:**

Holy Mary, Mother of God,   pray for _____.

Saint Joseph,   pray for _____.

Saint Peter,   pray for _____.

Saint James,   pray for _____.

Saint Mary Magdalene,   pray for _____.

Saint Lawrence,   pray for _____.

Saint Paul of the Cross,   pray for _____.

Saint Benedict of Nursia,   pray for _____.

Saint Teresa of the Andes,   pray for _____.

Saint Rafqa,   pray for _____.

Leader: All-powerful and ever-living God,
we find security in your forgiveness.
Give us serenity and peace of mind;
may we rejoice in your gifts of kindness
and use them always for your glory
and our good. We ask this in
the name of Jesus the Lord.

All: **Amen.**

Pastoral Care of the Sick 60C

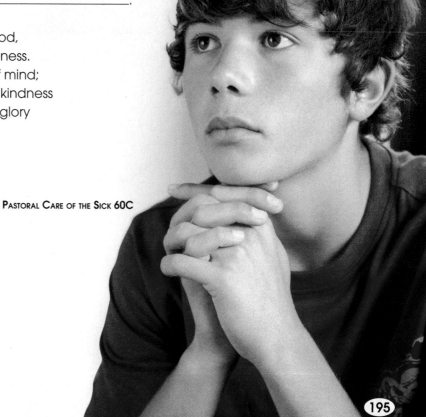

195

With My Family

This Week . . .

In Chapter 14, "Anointing of the Sick," your child learned:

▶ The healing ministry of Jesus was directed to those physically and spiritually in need.

▶ The Church continues Christ's healing ministry to those who are seriously sick and weak because of old age through the Sacrament of the Anointing of the Sick.

▶ The Church extends the gentle touch of Jesus through other ministries, like hospice care. Gentleness is a Fruit of the Holy Spirit that brings peace to others.

For more about related teachings of the Church, see the *Catechism of the Catholic Church*, 1499–1532, and the *United States Catholic Catechism for Adults*, pages 249–259.

Sharing God's Word

Read together James 5:14–15. Emphasize that the Church continues Jesus' ministry of healing in the Sacrament of the Anointing of the Sick.

We Live as Disciples

The Christian home and family form a school of discipleship. Choose one of the following activities to do as a family, or design a similar activity of your own:

▶ Talk about the ways in which your family cares for one another when sick. Include extended family members like grandparents, aunts, uncles, and other relatives.

▶ Form the habit of having your child accompany you when you visit someone who is elderly or experiencing an extended convalescence. Have your child make a small gift to bring cheer to that person. Teach by your example to be thoughtful, gentle, and kind.

Our Spiritual Journey

Dealing with end-of-life issues can be very difficult for both children and adults. Experiencing the support of family and the Church community is vital and can help prepare us. Celebrate frequently the heritage of the family, and recall fond memories of previous generations. This week, pray the litany on page 195 as a family.

For more ideas on ways your family can live as disciples of Jesus, visit **BeMyDisciples.com**

Looking Ahead

In this chapter, the Holy Spirit invites you to ▶

EXPLORE how a priest sought out the truth of the Church.

DISCOVER the three degrees of Holy Orders.

DECIDE decide on how you can live in Christ by serving others.

CHAPTER

15

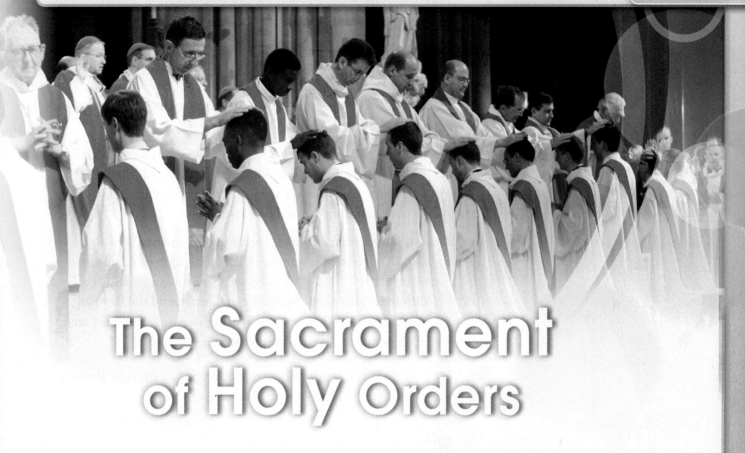

The Sacrament of Holy Orders

? In what ways do you serve others?

Jesus was not alone when he went out to proclaim the Gospel, nor did he minister to those in need by himself. Read about how Jesus ministered to the people:

> Jesus went around to all the towns and villages, teaching in their synagogues, proclaiming the gospel of the kingdom, and curing every disease and illness. At the sight of the crowds, his heart was moved with pity for them because they were troubled and abandoned, like sheep without a shepherd. Then he said to his disciples, "The harvest is abundant but the laborers are few; so ask the master of the harvest to send out laborers for his harvest."
>
> MATTHEW 9:35–38

? If you think of God as the "master of the harvest," who might his laborers be?

Disciple Power

Patience

One of the Fruits of the Holy Spirit is patience, which is the result of virtuous living. Being patient does not mean doing nothing. Patience involves the wisdom of knowing how to wait for truth while actively seeking grace.

Seeking to Serve

Every Catholic priest, as he ministers to people in need, travels on his own journey of faith. In the 1800s, John Henry Newman started one such faith journey. He was not a Catholic and his father was a banker. When he was a teenager, he decided that he did not believe in God at all. One day, a teacher suggested some Christian writings for him to read and they turned him towards God.

John Henry Newman began his journey as an evangelical Christian, then became an Anglican priest, and finally a Catholic cardinal. Throughout his life, Newman actively sought out the truth of God and the Church with humility and and patience.

While still in his early twenties, John Henry Newman became a leader of the Oxford Movement. This was a group of Anglican scholars at the University of Oxford, who sought to settle the differences between the Anglican Church and the Roman Catholic Church. Newman became an Anglican priest, an accomplished writer, and respected scholar.

? What kinds of questions do you ask yourself about faith? How can you find the answers?

A Journey in Faith

In 1845, Newman's journey of faith continued, when he was accepted into full communion with the Catholic Church. He was ordained a Roman Catholic priest a year later. He would go on to help Catholics in Ireland and England and continue to write about theological matters. Father Newman was instrumental in helping to expand the Catholic Church in England during a time when Catholics there faced prejudice and persecution. For this reason, the Church bestowed on him the honor of cardinal. This is a great honor. A year before his death, Cardinal Newman celebrated his last Mass on Christmas Day, 1889.

Cardinal Newman patiently served the Church throughout his faith journey in various roles. In his heart, John Henry Cardinal Newman preferred the life of a parish pastor. In Birmingham, England, where he was a parish priest for more than 30 years, Pope Benedict XVI beatified John Henry Newman on September 19, 2010.

Pope Benedict XVI during the Mass to beatify Cardinal John Henry Newman at Cofton Park, Rednal, Birmingham, England.

 How do you think Cardinal Newman was patient?

Activity   Which qualities do you think are necessary to be a priest? Discuss your ideas with a classmate and make your list here. Next to each quality, write the reason this quality is important.

Quality:_____

Importance:_____

_____

_____

Quality:_____

Importance:_____

_____

_____

Quality:_____

Importance:_____

_____

_____

FAITH FOCUS
What does it mean to serve God?

FAITH VOCABULARY
communion
Communion is the unity in Christ of all the members of the Church, the Body of Christ; the word is from two Latin words meaning "sharing with." Full communion refers to full initiation into the Church.

Consecrated in Christ's Name

True success comes from happiness—the happiness of a servant's heart. Jesus has set the standard for success, and it is quite different from the standards sometimes seen in the world. Jesus taught,

> [W]hoever wishes to be first among you will be the slave of all. For the Son of Man did not come to be served but to serve and to give his life as a ransom for many.

MARK 10:44–45

To serve God and others means that we must serve as Christ did. Success built on material goods, self-centeredness, and self-interests is not in God's plan. We are called to build a community and be ready to make sacrifices. Christian service means that we serve others by giving ourselves as Jesus did. In doing so, we share in the unity of Christ.

There are many ways to serve others. Two ways of living for the sake of others are celebrated with Sacraments. The Sacrament of Holy Orders and the Sacrament of Matrimony are the two Sacraments at the Service of **Communion**.

The Priesthood of Christ

Jesus Christ is the one true priest. The baptized can share in the priesthood of Christ in two ways. There is the priesthood of all the faithful and the ordained priesthood.

? How do you live out your baptismal call to share in the priesthood of Christ?

The Priesthood of the Faithful

Every Christian is joined to Christ in Baptism and is called to live a life of generous service to God and others as Jesus did. We are a people set apart, consecrated to serve God and others. This is what we mean by the common priesthood of the faithful.

The Ordained Priesthood

Those baptized men who receive the Sacrament of Holy Orders share in the ordained ministry of service or the ministerial priesthood. This means that these ordained men are at the service of the common priesthood—they are consecrated in Christ's name for the good of all the faithful. Their solemn promises are a sign of being consecrated for the sake of the Kingdom of God (see Matthew 19:11–12). Through them, Christ continues to build up and serve the Church.

? What does it mean when a man is ordained to the priesthood?

Catholics Believe

Male Ordination

As with all vocations, the life of the priest is a calling. The Church recognizes herself to be bound by Christ's choice of only men to form the ministerial priesthood. The priesthood is a sacramental sign of Christ. Men, called to this vocation in the Catholic Church, humbly submit to the authority of the Church in service to her.

> **Activity** Give three examples of ways that a man who is ordained a priest serves the people of God.
>
> _____
> _____
> _____
> _____
> _____
> _____
> _____
> _____
> _____
> _____
> _____
> _____

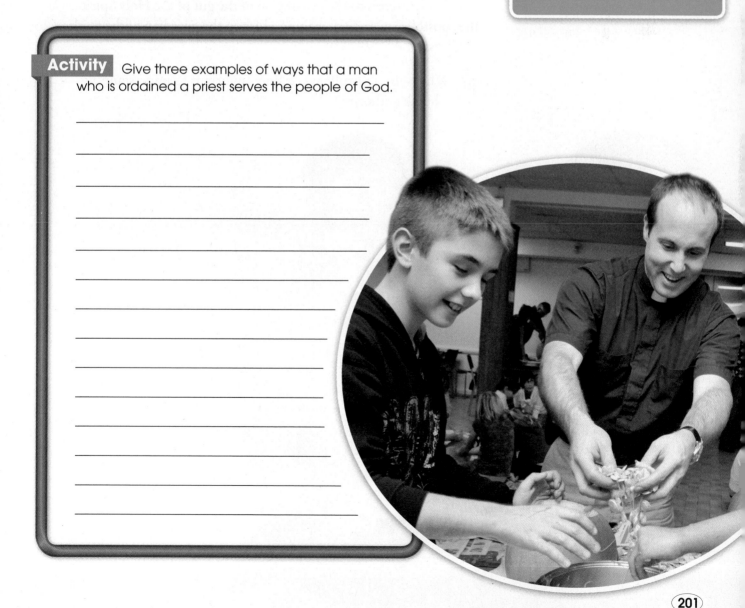

FAITH FOCUS
What does the Sacrament
of Holy Orders mean?

FAITH VOCABULARY
ordination
Ordination is the Sacrament
of Holy Orders in which
a baptized man is
consecrated to serve the
Church as a bishop, priest,
or deacon.

Degrees of Holy Orders

Holy Orders or **Ordination**, is the Sacrament in which a baptized man shares in a unique way the priesthood of God as a bishop, priest, or deacon. The three degrees of Holy Orders are the episcopate (bishops), the presbyterate (priests), and the diaconate (deacons). An ordained man becomes a member of the "order" of bishop, priest, or deacon through the Rite of Ordination as conferred by a bishop.

Unbroken Powers

Holy Orders is celebrated by the laying on of hands by a bishop on the head of a man to be ordained, which is followed by a prayer of consecration. Holy Orders, like Baptism and Confirmation, can be received only once and marks the man who is ordained with a spiritual character forever.

During the Ordination of a bishop, the powers conferred on the Apostles by Christ himself remain unbroken by the laying on of hands. The Church refers to this passing on of the gift of the Holy Spirit as the apostolic succession, making a bishop the guardian of the work of Christ.

? Why is the apostolic succession important to understanding Church authority?

Acting in the Person of Christ

Bishops and priests share in the priesthood of Christ in a unique way. The Sacrament of Holy Orders enables bishops and priests to act in the person of Christ. When they serve the Church, Christ himself is present to the Church. For example, at Mass when the priest says, "This is my Body," he is not referring to his own body, but Christ's. Through the priest or bishop, Christ says, "This is my Body."

Through the ordained ministry, the presence of Christ as Head of the Church is made visible to the faithful; however, this does not mean that the ordained man is not without fault or sin. This means that priests and bishops remind us of the reality that Christ himself is present when exercising the office of his ministry.

? What does it mean that a priest or bishop acts in the person of Christ?

Activity Complete the prayer below prayed during Ordination to ask God to be with the man being ordained. Only consonants are missing.

___ e ___ ely o ___

the ___ elp o ___

the ___ ord ___ od

and ou ___ Sa ___ io ___

___ e ___ u ___ Ch ___ i ___ t,

and ___ e ___ ___ oose this ___ an,

our bro ___ ___ er,

for ___ riest ___ ood in

the pres ___ ___ teral or___er.

ORDINATION OF A PRIEST

Faith-Filled People

Venerable Jean Gailhac

Father Jean Gailhac was born in France in 1802. In his early work as a priest, he served the poor and most marginalized of society. After he started his first shelter for women with nowhere to live, a wealthy widow, Appolinie Cure, joined him in his work. He founded a new religious community, the Institute of the Religious of the Sacred Heart of Mary. She took the name of Mother Saint Jean. She transformed the shelter for women into a place of safety for young girls at risk and started a boarding school. Today, the sisters serve in educational and social ministries in fourteen countries around the world, including France, Ireland, the United States, Brazil, and Zimbabwe.

203

Shepherds of the Flock

During the Rite of Ordination, the bishop is entrusted with the care of the Church. He is appointed by the Holy Spirit to attend to the whole flock, or the faithful of his particular diocese. The bishop carries a **crosier** as a sign of his authority.

A bishop is a teacher, priest, and shepherd. He promises to guide his people in the way of Salvation, showing kindness and compassion. Bishops seek out people who are lost and gather them into the fold for the Lord. With the help of God and until the end of his life, the bishop is to be faithful and constant in proclaiming the Gospel.

Continuing Apostolic Ministry

When a bishop is ordained, he receives the fullness of the Sacrament and continues the ministry of the Apostles. Bishops work in communion with the Pope, who is the bishop of Rome and successor of Saint Peter. A bishop serves as the visible head of a diocese and is a sign of her unity.

Bishops also have the duty to teach the faith; celebrate divine worship, above all the Eucharist; and guide their local churches as true pastors. The priests are the coworkers of the bishops, whereas the deacons are the helpers of the bishops. Each bishop shares the responsibility for the Universal Church with the Pope.

[?] What are some of the works of a bishop?

Pope Francis

Activity **Ask the Pastor**

Brainstorm with a small group some questions you would like to ask a priest about his work. Write your questions here. If possible, invite a pastor to visit your class so you can all ask your questions in person.

_____

_____

_____

_____

_____

_____

I FOLLOW JESUS

Every Christian is joined to Christ in Baptism and is called to live a life of generous service to God and others as Jesus did. The Church needs many more priests and religious sisters and brothers to meet the needs of the People of God.

MY SERVICE DIARY

Imagine that you are a priest or religious sister serving others here or in a missionary land. Write an entry in your journal describing a typical day in your life.

Date

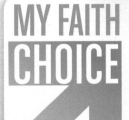

MY FAITH CHOICE

This week, I will patiently live my baptismal call to serve others as Jesus did.

I will

_____

_____.

Pray, "Lord Jesus Christ, true High Priest of all, teach me how to serve others with patience and out of love for you. Amen."

1. Every Christian is joined to Christ in Baptism and is called to live a life of generous service to God and others as Jesus did.

2. Holy Orders consecrates a baptized man to serve the whole Church as a bishop, priest, or deacon.

3. When a bishop is ordained, he receives the fullness of the Sacrament of Holy Orders.

Chapter Review

Recall

Fill in the circle next to the word or phrase that completes each sentence correctly.

1. The word ____ is used to point out the sharing of Christians in the life of Christ.

   ○ sacrifice ○ communion ○ service ○ Gentiles

2. The priesthood of all the faithful refers to the Sacrament of ____.

   ○ Marriage ○ Eucharist ○ Baptism ○ Holy Orders

3. The ordained priesthood refers to the Sacrament of ____.

   ○ Marriage ○ Eucharist ○ Baptism ○ Holy Orders

4. The ____ serves as the visible head of a diocese and is a sign of her unity.

   ○ Apostle ○ bishop ○ cardinal ○ pastor

5. Jesus Christ is the one true ____.

   ○ Apostle ○ bishop ○ cardinal ○ Priest

Reflect

What does it mean to you that you share in the priesthood of Christ today?

_____

_____

_____

_____

_____

_____

Share Work with a partner to explain what it means that bishops and priests act in the person of Christ.

Prayer for Vocations

Throughout the many dioceses in the United States, parishes pray for vocations to the priesthood and religious community life. Here is a prayer for vocations from the United States Conference of Catholic Bishops that you can pray as a class.

God our Father,
you will all men and women to be saved
and come to the knowledge of your Truth.
Send workers into your great harvest
that the Gospel may be preached
to every creature
and your people, gathered together
by the word of life
and strengthened by
the power of the sacraments,
may advance in the way
of salvation and love.

I ask this through our Lord Jesus Christ, your Son,
who lives and reigns with you
and the Holy Spirit, one God, forever and ever.
Amen.

With My Family

This Week . . .

In Chapter 15, "The Sacrament of Holy Orders," your child learned:

▶ God calls some members of the Church to live their baptismal calling by serving the whole Church through the Sacraments at the Service of Communion.

▶ Responding to one's vocation takes virtuous living. Patience, a fruit of the Holy Spirit, involves the wisdom of knowing how to wait for truth while actively seeking grace.

▶ In Holy Orders, a baptized man is ordained as a bishop, priest, or deacon to serve the whole Church by continuing the unique work of Jesus that was entrusted to the Apostles.

For more about related teachings of the Church, see the *Catechism of the Catholic Church*, 1533–1600, and the *United States Catholic Catechism for Adults*, pages 261–275.

■ Sharing God's Word

Read together Mark 10:42–45. Emphasize that each of us receives a special call or vocation from God to serve him and the whole community of the People of God, the Church.

■ We Live as Disciples

The Christian home and family form a school of discipleship. Choose one of the following activities to do as a family, or design a similar activity of your own:

▶ Review your parish bulletin or Web site to see in which ministries each family member can serve. Take time to find out about each and discern the best match.

▶ Include in your family prayers a particular blessing for your parish priests and local bishop. Remember also the Pope who serves the Universal Church.

■ Our Spiritual Journey

The use of the spiritual discipline of discernment enables us to come to know both our vocation and how to live it. Discernment is the prayerful reflection on our gifts and talents. It is coming to know who God created us to be and how we can live the dismissal command given at the end of Mass to glorify God by our lives. This week with your family, pray for vocations by praying the prayer found on page 207.

For more ideas on ways your family can live as disciples of Jesus, visit **BeMyDisciples.com**

Looking Ahead

In this chapter, the Holy Spirit invites you to ▶

EXPLORE the Church's hopes for newly married couples.

DISCOVER God's plan for love and life in marriage.

DECIDE how to be a true sign of Christ's love.

CHAPTER

16

The Sacrament of Matrimony

? What qualities are necessary to maintain a close friendship with someone? How would you define love?

Here is the way Saint Paul described for the community at Corinth what love is and what it is not.

> Love is patient, love is kind. It is not jealous, [love] is not pompous, it is not inflated, it is not rude, it does not seek its own interests, it is not quick-tempered, it does not brood over injury, it does not rejoice over wrongdoing but rejoices with the truth. It bears all things, believes all things, hopes all things, endures all things. . . . So faith, hope, love remain, these three; but the greatest of these is love.
>
> 1 CORINTHIANS 13:4–7, 13

? Have you heard this passage before? What does it tell you about the challenges of loving your family members or your friends?

Disciple Power

Chastity

When we exercise self-control with God's grace in our relationships, the Holy Spirit forms the virtue of chastity in us. This means that we can appropriately integrate the gift of our human sexuality according to God's calling for us. In other words, we respect each other as persons and not as objects to be used.

Pre-Cana Ministry

The Catholic Church requires that Catholic couples take part in a course or period of preparation before they can be married in a Catholic Church. Some of these programs are called Pre-Cana programs for marriage preparation. The name is rooted in the first miracle that Jesus performed at the marriage feast of Cana in Galilee (see John 2:1–12).

The time of preparation may vary from several sessions or conversations to six months of preparation. A priest, often assisted by married couples of the parish, usually conducts the marriage preparation meetings, or course. Topics covered may include: the nature of marriage; family planning; parenting; how to handle family finances; communication skills; and how to resolve conflicts.

By helping couples to plan for their lives together, the Church is helping them to build a marriage that will last a lifetime. The Church is preparing them to create a family that will be a living sign of Christ's love to each other, to their children, and to others.

? What are some things you think are important for a couple to learn about so they will have a successful marriage?

A Marriage Blessing

When a man and woman are married in the presence of a priest within the celebration of the Eucharist, the rite concludes with a solemn blessing. Here is a portion of that beautiful blessing:

May the peace of Christ live always in your hearts and in your home.

May you have true friends to stand by you, both in joy and in sorrow.

May you be ready and willing to help and comfort all who come to you in need.

And may the blessings promised to the compassionate be yours in abundance.

Amen.

May you find happiness and satisfaction in your work.

May daily problems never cause you undue anxiety, nor the desire for earthly possessions dominate your lives.

But may your hearts' first desire be always the good things waiting for you in the life of heaven.

Amen.

May the Lord bless you with many happy years together, so that you may enjoy the rewards of a good life.

And after you have served him loyally in his kingdom on earth, may he welcome you to his eternal kingdom in heaven.

Amen.

RITE OF MARRIAGE

Activity Think of an older married couple you know. Discuss with a partner what you notice about how they relate to one another. Then think of a newly married couple. Write a note or card to them expressing your hopes for them. Use the solemn blessing as your guide.

FAITH VOCABULARY

conjugal love
Conjugal love is the unique expression of sexual love between a husband and a wife, who freely give their whole selves to each other.

Matrimony
The Sacrament of the Church that unites a baptized man and a baptized woman in a lifelong bond of faithful love as a sign of Christ's love for the Church.

God's Plan for Love and Life

Think about the relationships we have in our lives. We have friends and relatives. With some people, we feel more comfortable sharing our deep feelings than with others.

Just as there are different types of relationships, there are different kinds of love. For example, there is the love between friends and siblings. There is also the love between parents and children, and there is yet another unique kind of love between a man and a woman who commit to an exclusive and faithful love over a lifetime in marriage.

Each kind of love expresses being a "gift of self" to another. When we love someone, we care about them. We are eager to help them when they need help and to comfort them when they are hurting. We will sacrifice what we want to help make them happy.

Every expression of love has at its source the love of God. One of the most special kinds of love is expressed through marriage. These are the kinds of relationships planned by God since the creation of Adam and Eve, our first parents.

? How do you express your love for your friends, for your siblings, or for your parents?

Expressions of Love

With each kind of relationship, there are certain appropriate ways to express love. The appropriateness of the expression depends on the kind of relationship. Friends, for example, might express their love with a handshake. This might show friends who walk on equal ground, enjoying each other's company.

Parents show love for their children by caring for them. This love can be expressed with a hug, kind words, or providing material needs and wants (like chocolate chip cookies!). Because parents are responsible for raising their children, the relationship is not one between equals.

There is also the love between spouses. When a man and woman have strong feelings and are sexually attracted to each other, God calls them to recognize this unique expression of their love in a marriage commitment (read Tobit 7:11–13). The unique expression of married love is called **conjugal love.** This mutual kind of love demands that a man and a woman share their lives together completely. They help each other, sacrifice for each other, and support each other.

Catholic couples celebrate the Sacrament of **Matrimony** to become married. The Sacrament of Matrimony is the celebration of a baptized man and a baptized woman who join themselves to each other in a lifelong bond of spousal and mutual love. The Sacrament of Matrimony is one of the two Sacraments at the Service of Communion.

? How is the Sacrament of Matrimony a Sacrament at the Service of Communion?

Catholics Believe

Marital Love

Marriage is both a natural institution and a sacred union. Marriage is God's plan for a man and a woman to express their spousal love in a lifelong loving relationship. In the Sacrament of Matrimony, Christ joins together the bride and the bridegroom in a holy bond that symbolizes the marriage of Christ and his Church.

Activity   Give examples of how someone might share the gift of themselves in the following relationships:

Friend _____

_____

Family _____

_____

Married couple _____

_____

FAITH FOCUS
What are the qualities demanded of Catholic couples by the Sacrament of Matrimony?

FAITH VOCABULARY
complementarity
Complementarity is living with and for each other as equal in dignity and unique in gender, helping each other according to God's plan for both genders.

A Married Couple's Bond

Marriage is like no other loving relationship. Through marriage, a man and a woman make the promise to love, before fully expressing their love. In doing so, they express their **complementarity** with respect and exclusively for each other.

Marital love is expressed according to the two unique genders. In this expression of love, spouses honor the equal dignity of being male and female. Their vowed loved is a complete giving of themselves to one another, the promise to love freely, faithfully, fully, and forever.

The marriage relationship is a covenant. Conjugal love is to be exclusive, permanent, unbreakable, and faithful. The couple's love expresses two important aspects of their relationship: the bond of their mutual love as a couple and their openness to accept and raise children.

A married couple is an example of love to those around them too. By the way they treat each other, they show others how to care, support and sacrifice in their own lives. The married couple becomes a sign of Christ's love for the Church. Christian married love, like Christ's love for the Church, is a sign of the faithful and unbreakable love of God for his people.

? How would you explain that a married couple becomes a sign of Christ's love for the Church?

Essential Qualities

In the Letter to the Ephesians, Paul encourages husbands to love their wives as Christ loves the Church. He equally encourages wives to respect their husbands. This mirrors the love and respect that exists between Christ and his Church (read Ephesians 5:21–27).

When a husband and wife nurture and cherish each other in this way, they become a living Sacrament. They are a living sign through which Christ works in the world. The married couple with their children are a domestic Church, or "Church of the home." The family listens to God's Word, prays together, and serves one another with generosity and compassion. All baptized Christians are called to serve as Jesus did, to be a living sign of God's saving presence, as the one family of God.

When selfishness and materialism replace service and communion, marriages and families are not successful. This can lead to separation or divorce. Because married love is mutual, it requires the cooperation of both spouses. Divorce is painful for not just the married couple but for the entire family. Sadly, divorce is a reality in many families. Many divorced persons wish to remain faithful to the Church and to raise their children in the Catholic faith. The Church continues to support them as baptized members and prays for a resolution of their difficulties.

[?] How does your family live like a "Church of the home"? In what ways do you contribute?

Faith-Filled People

Blesseds Louis and Zélie Martin

The parents of Saint Thérèse of the Child Jesus were only the second married couple beatified by the Catholic Church. They saw their engagement as being open to the will of God. Married in 1858, they dedicated their marriage to serve God. Blessed with nine children, they are honored as a true model of Christian spouses.

Activity Unscramble the key qualities that a marriage should have. Use these words to write a paragraph describing the relationship between a married couple.

cEveisulx _____

nnteamrPe _____

bbaaknreelU _____

lufaihtF _____

Sacred Union

In the Book of Genesis, God's plan for love and life is revealed when he created human beings in his image, both male and female as equal in dignity yet unique in gender (read Genesis 2:22–24). Christ the Lord raised marriage to the dignity of a Sacrament (John 2:1-11). Unlike any other Sacrament, in the Latin Rite, the couple to be married are the ministers of the Sacrament. By their free consent before the Church, a baptized man and a baptized woman offer themselves as a gift to each other. They become one according to God's plan. Jesus echoed this when he reminded the Pharisees of the words from the Book of Genesis:

> So they are no longer two, but one flesh. Therefore, what God has joined together, no human being must separate.
>
> MATTHEW 19:6

The marital love between spouses is a "saving reality" (read Isaiah 54:5–8, 10). This means that a husband and wife are to work for the good of each other and be open to life, to accept and raise children. Acts such as adultery, artificial contraception, divorce, and polygamy violate the nature and purpose of marriage.

Through the Sacrament of Matrimony, the married couple enters into a covenantal relationship in which their love is sealed and strengthened by the grace of God (read Hosea 2:21-25). The married couple is to become a communion of love following in the image of the Holy Trinity.

? How is the love of a married couple sealed and strengthened by the grace of God?

Activity With a partner, read one of these Scripture passages and report to your class what it taught you about Matrimony. Jot down your notes for your report.

Genesis 2:22-24
Hosea 2:21-22

_____

_____

_____

_____

_____

I FOLLOW JESUS

The domestic Church, or Church of the home, is the model for every Catholic household of faith. A Catholic family can be a living sign of Christ in the world. God dwells in all families even though no family is perfect. It is the responsibility of every family member to make Christ's love visible to those within and outside of the home.

MY CHURCH OF THE HOME

What would your family be like if it was a true sign of Christ's love? Write or draw your dreams here. Include the good things that are happening and the things you would like to see. Be sure to express your role.

_____

_____

_____

_____

_____

_____

_____

_____

_____

MY FAITH CHOICE

This week, I choose to express love to my family and friends according to God's plan for love and life. I will

_____

_____

 Pray, "Holy Spirit, guide me to be a chaste person who loves and serves other in your image. Amen."

1. Marriage is part of God's plan for love and life in which a man and a woman form a lifelong bond with openness to life.

2. Spousal love is to be exclusive, permanent, unbreakable, and faithful.

3. Matrimony unites a baptized man and a baptized woman to be a living sign of Christ's love for the Church.

Chapter Review

Recall

Answer the following questions in complete sentences.

1. What is the meaning and purpose of marriage?

_____

_____

_____

_____

2. What are the essential qualities necessary for conjugal love?

_____

_____

3. How is the sacred union of the marriage of a baptized man and a baptized woman like the love between Christ and the Church?

_____

_____

4. Why is the Sacrament of Matrimony a Sacrament of service?

_____

_____

Reflect

What are ways you can help your family be a sign of Christ's love?

_____

_____

_____

_____

Share Describe the Christian family as a domestic Church. Share your response with the class.

Signs of Christ's Love

Our prayers for married couples help them live their vocation to be signs of Christ's love in the world. This prayer recalls that blessing.

Leader: Let us pray for all who have been consecrated in the Sacrament of Matrimony to serve the Church.

Reader 1: May the peace of Christ live in their homes.
May they have true friends to help them.
May they be ready to help all who are in need.

All: Bless them, O Lord.

Reader 2: May they enjoy their work.
May they solve their daily problems.
May they not care too much about material things.

All: Bless them, O Lord.

Reader 3: May they find joy in God's gift of married life.
May they give witness to Jesus
by the goodness of their lives.

All: Bless them, O Lord.

Reader 4: May they praise God in the happy times
and rely on him in times of sadness.
May they take comfort in God's care and know
that he is with them every moment of their lives.

All: Bless them, O Lord.

Leader: We now pray aloud for the married couples we know.
(Pause for students to add intentions.)
May God reward them with a long life and with
eternal happiness.

All: Amen.

BASED ON THE *RITE OF MARRIAGE*

With My Family

This Week . . .

In Chapter 16, "The Sacrament of Matrimony," your child learned:

▶ Marriage is a natural institution and sacred union between a man and a woman, who share in a lifelong commitment.

▶ Spousal love is to be exclusive, permanent, unbreakable, and faithful.

▶ In Matrimony, a baptized man and a baptized woman are united in a lifelong bond of faithful love as a sign of Christ's love for the Church.

▶ Through the virtue of chastity, we respect each other as persons, not as objects to be used. We integrate the gift of our sexuality according to God's plan.

For more about related teachings of the Church, see the *Catechism of the Catholic Church*, 1601–1666, and the *United States Catholic Catechism for Adults*, pages 277–292.

■ Sharing God's Word

Read together Ephesians 5:1–32; 6:1–4. Emphasize that each of us is to live in the light of Christ. Husbands and wives are to imitate the sacrificial love between Christ and the Church. Parents and children are to love each other with honor and respect.

■ We Live as Disciples

The Christian home and family form a school of discipleship. Choose one of the following activities to do as a family, or design a similar activity of your own:

▶ During family talks, discuss with your children the joys and struggles of marriage and what you are doing to create a household of faith. Plan regular outings together to strengthen your family bonds.

▶ Help your child to be sensitive to their friends who may be experiencing difficulties at home. Allow them to participate in some of your activities.

■ Our Spiritual Journey

Christ's sacrifice is the paradigm of Christian living. Sacrifice, the giving of oneself freely out of love for another, gives expression to the paradox that Saint Francis of Assisi captured in the words, "It is in giving that we receive," which in turn reflects the infinite self-giving love of the Trinity, One Divine Person to the Other. With your family this week, bless the married couples your family knows by praying the prayer on page 219.

For more ideas on ways your family can live as disciples of Jesus, visit **BeMyDisciples.com**

Family Values

Mr. Harper and his sixth grade class were in an intense discussion about values. "What is a value?" he asked them.

"Something important," John answered. "A quality that is important," added Rosario.

"An ideal. A value is a belief we have about what is important," summarized Katie.

"Very good," said Mr. Harper. "So what values are important to you?" he challenged the class.

"Listening." "Respect." "Honesty." The class shouted out a lot of words.

"Now," Mr. Harper continued as he handed out a 3 x 5 inch card to each student, "write down what you think are the top five values in family life. Think about what is most important for families and what families want to hold up as their standard for how members treat each other."

When the class was finished, Mr. Harper collected the cards. He and the students tallied the responses. How do you think they responded?

WE LIVE IN COMMUNITY

In our families, we learn about and act on our values. We build up family life and promote Jesus' way of living by acting on Christian values.

MAKING CONNECTIONS

Mr. Harper posed some challenging questions to his class about which values are most important for family life. Family life is important to each of us, our society, and our Church. We are all responsible to help our families live as Jesus taught.

with MATH AND SCIENCE

Find out what the top five family values are for the students in your class. Write a short survey for the students in your class to complete. Find out what the most important values are for the students' families and how their families choose to live those values. Create a graph or data chart that shows the top five family values in your class. Discuss with your class the following question: What difference do these values make in your families, society, and the Church?

with SOCIAL STUDIES

Read a newspaper or an on-line newspaper. Find two stories about situations that demonstrate how people live a value in their lives. Determine the situation and the value expressed by the people involved. Now, choose a different value for each story. Describe how the situation will be different if the values of the people involved were different. Explain why Christian values, like Disciple Power virtues, are important in our lives.

with CREATIVE ARTS

Using the list of family values your class chose as important, act out scenarios showing those values being lived out in a home situation. Share with the class, if the value you are acting out, is one of the Disciple Power virtues or qualities that you have learned about this year.

Faith Action

There is a saying, "You have to walk the walk and talk the talk." This means that if we say we value something, our actions should reflect that value. Think about how your actions at home reflect what you value. Write two actions and identify the values they reflect.

_____

_____.

Unit 4 **Review**

A. Choose the Best Word

Read each statement and circle the best answer.

1. Which Sacrament uses the Rite of Anointing?

    A. Holy Orders   B. Penance and Reconciliation

    C. Matrimony   D. Eucharist

2. Which Sacrament strengthens our faith and trust in God when we are ill?

    A. Holy Orders   B. Anointing of the Sick

    C. Matrimony   D. Penance and Reconciliation

3. What are the Sacraments at the Service of Communion?

    A. Baptism and Holy Orders   B. Confirmation and Holy Orders

    C. Baptism and Matrimony   D. Matrimony and Holy Orders

4. Which of these does not include anointing with oil?

    A. Anointing of the Sick   B. Holy Orders

    C. Eucharist   D. Baptism

5. Which kind of love is to be exclusive, permanent, unbreakable, and faithful?

    A. conjugal love   B. marital love

    C. spousal love   D. all of the above

B. Show What You Know

Match the words in Column A to their definitions in Column B.

Column A	Column B
A. marriage	____ **1.** a degree of Holy Orders
B. mortal sin	____ **2.** a Sacrament at the Service of Communion
C. diaconate	____ **3.** God's plan for love and life
D. Holy Orders	____ **4.** gravely wrong action
E. Penance and Reconciliation	____ **5.** a Sacrament of Healing

C. Connect with Scripture

*Reread the Scripture passage on the first Unit Opener page.
What connection do you see between this passage and
what you learned in this unit?*

_____

_____

_____

_____

_____

D. Be a Disciple

1. *Review the four pages in this unit titled, The Church Follows Jesus.
What person or ministry of the Church on these pages will inspire
you to be a better disciple of Jesus? Explain your answer.*

_____

_____

_____

_____

_____

2. *Work with a group. Review the four Disciple Power virtues, or gifts,
you have learned about in this unit. After jotting down your own
ideas, share with the group practical ways that you will live these
gifts day by day.*

_____

_____

_____

_____

_____

Put On Love

Put on, then, as God's chosen ones, holy and beloved, heartfelt compassion, kindness, humility, gentleness, and patience bearing with one another and forgiving one another, if one has a grievance against another; as the Lord has forgiven you, so must you also do. And over all these put on love, that is, the bond of perfection.

COLOSSIANS 3: 12–14

What I Know

What is something you already know about these faith concepts?

Works of Mercy

_____

_____

_____

Natural Law

_____

_____

_____

Beatitudes

_____

_____

_____

Faith Terms

Put an X next to the faith terms you know. Put a ? next to faith terms you need to learn more about.

_____ holiness

_____ Cardinal Virtues

_____ Theological Virtues

_____ conscience

_____ Capital Virtues

_____ Golden Rule

_____ Shema

_____ canonization

Questions I Have

The Bible

What do you know about Jesus' teaching on the Great Commandment?

_____

_____

_____

The Church

What would you like to know about the requirements for sainthood?

_____

_____

_____

Questions I Have

What questions would you like to ask about moral decision making?

_____

_____

_____

Looking Ahead

In this chapter, the Holy Spirit invites you to ▶

 **EXPLORE** simple ways to work for justice.

 **DISCOVER** how God calls us to live with grace and freedom.

 **DECIDE** how you can grow through the Works of Mercy.

CHAPTER

17

Our Call to Holiness

? What is something unique about you?
What do your actions say about you?

God's actions among his people revealed something about God. Listen to the psalmist's prayer of praise of God.

> *O mighty king, lover of justice,*
> *   you alone have established fairness; . . .*
> *From the pillar of cloud God spoke to them;*
> *   they kept the decrees, the law they received.*
> *Exalt the LORD, our God;*
> *   bow down before his holy mountain;*
> *   holy is the LORD, our God.*
>
> PSALM 99:4, 7, 9

? What examples of God's justice do you know from the Scriptures?

Disciple Power

Understanding

This Gift of the Holy Spirit helps us to know ourselves better as we grow in our relationship with God. Saint Augustine said of this gift, "That I may know You, may I know myself." Ruth in the Old Testament understood the needs of others, and her actions showed it (read Ruth 1:11–18).

The Gleaning Network

The work of the Gleaning Network tells us much about their focus on justice. This group of dedicated people value and live Christ's command to love one another.

The Gleaning Network is an organization that responds to the needs of many people who are without food. Its thousands of volunteers provide millions of servings of nourishing food to feed the hungry in the United States each year. These people call themselves, "gleaners." Do you remember Ruth in the Old Testament who stood by her mother-in-law, Naomi? Listen to the conversation between Ruth and Naomi.

> Ruth the Moabite said to Naomi, "Let me go and glean ears of grain in the field of anyone who will allow me that favor." Naomi said to her, "Go, my daughter," and she went.
>
> RUTH 2:2–3

The Gleaners chose their name to honor Ruth, who gleaned from the fields crops not harvested to support her and her family.

How do you think the Gleaning Network is different from the food pantries?

Living Holiness

The Gleaners in the Midwest saw that their fertile region produced an abundance of crops, such as tomatoes, oranges, onions, and carrots. Some of this food went to waste. The Gleaners contacted local farmers to help them collect the unused crops.

The Gleaners grew larger and larger, involved members of other churches, and they purchased their own buildings. They now bring in fresh produce and canned goods from grocery stores and from food drives. They distribute food not just to people in their own communities but to the needy throughout the country in which they live. Gleaners in your community are living the call to holiness and justice. They take up the challenge to feed the poor and live the Works of Mercy.

 What do you think are ways that we can live God's call to holiness?

Activity List items that you have in abundance that you can "glean" for those in need. Who would gain from the gleaning from your abundance?

_____

_____

_____

_____

_____

_____

_____

_____

_____

_____

_____

FAITH VOCABULARY

holiness
The quality, or condition, of a person who is living in communion and in right relationship with God, with others, and with all of creation; being in the state of grace.

Theological Virtues
The virtues of faith, hope, and charity; gifts of God that enable us to live a life of holiness, or a life in communion with the Holy Trinity.

Called to Be Saints

Our life's job description is to share in God's **holiness**. God created us to be holy as he is holy. He created us to know him, to love him, to serve him, and to live with him forever in eternal happiness. God's command to the Israelites is a command to all his people:

"For I, the LORD, am your God; and you shall make and keep yourselves holy, because I am holy. . . . Since I, the LORD, brought you up from the land of Egypt that I might be your God, you shall be holy, because I am holy."

LEVITICUS 11:44–45

On the day, we were baptized, we received one vocation: to be holy. In our everyday lives we have responsibilities, such as studying, cleaning our rooms, and helping our families. As adults we may raise children and go to work. Whatever we do and wherever we go, we need to keep God in our lives because God created us to be holy as he is holy. Saint Paul tells us in his letter to the Corinthians,

". . . to you who have been sanctified in Christ Jesus, called to be holy, with all those everywhere who call upon the name of the Lord Jesus Christ, their Lord and ours." 1 CORINTHIANS 1:2

The ability and freedom to live a holy life is a gift from God. He not only invites us to live a life in communion with him but also gives us the strength to live that life.

Why do you think the title of this page states that we are called to be Saints?

Faith, Hope, and Charity

God gives us the **Theological Virtues**, which help us to live as his children. The Theological Virtues enable us to grow stronger in holiness, the life of God within us. They are those strengths that begin in God and direct us toward holiness. There are three Theological Virtues: faith, hope, and charity.

You may recall that Saint Paul concludes his great hymn to love with this memorable verse,

> So faith, hope, love remain, these three; but the greatest of these is love.
>
> I Corinthians 13:13

These virtues are gifts from God. They connect us with the Holy Trinity—Father, Son and Holy Spirit—in a very direct way. The more we choose to live according to these virtues, the more we grow in holiness.

? What are the ways the Theological Virtues help us live holy lives?

Catholics Believe

Sacramentals

Sacramentals are sacred signs that help us give praise to God and live holy lives. The Church uses sacramentals to remind us of God's presence with us. One of the most important sacramentals is blessings. Blessings include praising God for his works and gifts, and the Church's intercessions for people to use God's gifts according to the Gospel.

Activity Draw a symbol that shows your understanding of faith, hope, and love.

FAITH FOCUS
What role does grace play
in our lives of holiness?

Grace and Freedom

With Christ, everything changed. Before Christ's life, Passion, Death, Resurrection, and glorious Ascension, humanity was under the power of sin and death. By dying, he destroyed our death and freed us from sin's power. By rising from the dead, he restored our life of holiness. Through Christ we receive the grace of the Holy Spirit that makes us holy and gives us the power to live holy lives. The grace of Christ makes us right with God again. We join with the Church and proclaim this faith at Mass when we sing or pray aloud:

Save us, Savior of the world,
for by your Cross and Resurrection
you have set us free.

EUCHARISTIC PRAYER, *ROMAN MISSAL*

At Baptism, we are joined to Christ and are made sharers in his work of Salvation and Redemption. We are made sharers in the saving act of God setting humanity free from slavery to sin and from death through the power of the sacrifice of Jesus Christ on the Cross.

We receive the grace of holiness called sanctifying grace. We are made right with God the Father in Christ. We receive the gift of the Holy Spirit to live holy lives. God freely gives us the gift of Salvation in Christ. Salvation is not something we could ever earn on our own.

It is due to him that you are in Christ Jesus, who became for us wisdom from God, as well as righteousness, sanctification, and redemption.

1 CORINTHIANS 1:30

? In what ways do you share in the work of Christ?

Growth in Holiness

With the sanctifying grace of the Holy Spirit, we are made holy again. The grace of the Holy Spirit calls us to use responsibly the gift of freedom and to grow in holiness.

> In the sin of his lips the evil man is ensnared,
>   but the just comes free of trouble.   PROVERBS 12:13

With the grace of the Holy Spirit, we grow in our ability to make the right choices and to live as adopted children of God the Father. We turn toward God and away from sin. We accept forgiveness and the gift of having our communion and life with God restored.

? How does grace help us to be free?

Faith-Filled People

Job

The story of Job is told in the Old Testament. Job was wealthy and faithful to God. He lost all his wealth and became ill with a serious disease. In all of this trouble, he did not blame or reject God even when his friends tried to convince him to do so. Job's story is one of grace, freedom, faith, and hope.

Activity List the things in your life that really help you live a holy life. Then explain why it helps you.

Helps to Live a Holy Life	Why

FAITH FOCUS
How do the Works of Mercy
guide us in living holy lives?

FAITH VOCABULARY
Works of Mercy
Virtuous actions that we
do to help others in need,
grouped as Corporal
(bodily needs) and Spiritual
(spiritual needs).

Growth in Holiness

God's gift of holiness is not just for us as individuals. It is not something we keep for ourselves. As God shares his life and love with us, we also share our life and love with others. Our growth in holiness involves the way that we live with other people. Holiness is about how we act with others.

Saint Paul teaches,

Put on then, as God's chosen ones, holy and beloved, heartfelt compassion, kindness, humility, gentleness, and patience, bearing with one another and forgiving one another. . . . And over all these put on love, that is, the bond of perfection.

COLOSSIANS 3:12–14

The Church gives us the Spiritual and Corporal Works of Mercy to guide us in living the life of mercy and compassion that Saint Paul describes. These **Works of Mercy** are part of the Church's social teachings—a collection of principles that guide us to moral living as a holy community. Yet the Works of Mercy are not just an idea; they are concrete, practical things that we can do to live the Gospel. They clearly show that holiness is not just an idea but something we must practice everyday. Holiness is a life of true courage, a life that requires God's grace.

 In what ways does your growth in holiness involve others?

Activity **Works of Mercy**

Read the lists of Corporal and Spiritual Works of Mercy on page 371. Under each picture, write the Work of Mercy it illustrates. In the space provided, draw or write how you can live one of the Works of Mercy.

_____

_____

_____

_____

_____

_____

I FOLLOW JESUS

Ruth told her widowed mother-in-law, Naomi, "Wherever you go I will go" (Ruth 1:16). Focus on trying to understand how God desires for you to live your life. Go where God wants you to be. Living the Works of Mercy is a way you can strive to live a holy life. See God in each person you help, for each of us is created in the image and likeness of God.

HOLY LIFE IN ACTION

Develop a list of three activities that you could do with others that would help you to live a holy life. Choose one and draw up a plan to put it into action.

Which Work of Mercy?	With whom?	What will we do?	When will we do this?	What will we need to do it?
1.				
2.				
3.				

MY FAITH CHOICE

This week, I will focus on understanding God's will for me so that I can know myself more and live a life of holiness. I will

_____

_____

 Pray, "Lord, help me to know you more so that I may know myself better and know your will for my life. Amen."

1. The Theological Virtues are gifts from God that connect us with him and strengthen us to live lives of holiness in communion with God.

2. The grace of the Holy Spirit helps us grow in our ability to freely make choices to grow in holiness.

3. Living the Works of Mercy is a sign that we are trying to live holy lives.

Chapter Review

Recall

Match each term with its description.

Faith Term

_____ 1. holiness

_____ 2. virtues

_____ 3. faith

_____ 4. hope

_____ 5. charity

Description

A. The virtue by which we love God above all else and love our neighbor as ourselves.

B. Good habits that enable us to grow stronger in the God-life that dwells within us.

C. The virtue by which we believe in God.

D. God's presence in us and our fidelity to him.

E. The virtue by which we trust that God is looking after us.

Reflect

What are some ways that God helps you to live a holy life?

_____

_____

_____

_____

_____

_____

_____

_____

Share   Work with a partner to name and explain the Theological Virtues. Share ways you live these virtues.

The Road Ahead

The road to living a holy life is not always an easy road to travel. Yet God always leads us along that road. Quiet yourself and place your trust in God, praying this prayer. Pray it often.

Group 1: Happy are those whose way is blameless,
who walk by the teaching of the LORD.

Group 2: Happy are those who observe God's decrees,
who seek the LORD with all their heart.

Group 1: May my ways be firm
in the observance of your laws!

Group 2: I will keep your laws;
do not leave me alone.

Group 1: With all my heart I seek you;
do not let me stray from your commands.

Group 2: Open my eyes to see clearly
the wonders of your teachings.

Group 1: Give me insight to observe your teaching,
to keep it with all my heart.

Group 2: Let your love come to me, LORD,
salvation in accord with your promise.

Group 1: I will keep your teachings always,
for all time and forever.

Group 2: I delight in your commands,
which I dearly love.

Group 1: Teach me wisdom and knowledge,
for in your commands I trust.

Group 2: Your word is a lamp for my feet,
a light for my path.

PSALM 119:1–2, 5, 8, 10, 18, 34, 41, 44, 47, 66, 105

With My Family

This Week . . .

In Chapter 17, "Our Call to Holiness," your child learned:

▶ Each of us is called to live the way of holiness that Jesus lived and taught to his disciples.

▶ We are joined to Christ and receive the gift of the Holy Spirit and the grace to live as adopted children of God the Father.

▶ As we strive to understand more about God, we come to know more about ourselves and how we can respond to his call of holiness.

▶ Living the Works of Mercy is one way that we cooperate with the Holy Spirit and strive to live holy lives.

▶ Understanding, a Gift of the Holy Spirit, helps us know ourselves better and grow in our relationship with God.

For more about related teachings of the Church, see the *Catechism of the Catholic Church,* 1699–1715, 1730–1748, 1803–1845, 1987–2029, and the *United States Catholic Catechism for Adults,* pages 307–313, 315–321, 328–330.

Sharing God's Word

Read together Leviticus 11:44–45. Emphasize that every person is created by God and is to live a holy life.

We Live as Disciples

The Christian home and family is a school of discipleship. Choose one of the following activities to do as a family, or design a similar activity of your own:

▶ Write a family pledge to live holy lives. Be sure that the pledge describes specific behaviors and attitudes that constitute holiness.

▶ During family prayers, remind everyone that God is with you as you journey on the road of holiness.

Our Spiritual Journey

Trusting God may not be easy, especially during times of distress and anxiety. During such times, God is there. He might be inviting you to help others in need through Works of Mercy. In doing so, we take up our cross for the sake of others and receive the grace to persevere. This week as a family pray together Psalm 119:105, "Lord, your word is a lamp for my feet, a light for my path. Amen."

For more ideas on ways your family can live as disciples of Jesus, visit **BeMyDisciples.com**

Looking Ahead

In this chapter, the Holy Spirit invites you to ▶

EXPLORE how two boys mixed faith and fun.

DISCOVER how to make moral decisions as a disciple of Jesus.

DECIDE on ways you can form a good conscience.

CHAPTER
18

Making Moral Choices

? What are some skills that you would like to develop? What are some qualities about yourself that you would like to improve?

The Book of Proverbs is a summary of maxims, short sayings that guide us in living a moral life. In this proverb, we read about the value of wisdom:

> "Happy the man who finds wisdom,
>   the man who gains understanding!
> For her profit is better than profit in silver,
>   and better than gold is her revenue. . . .
> She is a tree of life to those who grasp her,
>   and he is happy who holds her fast." Proverbs 3:13–14, 18

? What is this proverb saying about the role of wisdom in making good decisions? In what ways do you seek wisdom?

Disciple Power

Prudence

This Cardinal Virtue is also referred to as wisdom. Saint Thomas Aquinas defined prudence as "right reason in action." With experience comes wisdom, and prudence is often the guide for growing in wisdom.

Mixing Faith and Fun

For the Hebrew people, proverbs were a source of wisdom. In this story, some contemporary students find value in the proverbs too.

In honor of Saint John Bosco, who was known for mixing faith and fun, the boys at Don Bosco High School have a tradition in which they challenge each other by quoting Scripture while juggling. It keeps their minds sharp and their bodies coordinated. Plus, the fun is a nice distraction from the poverty and turmoil of their inner-city lives. The one who lasts the longest is the "new Don." This respectful title means "nobelman" in Italian. A sense of brotherhood among the boys results from the challenge.

"Yeah! Dominic! Get ready to call me Don Roberto!" shouted Robert. "You are on!" Dominic hollered back. "So you think you've got what it takes?" Dominic said, ready to juggle.

Robert and Dominic squared up in front of each other, while other boys circled around them in anticipation of who would be first to drop out. They began to juggle, and Robert started quoting first since he was the challenger.

? What are some proverbs that you may remember? What do they mean to you in your life?

A Source of Wisdom

Now the boys started quoting proverbs very quickly.

"Proverbs 29:8—Arrogant men set the city ablaze, but wise men calm the fury!" Robert said confidently. The crowd cheered. Still juggling, Dominic went next, "Proverbs 16:8—Better a little with virtue, than a large income with injustice."

"Proverbs 11:19—Virtue directs toward life, but he who pursues evil does so to his death," Robert said, as he almost dropped a juggling ball. Dominic then moved closer to Robert saying, "Proverbs 15:4—A soothing tongue is a tree of life, but a perverse one crushes the spirit." The crowd waited for Robert's return.

Robert stood his ground saying, "Proverbs 24:3—By wisdom is a house built, by understanding is it made firm." Just then, Dominic lost his balance, and the juggling balls scattered. Dominic was disappointed, but he went over to Robert and said, "Nice one, Don Roberto!"

 Who helps you to make good moral choices?

Activity Using your Bible, work with a classmate to discover the second line of each of the proverbs listed below. Write a proverb that you choose. Then memorize two of the proverbs and practice saying them with each other.

Proverbs 10:6   Blessings are for the head of the just

_____

Proverbs 12:15   The way of the fool seems right in his own eyes

_____

Proverbs 15:30   A cheerful glance brings joy to the heart;

_____

Proverbs 16:9   In his mind a man plans his course,

_____

Proverbs _____   _____

_____

_____

_____

Christian Morality

Each day, we make many choices. The decisions we make as disciples of Jesus to live holy and moral lives are called moral decisions. Our lives are a journey of faith, hope, and love. It is a response to God's invitation and to the grace he gives us as we make our journey.

Where do we go when we need information about making prudent and wise moral decisions? Here are some guides for our journey:

The natural law, or the laws inscribed in creation and written on the human heart. For example, "Do good and avoid evil" and "Treat others as you want them to treat you."

The Bible, especially the Great Commandment and the Ten Commandments.

The life and teachings of Jesus Christ and the teachings of the Church.

Knowing what determines the **morality,** that is, the goodness or evil of human acts will also help us make wise moral decisions.

❓ Why do you think the sources listed above can help you to make wise moral decisions?

The Sources of Moral Actions

Three things determine the morality of an act. They are the object of the act, the intention of the agent (the one who is acting), and the circumstances surrounding the act.

The Object. The object of the act is what we do. It is the good or the bad we do or say. Some things are good in themselves, such as praying. Other things such as murder are evil in themselves. Many evil acts, such as lying, cheating, and stealing, are prohibited by the Ten Commandments.

The Intention. The intention is what the person doing the act wants, or desires to do. Intention is the purpose for doing or saying something. A good intention cannot change an evil act into something good. For example, if a person steals something to give it to someone else as a gift, the act of stealing is still wrong, even if the person had a good intention.

The Circumstances. The circumstances of the act are those things that surround the decision. Circumstances do not change the goodness or evil of an act. They can make something we do or say better or worse. For example, if a person steals out of fear or ignorance, the act is still evil and wrong, but they may not be as responsible for the act.

A morally good act requires all three aspects: the goodness of the object, a good intention in doing the act, and its circumstance.

? How do you determine a wise moral decision?

Activity List three examples of circumstances that might make it difficult for people to choose to do something they know is right. Write a sentence explaining your reasoning for each.

_____

_____

_____

_____

_____

_____

_____

FAITH FOCUS
What happens when we
make sinful moral decisions?

Sin: Turning Away from God

The Cardinal Virtues, such as prudence, help us make good
moral decisions, which are necessary to live a holy and moral life.
The decisions we make, however, are not always easy. Sometimes we
come close to doing what we know is against God's Law and choose
not to do it. At other times, we give in to temptation and choose to
do something that we know is wrong.

We sin when we deliberately turn away from God and his love.
In doing so, we offend him. Sin includes both the wrong we do as
well as the good we choose not to do. To help us understand more
clearly what sin is about, the Church speaks about Capital Sins,
mortal sins, and venial sins.

Capital Sins. These are sins that lead to other sins. There are
seven Capital Sins (read Proverbs 6:16–19; Matthew 15:18–20). They
are usually listed as pride, greed, envy, anger, lust, gluttony, and
sloth or laziness. Each of these Capital Sins has a corresponding
Capital Virtue to help resist the temptations of these sins. The
Capital Virtues are humility, loving kindness, patience, chastity,
temperance, generosity, and diligence (read Galatians 5:19–26).

Mortal Sins. These are serious offenses against God that break our
relationship with him (read Mark 10:17–22). If we die in this state
of separation from God, we remain separated from him forever by
our own choice. Being forever separated from God is what we call
hell. When we are aware of being in a state of mortal sin, we are
to seek God's grace and forgiveness in the Sacrament of Penance
and Reconciliation.

Three things are necessary for a sin to be mortal. They are:

- The action involves a grave or serious matter.
- The choice is made with full knowledge of the seriousness
  of the choice.
- The choice is made freely.

❓ How can the virtue of prudence help you resist the sin of anger?
How can the virtue of humility help you resist the sin of pride?

Sin and Forgiveness

Venial Sins. These are less serious offenses against God. Because all sins turn our hearts away from God's love, we should seek forgiveness of all sins, including venial sins (read 1 John 5:16–17).

In the First Letter of John, we read,

If anyone sees his brother sinning, if the sin is not deadly, he should pray to God and he will give him life.

1 JOHN 5:16

Never forget that God wants to forgive us. If we are truly sorry for what we have done, we can always find forgiveness.

❓ Why do we need to seek forgiveness when we sin?

Faith-Filled People

Saint Alphonse de Liguori

Alphonse is a Doctor of the Church and the founder of a religious community called the Redemptorists. He was a poet, musician, and author. His writings on the moral life include practical answers to questions about moral decisions for daily living. He is the patron Saint of confessors and teachers of moral theology. His feast day is August 1.

Activity Draw a line to match the virtue that helps us resist the sin.

SINS	VIRTUES
pride	diligence
greed	chastity
gluttony	generosity
lust	temperance
sloth	loving kindness
anger	humility
envy	patience

Choose two of the virtues to help you live a holy life. Write a plan of action using these virtues to help you.

Virtues _____

Action Plan _____

_____

_____

_____

FAITH FOCUS
Why is it important to form
a good conscience?

FAITH VOCABULARY
conscience
The gift of God that is part
of every person that guides
us to know and judge what
is right and wrong.

Conscience

Our lives are filled with so many things that compete for our attention. We juggle facts and ideas to make our decisions. How do we know what is good and what is evil?

Every human being has another "voice" that constantly calls for our attention. It is our **conscience**. Our conscience helps us to judge what is right and what is wrong. We have the responsibility to train our conscience and obey our well-formed conscience. The better we train, or form, a good conscience, the better we will be at making decisions that help us live as followers of Jesus Christ.

People can have a conscience that does not correctly judge something to be good or evil. Such a conscience is called an erroneous conscience. It is a conscience that is filled with errors. An erroneous conscience provides someone with information that leads to decisions that are against God's law. When a person deliberately chooses not to work at forming a good conscience, that person is responsible for his or her erroneous conscience. That means that the person is also responsible for the wrong caused by actions that are due to erroneous conscience. However, if a person has never been taught what is right or is not mentally able to choose, then that person cannot be held accountable for the evil he or she does.

 What is an example of an erroneous conscience?

Activity **What to Do?**

Solve this dilemma. Your friend approaches you with the answers to an upcoming test. What do you do?

1. What is your first response?

_____

_____

2. What will you do?

_____

_____

3. Why would you do it?

_____

_____

4. What might be the consequence of your decision?

_____

_____

I FOLLOW JESUS

You make many moral decisions each day. Some are easy to make; others are more difficult. The Holy Spirit is always with you to teach you and to guide you in making good moral decisions. Forming a good conscience will help you make wise and morally good choices.

CONSCIENCE BUILDERS

Look over this list of conscience builders. Mark a ✔ next to the actions you use to help build, or form, a good conscience.

☐ Read Sacred Scripture.

☐ Pray to the Holy Spirit.

☐ Study and follow the teachings of the Church.

☐ Learn from the stories of people of faith, like the saints.

☐ Seek the advice of people of faith whom I trust.

How might using these conscience builders help you make good moral decisions?

_____

_____

_____

_____

_____

_____

MY FAITH CHOICE

This week, I will practice the Cardinal Virtue of prudence and make moral decisions thoughtfully and responsibly. I will

_____

_____

 Pray, "Holy Spirit, be my advocate and guide me in making good decisions. Amen."

Chapter Review

Recall

Read this situation. Name the object, intention, and circumstances. Then answer the questions.

Sarah and her teammates were playing in the championship game. In the final minutes of the game, Sarah swept by the defender. As she kicked the ball, trying to break the 0–0 score, she slipped on the wet grass, and the ball struck the goalkeeper in the face. Stunned from the fall, she looked toward the goal and saw the goalkeeper running toward her.

1. Object: _____

_____

2. Intention: _____

_____

3. Circumstances: _____

_____

4. Was the ball striking the goalkeeper in the face a sin? Why

or why not? _____

_____

5. What choice does Sarah now face? _____

_____

Reflect

Why do you think it is important to form a good conscience?

_____

_____

_____

_____

Share | With a partner, explain the purpose of an examination of conscience. Describe the ways it can help you.

Examination of Conscience

Thinking about and evaluating our moral decisions is important.
One way we do this is by examining our conscience.

Leader: Let us look into our hearts and think about the way we have loved or failed to love God and our neighbor as Jesus taught us.

All: **Happy those who observe God's decrees, who seek the Lord with all their heart.**

PSALM 119:2

Leader: Reflect in silence after each question.

Reader: How have you kept God first in your life? *(Pause)*
How have you shown respect to your parents and teachers? *(Pause)*
How have you been kind and helpful to other people? *(Pause)*
How have your words and actions shown respect for your body and the bodies of others? *(Pause)*
How have you respected the truth and been honest in your dealings with others? *(Pause)*
How have you respected the property of others? *(Pause)*
How have you dealt with any feelings of anger, hatred, or envy? *(Pause)*

All: **Happy those who observe God's decrees, who seek the Lord with all their heart.**

PSALM 119:2

With My Family

This Week . . .

In Chapter 18, "Making Moral Choices," your child learned:

▶ The Church guides us in making wise decisions to live as faithful followers of Jesus Christ. Prudence is the Cardinal Virtue that helps us make good moral choices.

▶ When we freely and knowingly choose an act that is evil, we sin; we turn away from God and offend him.

▶ These three things determine the morality of our actions: the object of the act, our intention in doing the act, and the circumstances surrounding the act.

▶ A good conscience helps us to judge if an act is good or evil; and guides us in avoiding evil and doing good.

For more about related teachings of the Church, see the *Catechism of the Catholic Church*, 1750–1761, 1776–1876, and the *United States Catholic Catechism for Adults*, pages 311–321.

■ Sharing God's Word

Spend time reading through sections in the Book of Proverbs with your child. Select proverbs together to memorize. Keep them in your mind and your heart as you make daily choices in life.

■ We Live as Disciples

The Christian home and family is a school of discipleship. Choose one of the following activities to do as a family, or design a similar activity of your own:

▶ Discuss as a family how this statement applies to making moral decisions: "Right is right even if everyone is against it; and wrong is wrong even if everyone is for it."

▶ Spend one-on-one time with your children doing an activity they enjoy. Offer bits of advice or "kernels of wisdom" to help them in life.

■ Our Spiritual Journey

Discernment is vital to living a moral life and making our spiritual journey. An examination of conscience is one traditional tool that facilitates our use of the spiritual discipline of discernment. In this chapter, your child used an examination of conscience as part of the closing prayer. Use this or another form of an examination of conscience every day. This week as a family, pray this Scripture verse from Psalm 119:2 on page 249.

For more ideas on ways your family can live as disciples of Jesus, visit **BeMyDisciples.com**

Looking Ahead

In this chapter, the Holy Spirit invites you to ▶

EXPLORE the life of a person who loved others as Jesus taught.

DISCOVER that living as a child of God is to follow the Law of Love.

DECIDE how you can live according to the Golden Rule.

CHAPTER
19

The Law of Love

? How do friends treat one another? How do enemies tend to treat one another?

Read how Jesus challenges his disciples to be perfect as the Father is perfect, to love as God loves:

> "But I say to you, love your enemies, and pray for those who persecute you . . . For if you love those who love you, what recompense will you have? . . . And if you greet your brothers only, what is unusual about that?"
>
> MATTHEW 5:44, 46–47

? How did Jesus show love to his enemies? Why should we love our enemies?

Disciple Power

Charity

To love as God loves is what we call charity or caritas in Latin. This is the standard by which all of us are to live and as Saint Paul says charity is the greatest of the three Theological Virtues (read 1 Corinthians 13:13).

Witness of Love

Josephine Bakhita was an African girl from Sudan. She was taken into slavery as a child and became a Saint of the Catholic Church. Read these selections from her imaginary diary to learn about her life.

7:30 a.m. October 15, 1878

I write my first journal entry . . . trying to remember my name. I am only nine years old. My friend, Elham, and I were walking around the fields. We noticed we were far from home. Suddenly two strangers appeared from behind a fence. One of them asked me to pick some fruit for him in the forest. I did so out of respect for those older than I. They did not respect me. While in the forest, he grabbed me and threatened me with a knife. He told me, "If you cry, you'll die! Follow us!" They call me "Bakhita." I am now their slave.

9:00 p.m. February 2, 1881

Escape seems impossible. I think tonight I will die. I do not know if I can take any more cuts. My masters tattooed on my body my age, 13. It still hurts from when they rubbed the salt into my wounds. Why do they do this to me? I feel humiliated.

5:00 a.m. January 10, 1890

Heavenly Lord! I know that you have let me live because you have called me to do great things. My life is so different. I have now learned about God and the Christian faith. I am baptized and my name is now Josephine. Not only this, but a court in Italy has ruled that since slavery is illegal in Italy, I have been free ever since I came here! Loving Father, you have always been in my heart, but now I know your name. May I love everyone as you have always loved me. Perhaps I will become a sister like the ones who instructed me.

How do you think Bakhita lived a life of holiness?

Daughter in Christ

Saint Josephine Bakhita
Canossian Daughter of Charity

7:00 a.m. February 7, 1947

Almighty Father, I am not afraid to see you. You have blessed me greatly. All these years I have been a Canossian sister, living the life of a religious. Please loosen these chains, they are so heavy! I realize that the pain and suffering all my life, even as I lay dying, has been like your Son, Jesus. I am truly your daughter in Christ. All that I am belongs to you. As you desire, my Master.

Saint Josephine was canonized in October 2000.

? How did God bless Josephine in spite of her suffering?

Activity Imagine how Saint Bakhita felt toward the kidnappers who enslaved her. Write a diary entry explaining how she sees this event through the eyes of faith.

Journal Entry Time_____ Date_____

_____

_____

_____

_____

_____

_____

_____

_____

FAITH FOCUS
What rules or laws does
Jesus ask us to live by?

FAITH VOCABULARY
natural law
The foundation of the moral
life for everyone. It enables
us by human reason to know
what is good and what is evil.

Love Like God

Before Josephine learned about God, she tells us that she knew him in her heart. God created us in his image and likeness, calling us to love like him. In God's fatherly love for us, he has imprinted into our hearts and minds a law that guides us in living as his images in the world.

There is something about the way God has created us that moves us naturally to choose what is good for us and for others. The Church calls this the **natural law**. This law, a pattern or design, helps us to discover the way to the true happiness that God has promised us. This law also helps us to recognize evil, which leads us away from happiness and away from God.

Here are three principles of the natural law:

- Do good and avoid evil.

- Tell the truth to each other.

- Be respectful toward one another.

These principles or rules detail our responsibilities and expectations of standards on our conduct.

? How would you explain what the natural law means?

The Ten Commandments

When God entered into the Covenant with Moses and the Israelites, he gave Moses the Ten Commandments. These Commandments reminded the people of the laws that God had written on their hearts. The Ten Commandments named the important ways God wants his people to live so that they can create a community of care and respect (read Exodus 20:1–17).

Jesus told his disciples they were to live the Commandments. Jesus said,

"Do not think that I have come to abolish the law or the prophets. I have come not to abolish but to fulfill."

MATTHEW 5:17

? What are the ways the Ten Commandments help us to live holy lives?

Activity Which U.S. laws or customs appear to reflect the principles of natural law? Write your thoughts in the space below.

_____

_____

_____

_____

_____

_____

_____

FAITH VOCABULARY
Shema
The Shema is a prayerful
rule revealed by God in
the Covenant that there
is only One God, and the
Lord is God.

Golden Rule
A rule to live by that is
knowable by human
reason. It is to do unto
others as you would have
them do unto you.

The Great Commandment

Jesus told us to live the Commandments as he did. We are to love God and one another as he did. Jesus' way of love is the Christian way of life. When the Pharisees, scholars of the Law, gathered to hear Jesus speak, one of them asked him which of all the laws is the greatest. Jesus said:

"You shall love the LORD, your God, with all your heart, with all your soul, and with all your mind. This is the greatest and the first commandment. The second is like it: You shall love your neighbors as yourself. The whole law and the prophets depend on these two commandments."

MATTHEW 22:37–40

In teaching the Great Commandment, Jesus revealed his authority on the Law. The Great Commandment is a combination of the **Shema** and the **Golden Rule**. The Shema, from the Jewish tradition, is a prayerful reminder of the First Commandment that the Lord is God and God is One.

"Hear O Israel!
The LORD is our God, the LORD alone!
Therefore, you shall love the LORD, your God,
with all your heart, and with all your soul,
and with all your strength."

DEUTERONOMY 6:4–5

Jewish people pray the Shema every day. This prayer reminds them that God is to be most important in life.

? What is one way you keep God most important in your life?

A Rule for Everyone

Over the centuries, people have lived by different laws both just and unjust. Nevertheless God has clearly shown us, how to live justly by living the Commandments. Within the Great Commandment, we can detect the natural law at work. To love our neighbor as ourselves comes from what has been called the Golden Rule, a principle of the natural law.

Almost every religion has taught and continues to teach some form of the Golden Rule. It is phrased in different ways in the Bible (read Tobit 4:15; Matthew 7:12). Essentially the rule states that we should "do to others as you would have them do to you" (Luke 6:31).

Jesus teaches that those who faithfully follow him and live the Great Commandment will be invited to join him in the Kingdom that God has prepared since the beginning of creation (read Matthew 25:31–40). This is possible for everyone. God leads us to happiness here on Earth within the Church. Yet complete happiness is everlasting life with God, Mary, and all the Saints.

? How is the Great Commandment a combination of the Shema and the Golden Rule?

Activity

Read these three passages from the Bible. Next to each, write if it is like the Shema, The Golden Rule, or the Great Commandment.

Rule	Scripture Passage
Golden Rule	"Do to no one what you yourself dislike." TOBIT 4:15
Shema	"[Y]ou shall love the Lord, your God, with all your heart, and with all your soul, and with all your strength." DEUTERONOMY 6:5
Great Commandment	"This is my commandment: love one another as I love you." JOHN 15:12

Describe how each of these rules are the same. Share with your class.

"Remain in My Love."

Happiness with God comes through the grace of love and the freedom found in following God's Law. This grace of love is the grace of the Holy Spirit given to us as members of the Church. When we act out of charity, we are using the grace of love. And we follow Jesus' New Commandment, to "love one another" (John 13:34). The New Commandment is the Law of Love. By following this law, we show others that we are Jesus' disciples (read John 13:35).

The Holy Spirit gives us the grace to follow the Law of Love. Jesus taught, "As the Father loves me, so I also love you. Remain in my love. If you keep my commandments, you will remain in my love, just as I have kept my Father's commandments and remain in his love" (John 15:9–10). By following the Law of Love, we are not just being a disciple of Jesus; we are his friends (read John 15:14). By loving God, we are able to love one another, even our enemies.

"I Have Called You Friends."

Loving one another frees us to be who God created us to be—an image of God! This why Jesus says, "I no longer call you slaves, because slave does not know what his master is doing. I have called you friends." (John 15:15). Saint Josephine Bakhita understood Jesus' New Commandement, the Law of Love. She understood her freedom came from her relationship with God. Despite her childhood experience of being a slave, Josephine remained in the love of Christ. She was able to see herself as a friend of Jesus and a daughter of God the Father.

? How do you remain in the love of Christ?

Christ,
Rembrandt Harmenszoon van Rijn, c.1648/50 (oil on oak panel)

Activity When is it easy to apply the Law of Love to others, and when is it hard to do? Describe a situation in which someone applies the Law of Love when it is not easy to do. With a classmate, act out the situation for your class.

I FOLLOW JESUS

Part of being a Christian means to love others as God loves you. Each day, you cooperate with the Holy Spirit to show love and respect to yourself and others. Making such decisions according to the Law of Love builds friendships.

LIVING THE GOLDEN RULE

Write several ways you would like others to treat you. Then think of a situation in your school, family, or neighborhood where you could treat someone else in the way you like to be treated. Write or draw the situation here.

_____

_____

_____

_____

_____

_____

_____

MY FAITH CHOICE

This week, I will look for opportunities to live the Law of Love according to the Golden Rule. I will

_____

_____

 Pray, "Jesus, you call me friend. Help me to be a friend to others as you are to me. Amen."

▶ **TO HELP YOU REMEMBER**

1. Do good and avoid evil is a principle of the natural law

2. Love of God and love of neighbor is essentially the Great Commandment.

3. The Law of Love is the way we are called to be friends with Jesus and with one another.

Recall

Match the term in the left column with the description on the right.

____ **1.** Ten Commandments   **a.** the laws God gave to Moses

____ **2.** Shema   **b.** the law written in our hearts

____ **3.** natural law   **c.** Love God, and your neighbor as yourself

____ **4.** Great Commandment   **d.** a prayerful rule revealed through the Covenant

____ **5.** Law of Love   **e.** to love others

Reflect

Describe what your life would be like if you put God above all else in your life.

_____

_____

_____

_____

_____

_____

_____

_____

_____

_____

Share   Design a symbol that will remind you of the Law of Love. Share it with your class to help in the design of a class symbol.

The Shema

The Shema is prayed as a morning and evening prayer by Jewish people today. Praying the Shema is the ancient tradition found in the Old Testament. Below is an abbreviated version of the prayer in English and Hebrew. Pray these words with your class in English.

Leader: In the morning the Jewish people pray, in part:
"Hear, O Israel, the Lord is our God, the Lord is One."
Sh'ma Yisrael Adonai Elohaynu Adonai Echad.

In the evening they pray, in part:
"Blessed be the Name of His glorious kingdom for ever and ever."
Barukh Shem k'vod malkhuto l'olam va-ed.

Let us pray in the spirit of the Shema, using King David's prayer from the First Book of Chronicles.

Group 1: "Blessed may you be, O LORD,
God of Israel our father,
from eternity to eternity.

Group 2: Yours, O LORD, are grandeur and power,
majesty, splendor, and glory.

All: **Blessed may you be, O LORD.**

Group 1: In your hand are power and might;
it is yours to give grandeur and strength to all.

Group 2: Therefore, our God, we give you thanks
and we praise the majesty of your name.

All: **Blessed may you be, O LORD.**

1 CHRONICLES 29:10–13

With My Family

This Week . . .

In Chapter 19, "The Law of Love," your child learned:

▶ God etched in our hearts the natural law. This law helps us to do good and avoid evil.

▶ Jesus taught us that we are to love God and to love our neighbor. This is the Great Commandment.

▶ Jesus challenges us to be perfect as the Father is perfect. We can do this with the grace of the Holy Spirit who enables us to love others as God loves us.

▶ Charity calls us to love others as God loves us.

For more about related teachings of the Church, see the *Catechism of the Catholic Church*, 1949–2029, and the *United States Catholic Catechism for Adults*, pages 310–311, 315–318, 327–330.

■ Sharing God's Word

In John 15:1–17, Jesus teaches the parable of the Vine and the Branches. Read this Scripture passage with your family, reflecting on how this imagery is relevant today. Discuss how your family remains in the love of Christ.

■ We Live as Disciples

The Christian home and family is a school of discipleship. Choose one of the following activities to do as a family, or design a similar activity of your own:

▶ Post in your home the family rules. Be sure that each of the family rules follows the Law of Love.

▶ During family mealtime, talk about some major events in the lives of your children. Discuss how the Law of Love is followed or violated.

▶ Select new ways to participate in the life of your parish and greater community that demonstrate the Law of Love.

■ Our Spiritual Journey

Often we struggle with the need to make sacrifices in life. This can limit us in our ability to fully respect others, especially those whom we might consider undeserving. Almsgiving is an ancient practice in which sacrifice and charity come together for the good of those in need, as well as for the good of ourselves. Find new ways to give to the needy this week. This week, pray together as a family, "Blessed may you be, O Lord."

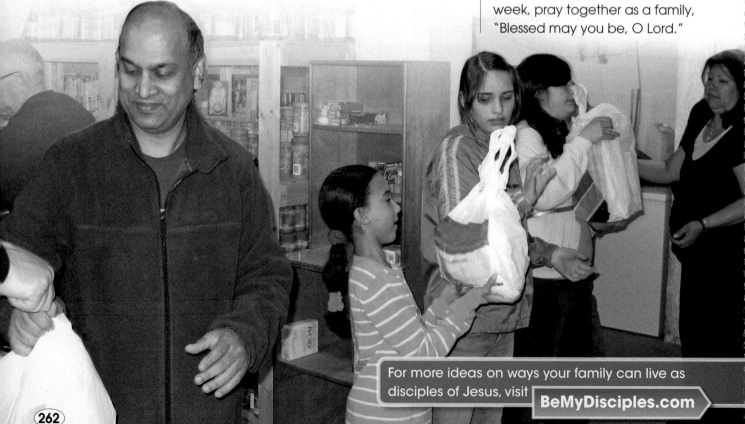

For more ideas on ways your family can live as disciples of Jesus, visit **BeMyDisciples.com**

Looking Ahead

In this chapter, the Holy Spirit invites you to ▶

EXPLORE the impact of Blessed John XXIII's spirit of joy upon the Church.

DISCOVER how following the Beatitudes is living a life of holiness.

DECIDE how you can live the Beatitudes to gain a sense of joy.

Ways of Happiness

? What do you do to bring happiness to others?

While ministering to a great multitude, Jesus taught how to live as one of his disciples. Listen for the attitudes of discipleship.

> "Blessed are the poor in spirit,
>   for theirs is the kingdom of heaven. . . .
> Blessed are the merciful,
>   for they will be shown mercy.
> Blessed are the clean of heart,
>   for they will see God.
> Blessed are the peacemakers,
>   for they will be called children of God. . . ."
>
> MATTHEW 5:3,7-9

? According to Jesus' words, who are blessed by God? What do you think people thought when they heard these words?

Disciple Power

Joy

One of the Fruits of the Holy Spirit, joy demonstrates that we live according to the Spirit (see Galatians 5:22–23). Joy results from moral living and believing in the hope of eternal life.

A Spirit of Peace

A great sense of joy and anticipation filled the air as the bishops began the Second Vatican Council in 1962. Saint John XXIII called this meeting of all the bishops of the Church to renew the Church with the light of Christ. The Council continued until 1965. Despite the unexpected death of Pope John XXIII on June 3, 1963, the Pope's spirit of joy and peace reinvigorated the entire Church.

Not long before his death in 1963, Pope John XXIII released *Pacem in Terris*, or "Peace on Earth." *Pacem in Terris* is an encyclical. It is more than a letter. It is a document to the Church from the Pope. Saint John XXIII wrote this encyclical, not only to Catholics, but to all people to remind the world that all human life, without exception, is sacred. The Pope was concerned about the many ways human life was being abused.

Pacem in Terris listed the rights of all human beings to life, respect, freedom, and education. It also addressed the need to do away with nuclear weapons. Pope John pointed out that when people are left to be poor, when governments misuse power and make people less free, God's plan for humanity is abused. We must work to correct these injustices and build the kingdom of peace that Jesus announced. We must love one another as Jesus did according to the natural rights given to us by God.

❓ If you were Pope, what kind of message, or encyclical, would you write to the Church?

Pope John XXIII

Joy to the World

The road to peace leads to joy. When, as individuals and groups, we respect the life and dignity of everyone as sacred, we pave the way for justice in the world. The Holy Spirit teaches us Christ's way of justice. The more we listen, accept his help, and act justly, the more we are building a world of peace as Saint John XXIII taught.

Pope John Paul II claimed that Vatican II was one of the greatest religious events of the 20th century. Today the Church continues Christ's way of justice with a joy-filled spirit.

? What do you think needs to be done to bring more joy into the world?

Activity Think of three situations from your community or from the news in which people are building a world of peace. Write one headline for each of their efforts.

FAITH FOCUS
What is the relationship between happiness and living as disciples of Jesus?

FAITH VOCABULARY
Beatitudes
The teachings of Jesus from his Sermon on the Mount that describe the attitudes and actions of people blessed by God; a word meaning "ways of happiness."

Living as Disciples

In his encyclical *Pacem in Terris,* Pope John XXIII taught that the happiness we all seek is not fully possible here on Earth. Because God created us with spiritual souls as well as physical bodies, life on Earth can never fully satisfy us. God created all of us to be with him forever. While we remain on Earth, our work is to prepare the way for God's kingdom by our works of love, justice, and peacemaking. Following the **Beatitudes** shows us how to do what God intends (read Matthew 5:3–11).

The Beatitudes summarize the attitudes and actions of a person living a life of holiness. Each Beatitude begins with the word "Blessed." For example, the first Beatitude reads,

*"Blessed are the poor in spirit,
    for theirs is the kingdom of heaven."*

MATTHEW 5:3

The word *blessed* means "made holy." The Beatitudes bless those who are humble, work for peace, are merciful, and are willing to be persecuted for doing right. The Beatitudes also describe the characteristics of the people in the Kingdom of God.

The Gospel of Matthew tells the story of the Sermon on the Mount. With a crowd of people gathered around him, Jesus taught the Beatitudes. His teachings are a summary of what it means to live as his disciple. When we follow his way, we are promised the gift of eternal life with God in Heaven.

❓ What is one way that your school community supports the parish in living the Beatitudes?

Understanding the Beatitudes

The Beatitudes give us a grace-filled way to seek true and lasting happiness. They reveal the way to Heaven. If we think of each Beatitude as a step on a ladder, we can see our path to God. Jesus teaches us that the first step to eternal happiness is being "poor in spirit." This is the way of the lowly and humble, who recognize their complete dependence on God. This is how we are to live, too. They who mourn a loss also will be comforted by God. Those who are meek will inherit the Kingdom of God.

Several of the Beatitudes speak of "righteousness." To be righteous means to be in right relationship with God and other people. This word is related to the Kingdom of God. A righteous person is one who is working to fulfill God's will to prepare the way for the Kingdom to come in its fullness. The "clean of heart," as well, are those who are single-minded in their pursuit of the will of God. They are undistracted by anything that could separate them from their desire for God. By taking the Beatitudes as our guide, we can be happy here on Earth while we await the promise of eternal life with God the Holy Trinity.

 What new understanding of the Beatitudes did you gain from these two pages?

Activity Read the Scripture passage from the Sermon on the Mount, Matthew 5:3-11. Explain each Beatitude in your own words.

Poor in spirit _____

_____

Mourn _____

_____

Meek _____

_____

Righteousness _____

_____

Merciful _____

_____

Clean of heart _____

_____

Peacemaker _____

_____

Persecuted _____

_____

"Rejoice and be glad, for your reward will be great in heaven."

Matthew 5:12

Living the Beatitudes

You can think of the Beatitudes as the way to live the Law of Love. We cannot earn Heaven. That is why Christ won it for us. In Christ, all our actions are made worthy. We live the Law of Love joyfully because we are so grateful for what has been done for us.

The Beatitudes help us to walk in Jesus' footsteps. The Beatitudes tell us what it is like to live in the Kingdom of God. As Jesus' followers, we live in hope of the fulfillment of God's promise to bring forth his kingdom.

We all want to be happy and know that Jesus can lead us to a life of holiness. The Beatitudes enable us to experience some of the blessings that God intends for us.

When we live by the Beatitudes, we are participating in the coming of God's kingdom. In our own way, we are cooperating with God's plan and helping to transform the world. When we live as Jesus taught us, we are one with all people throughout the world. We enter into the joy of the Trinity.

? What do you think the Beatitudes tell you about the Kingdom of God?

In the Footsteps of Christ

As we live the Beatitudes, we are walking in the footsteps of Christ. The way of Jesus is not always an easy one. Jesus does not hide the fact that the way to eternal happiness often involves hardship and sometimes persecution. Living the Beatitudes strengthens and protects us with the knowledge of God's everlasting love. We can experience joy amidst our hardships because we have accepted the words of Jesus that our joy will be forever.

? What do you think are some of the hardships that will be faced by someone who is trying to follow Christ?

Activity On the sole of the left shoe write the name of one of the eight kinds of people blessed by God. Then, on the sole of the right shoe, write one way you have tried to live the message of this Beatitude.

Holy Men and Women

There are many people who have walked the way of Jesus with the joy and love of God in their hearts. As faithful members of the Church, they have lived lives of heroic virtue. Some have even died for their faith in Jesus Christ. The Church refers to this faithful group as part of the Communion of Saints. Some of them are officially recognized in the process called **canonization**.

These holy men and women lived the Beatitudes and acted in imitation of Christ. They lived worthy lives because they accepted God in their lives, lived according to his Law, and knew that with faith in Christ, all things are possible.

Saint Paul knew well the way of Christ. He believed that all things are possible with God (read Mark 9:23). He instructed the Church in Philippi that the ways of happiness involve the joy and peace of Christ.

"Rejoice in the Lord always. I shall say it again: rejoice! Your kindness should be known to all. The Lord is near. . . . whatever is true, whatever is honorable, whatever is just, whatever is pure, whatever is lovely, whatever is gracious, if there is any excellence and if there is anything worthy of praise, think about these things. . . . I have the strength for everything through him who empowers me."

PHILIPPIANS 4:4, 8, 13

? Who is your favorite Saint? What do you think you can learn from him or her?

Activity Attitude Check

Use this checklist to evaluate the current state of your attitude. I have an attitude:

- ☐ in which I put God first in my life.
- ☐ where I respond with gentleness when I am hurt.
- ☐ that seeks the truth of God's plan for love and life.
- ☐ that leads me to call for peace when I see conflict.

I FOLLOW JESUS

As we live according to the Spirit, the fruit of joy will bring us happiness. In the Beatitudes, Jesus taught that purity of heart and being a peacemaker are essential aspects of the Christian life.

THE JOY OF BRINGING PEACE

Think of a situation to which someone could bring peace. Sketch your idea in the three frames. In the first, show the situation. In the second, show what you could do. In the third, show the outcome.

MY FAITH CHOICE

This week, I will focus on being a peacemaker. I will:

_____

_____

 Pray, "Holy Spirit, may your love dwell in my heart. Help me to keep a spirit of joy. Amen."

1. The Beatitudes are teachings of Jesus from his Sermon on the Mount that describe the attitudes and actions of people blessed by God.

2. Living the Beatitudes is the way to follow the Law of Love.

3. The spirit of joy comes from the love of God being the treasure kept in our hearts.

Chapter Review

Recall

Complete each sentence based on the eight Beatitudes found in Matthew 5:3–12.

1. Blessed are the _____, for theirs is the kingdom of heaven.

2. Blessed are the _____, for they will inherit the land.

3. Blessed are the _____, for they will see God.

4. Blessed are the _____, for they will be called children of God.

5. Blessed are the _____, for they will be shown mercy.

6. Blessed are they who mourn, for they will be _____.

7. Blessed are they who hunger and thirst for righteousness, for they will be _____.

8. Blessed are they who are persecuted for the sake of righteousness, for theirs is the _____.

Reflect

Why do you think living the Beatitudes brings joy?

_____

_____

_____

_____

_____

_____

_____

_____

Share With a partner, describe the characteristics of a person who lives the Beatitudes as a way to follow the Law of Love.

Praise the Lord, My Soul

The Book of Psalms is filled with different kinds of psalms. One type is a psalm of praise. Use the following prayer to praise God for the spirit of joy in your heart.

All: **Praise the Lord, my soul;**
I shall praise the Lord all my life,
sing praise to my God while I live.

Group 1: Happy those whose help is Jacob's God,
whose hope is in the Lord, their God.

All: **Praise the Lord, my soul;**
I shall praise the Lord all my life,
sing praise to my God while I live.

Group 2: The Lord shall reign forever,
your God, Zion, through all generations!
Hallelujah!

All: **Praise the Lord, my soul;**
I shall praise the Lord all my life,
sing praise to my God while I live.
Amen.

Psalm 146:2, 5, 10

With My Family

This Week . . .

In Chapter 20, "Ways of Happiness," your child learned:

▶ The Beatitudes are teachings of Jesus from his Sermon on the Mount that describe the attitudes and actions of people blessed by God.

▶ Living the Beatitudes is the way to follow the Law of Love. Canonized Saints are models of people who faithfully lived the Beatitudes.

▶ Blessed Pope John XXIII is one example of this. He was a great proponent of creating a just society so that peace can reign in the world.

▶ The spirit of joy comes from our knowledge of the love of God, the treasure kept in our hearts.

For more about related teachings of the Church, see the *Catechism of the Catholic Church*, 1716–1729, 1812–1819, 1830–1845, 1965–2029, and the *United States Catechism for Adults*, pages 307–311, 318.

■ Sharing God's Word

There are two Gospel accounts of the Beatitudes. The Sermon on the Mount version is found in Matthew 5:3–12. The Sermon on the Plains version is found in Luke 6:20–26. Spend time breaking open the Word of God to let the light of the Gospel shine in your heart so your actions may be worthy of Christian living.

■ We Live as Disciples

The Christian home and family is a school of discipleship. Choose one of the following activities to do as a family, or design a similar activity of your own:

▶ On occasion during family prayers, instead of reciting a traditional prayer, read the Beatitudes from the Sermon on the Mount.

▶ When there is conflict in the home, take time to pause to reflect on the attitude in your heart. Then act, seeing yourself and the other as children of God.

▶ Randomly celebrate a "Beatitude Day" by marking the calendar as such. This celebration is choosing joy no matter what is happening throughout the day and letting the actions of the Beatitudes guide your choices. At the end of the day, discuss your experiences as a family.

■ Our Spiritual Journey

Consider enacting the Works of Mercy as the way to act out the Beatitudes. Let the loving attitude in your heart guide you in offering to others God's merciful love. For example, when you comfort people who suffer, do not attempt to rush them through their sadness. Simply stand with them and let them know you share their sorrow. This week, as a family, pray together the prayer found on page 273.

For more ideas on ways your family can live as disciples of Jesus, visit **BeMyDisciples.com**

An Unexpected Gift

Mr. D'Agostino's sixth grade class had decided that they would visit Sweet Meadows nursing home for their class service project. The day before the visit, they made small bouquets of flowers nestled in colorful cups to be distributed as a gift to the residents.

When they arrived, they carried the cardboard trays full of flowers into the lobby, where they met Miss Karen, the administrator of the nursing home. After greeting them, she explained that they would be visiting the residents on the third floor. They should stay in pairs, and not run or shout in the hallways. The students nodded.

"I'm scared to do this," Kristen whispered to Marina.

"So am I," said Marina. "I didn't think I would be, but I am."

"You don't have to talk to them. Just put the flowers down and leave," Jesse said.

The students discovered, though, that most of the residents were glad to see them and very friendly. Kristen and Marina found it easy to start a conversation just by saying hello and explaining that they had brought a gift because it was Spring. If a resident did not seem to want to talk, they just left the flowers and went on to the next room.

After distributing the flowers, the class met in the lobby again. They had lots of stories to share about the residents whom they had met. As they left the nursing home, the students were already planning their next visit.

WE DEFEND THOSE WHO CANNOT DEFEND THEMSELVES

Our God is a God of justice. To act justly and defend those who cannot defend themselves, is to give witness to the Kingdom of God.

MAKING CONNECTIONS

Only one third of people aged 65 or older will spend any time in a nursing home. However, two-thirds of nursing home residents have no immediate family members. Reaching out to those who are lonely and vulnerable is one of our most important social teachings.

with MATH & SCIENCE

The total elderly population, aged 65 and older, is 13 percent of the total population in the United States. 43% of those people who are 65 are older will be cared for or live in a nursing home during their lives. 1 in 3 will spend three months or more in a nursing home; 1 in 4 will spend a year or more; and 1 in 11 will spend five years or more. About 70% of all nursing home patients are women. There are 1,813,665 total beds in nursing homes across the United States. These beds are found in a total of 16,995 nursing homes. The average nursing home has 107 beds. Based on this information, determine the number of people who live in a nursing home each year and how many are female and male.

Review the data with your class. Based on the data, determine ways your school, parish, or family can find ways to help the elders in your community. Choose one way and act on it!

with LANGUAGE ARTS

Research a nearby nursing home in your area. Then write a story that describes the day in the life of a nursing home resident. Include examples of activities, food, and the staff with whom residents interact. You might choose to write the story as a play or skit.

with SOCIAL STUDIES

Working with a partner, find out how elderly people aged 65 and over are treated in other countries, such as Canada or Mexico. Write a report on your findings, including the number of senior citizens in the country you researched, and what kind of nursing care they are likely to receive. What can we learn from that country and the ways they care for their elders? What can that country learn from us about the care we give to our elders?

Faith Action

Plan a service project with your class to address the needs of the elderly in your community. You might choose to remember the elderly during a holiday or raise money for a badly needed resource. Jot down your ideas and put them into action.

_____

_____

Unit 5 **Review**

A. Choose the Best Word

Fill in the blanks to complete each sentence of the paragraph.
Use the words from the word bank

Cardinal	conscience	holiness
moral	mortal	venial

God gives each person the grace to make prudent decisions

and to live a life of _____ . Making decisions to

live according to God's will is called living a _____ life.

By developing and practicing the four _____ Virtues, we

develop good habits and grow in holiness. Our _____
guides us in judging whether an act is right or wrong. When we
deliberately choose to do or say something that we know

is against God's Law, we sin. _____ sins are grave or

serious sins that break our relationship with God. _____
sins weaken but do not break our relationship with God.

B. Show What You Know

Read each question and circle the best answer.

1. Which of these virtues is one of the Theological Virtues?

    A. wisdom   B. prudence

    C. faith   D. courage

2. Which of one of these describe the morality of an act?

    A. object, intention, circumstances   B. intention, reason, effect

    C. object, intention, purpose   D. object, circumstances, effect

3. Which one of the following is not the result of an informed conscience?

    A. Judging what is right and wrong   B. Choosing to do what is against
                                                God's Law

    C. Living as a follower of Jesus Christ   D. Making good moral decisions

C. Connect with Scripture

Reread the Scripture passage on the first Unit Opener page. What connection do you see between this passage and what you learned in this unit?

_____

_____

_____

_____

_____

D. Be a Disciple

1. *Review the four pages in this unit titled, The Church Follows Jesus. What person or ministry of the Church on these pages will inspire you to be a better disciple of Jesus? Explain your answer.*

_____

_____

_____

_____

_____

2. *Work with a group. Review the four Disciple Power virtues, or gifts, you have learned about in this unit. After jotting down your own ideas, share with the group practical ways that you will live these gifts day by day.*

_____

_____

_____

_____

_____

Depend on God

Jesus taught the crowds who followed him about prayer. During his Sermon on the Mount, he said,

"Ask and it will be given to you; seek and you will find; knock and the door will be opened to you. For everyone who asks, receives; and the one who seeks, finds; and to the one who knocks, the door will be opened."

MATTHEW 7:7–8

What I Know

What is something you already know about these faith concepts?

Ten Commandments

_____

_____

_____

temperance

_____

_____

_____

hope

_____

_____

_____

Faith Terms

Put an X next to the faith terms you know. Put a ? next to the faith terms you need to learn more about.

_____ idolatry

_____ worship

_____ culture of life

_____ culture of death

_____ almsgiving

_____ stewardship

_____ adoration

_____ contemplation

Questions I Have

The Bible

What do you know about Jesus' teaching on the Lord's Prayer?

_____

_____

_____

The Church

What Saint or organization of the Church would you like to learn more about?

_____

_____

_____

What questions would you like to ask about worshiping God?

_____

_____

_____

Looking Ahead

In this chapter, the Holy Spirit invites you to ▶

EXPLORE the sacred space to nurture the gift of piety.

DISCOVER that the first three Commandments teach us to love God.

DECIDE how you will keep God above all else in your life.

CHAPTER
21

Love of God

? Do you think laws are necessary for people to be happy? Why or why not?

Laws, decrees, and precepts are guidelines to help us keep what is important in life a priority. This psalm attributes God as the source of all that is truly important.

> "The law of the LORD is perfect,
>   refreshing the soul.
> The decree of the LORD is trustworthy,
>   giving wisdom to the simple.
> The precepts of the LORD are right,
>   rejoicing the heart."
>
> PSALM 19:8–9

? How are God's Laws "refreshing" to the soul? How can you tell that a person places God first in his or her life?

Disciple Power

Piety

When we worship God, we exercise the gift of piety. Piety is one of the seven Gifts of the Holy Spirit. It helps us give devotion to God. The attitudes of reverence and respect accompany piety and pious activity.

The Collection at Mass

When we take part in the celebration at Mass, we show our love both for God and for others. The collection of money at Mass is one sign of that love. This ancient tradition of the Church is one way we generously show our thanks to God and provide for the material needs of the Church.

From the earliest days of the Church, wealthy people gave money to the Church. Others brought cheese, hand-woven cloth, grain, animals, vegetables, bread, and other goods. After gathering at the entrance of the church, they walked in procession to an area near the altar where they left their gifts. After the celebration of the Mass concluded, these gifts were brought and shared with people in need. In some countries of the world today, that custom is still followed.

? In what ways does the Sunday collection at Mass show love for God?

Knights of Columbus

At the celebration of the Mass, we collect money to help share God's love for others. There are other ways people work together to support the Church too. People who try to live their faith often gather together to start organizations to help others in need. In 1881, at St. Mary Church in New Haven, Connecticut, a group of men and Father Michael J. McGivney, the assistant pastor, started an organization to help families and others in the community. This organization is called the Knights of Columbus.

Over the years, the Knights of Columbus grew from parish to parish and even from country to country. After this organization began, the Knights of Columbus started a life insurance program to help families provide funerals for family members. They raised money to help repair parish buildings, build Catholic schools, and support the Church in spreading the love of God.

Still active today, the Knights of Columbus help to support children with special needs by raising funds for educational programs assisting students and their families. They help war veterans and support the Church in helping with some of the social needs in the community.

The Knights of Columbus support the People of God to live their faith and share God's love by serving others.

? What are other organizations that show respect for God by serving others?

Venerable Father
Michael J. McGivney

Activity Design a Web page that shares how the People of God show respect for God by serving others. Include the title of your Web page and key features to explain how serving others is serving God.

FAITH FOCUS
How does the First
Commandment guide us to
love God above all else?

FAITH VOCABULARY

worship
Honor and respect we give
to God above all else; faith
in, hope in, and love for God
above all else is worship.

idolatry
This is the substition of
someone or worshiping a
creature or thing (money,
pleasure, power, etc.)
instead of God the Creator.

Precepts of the Lord

God gave us Commandments to remind us what is most important in life. The first three Commandments teach us ways that we are to love the Lord our God with our whole heart, soul, and mind (see Matthew 22:37). God gave his Commandments to Moses, and this was the first and most important of all:

"I, the LORD, am your God, who brought you out of the land of Egypt, that place of slavery. You shall not have other gods besides me."

EXODUS 20:2–3

The First Commandment

This First Commandment teaches us that we are to **worship** only God. We are to place our faith and hope in God and to love him above all else. God is due our honor and praise. Atheism, or denying the existence of God, is a sin against the First Commandment.

This commandment also warns us not to participate in activities that place our trust on anything other than God. It warns us about **idolatry.** Idols are those people or things that we place before God. Idols in our lives could be things like power, fame, material possessions, money, or even a person. We all know how easy it is to love these things to excess and allow them to take over our lives. Jesus was tempted in the desert by the devil three times to use his divine power for earthly gain. But Jesus remained faithful to God, the Father (see Luke 4:1–13).

How would you rewrite the First Commandment in your own words?

Moses Presenting the
Ten Commandments
by Raphael

Our Top Priority

There are many things in life that give us a feeling of great pleasure and excitement, especially when they place us in the center of life. Sometimes they may be the newest gadget, the latest trend, or the desire to be the "star" of a team. In and of themselves, they are not bad. But when they become our top priority in life, we worship them or ourselves as an idol. Idols consume our time and energy, enslaving us. When God is our top priority, we are not enslaved but become truly free to seek happiness.

? Why do you think God should be people's top priority?

Activity Work with a small group. Create a list of all the false idols that a person your age might worship. Then think of some practical steps people could take to redirect themselves toward God.

Idols	Solutions
_____	_____
	_____
	_____
	_____
_____	_____
	_____
	_____
_____	_____
	_____
	_____

Write one action that will help you keep God as your top priority in life.

_____

_____

In the Name of the Lord

As we prioritize things in our lives, we seek to order our lives with the hope that life becomes not just manageable but enjoyable. Often the words we use speak volumes about our attitude toward life.

The Second Commandment

Words reveal the kind of person we are, what is important to us, and how we look at life. The Second Commandment challenges us about some of the words we might use.

"You shall not take the name of the LORD, your God, in vain. For the LORD will not leave unpunished him who takes his name in vain."

EXODUS 20:7

The Second Commandment teaches us that we are to use the name of God and the names of Jesus, Mary and the Saints reverently and respectfully. Blasphemy is the use of the names of God, of Jesus Christ, of the Virgin Mary, and of the Saints in an offensive way. In fact, all the words we use and why we use them show what is really in our hearts.

This Commandment also teaches that we are to take an oath only when it is necessary, as in a court of law. Whenever we call God as our witness, we must tell the truth. To use the name of God or Jesus when we are angry, to show off, or to casually say "I swear to God" is against the Second Commandment.

How do words show respect or disrespect to God and to others?

The Power of Words

Each of us knows that our words do affect others, not just because of how we say them but how we use them. We can use words to praise, honoring the sacred such as God and one another. We can also use words to curse, hurting others with our profanity. Some words evoke such an impact when used that, regardless of our intention, they are powerful.

The name of God and Jesus Christ are examples of powerful and sacred words. God, above all, deserves our respect and worship.

 What influences in the world around you show disrespect for the names of God and Jesus? What can you do to stand up to them?

Activity Give examples of the influences in the world showing disrespect to God and Jesus. Then write one action that could help change the influence. What difference will it make in your life or the lives of others?

Faith-Filled People

Moses

Moses believed in God above all else. While Moses was on Mount Sinai, the people persuaded Aaron, the brother of Moses, to gather and melt all the gold the people had and create a golden calf. Aaron and the people worshiped the golden calf as the god who freed them from Egypt. Hearing the people dancing and singing, Moses came down from Sinai. He took the golden calf and threw it into a fire (read Exodus 32).

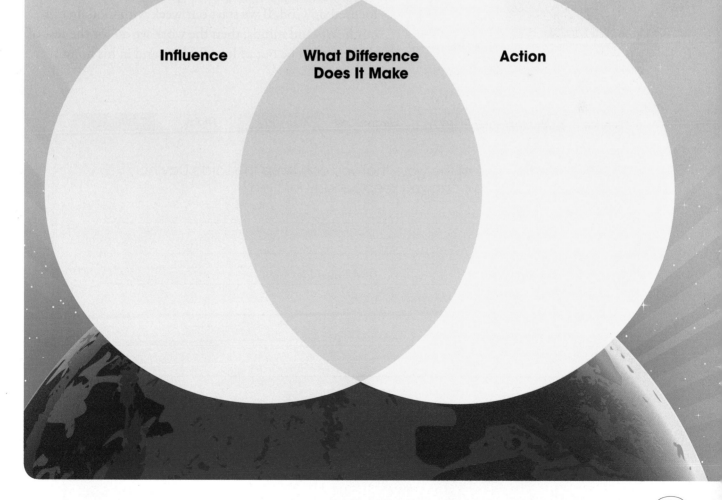

Influence

What Difference Does It Make

Action

FAITH FOCUS
What does the Third
Commandment teach us?

The Third Commandment

In the Old Testament, God rested from the work of creation on the seventh day, or the Sabbath. He commanded his people to do the same.

Remember to keep holy the sabbath day. Six days you may labor and do all your work, but the seventh day is the sabbath of the LORD, your God.

EXODUS 20:8–10

The Sabbath is to be set aside from all the other days of the week as the Lord's Day.

Sunday is the Lord's Day for Christians. It is the day on which the Lord Jesus was raised from the dead. It is the first day of the new creation of the world in Christ. It is the day on which we focus on keeping God first in our lives.

Sunday is to be kept as the most important holy day of obligation. Catholics have the obligation to take part in Mass on Sunday and on other holy days of obligation. We rest from all work that is not necessary. We are to use Sunday as the day to help us keep our hearts and minds focused on God. If we start our week with God first in our hearts and minds, then the work we do for the rest of the week can be out of love for him and in his honor.

| Sunday | Monday | Tuesday | Wednesday | Thursday | Friday | Saturday |

Activity   Name some of the ways that you can keep the Lord's Day holy. Log them here. How can you keep Sunday for God?

_____

_____

_____

_____

_____

_____

_____

_____

I FOLLOW JESUS

The Holy Spirit is always inviting you to place your faith, hope and love in the Holy Trinity above all else. This may not always be easy to do. Recognize the temptations and idols in your life that make it difficult to keep God first. Use the gift of piety to help you keep God above all else.

KEEPING GOD FIRST

Think of the obstacles to keeping God first that you brainstormed on page 285. Which of these things is the greatest temptation for you? Write it on the pedestal. Then write how you can overcome that obstacle.

I can overcome this obstacle . . .

_____

_____

_____

_____

_____

_____

_____

_____

MY FAITH CHOICE

This week, I will make God the top priority in my life. I will:

_____

_____

_____.

Pray, "Lord, you are above all else in my life. Help me to keep you first in my heart so that all I do and say gives honor and praise to you. Amen."

TO HELP YOU REMEMBER

TO HELP YOU REMEMBER

1. The First Commandment teaches us to worship only God and to believe in, hope in, and love God above all else.

2. The Second Commandment teaches us to use the name of God reverently and respectfully.

3. The Third Commandment teaches us to keep the Lord's Day as a holy day, a day set aside for God. Sunday is the Lord's Day for Christians.

Recall

Write First, Second, or Third beside the phrases that best describe the Commandments.

1. _____ We call God to be our witness to the truth of what we are saying.

2. _____ We worship only God.

3. _____ Catholics take part in Mass on Sunday.

4. _____ We speak the name of God reverently and respectfully.

5. _____ We love God above all else.

Reflect

What are some of the idols that keep you from putting God first in your life? Think of a way you can put God first.

_____

_____

_____

_____

_____

_____

_____

_____

_____

_____

_____

Share Work with a partner to list ways to keep Sunday as the Lord's Day. Share these ways with your class.

Act of Love

There are many traditional prayers that Catholics are asked to memorize. One of these is called the Act of Love, which is found at the end of this prayer celebration. If you do not already know this prayer, memorize it so that you will always remember your love of God.

Leader: Let us pray together praising the Lord by praying verses from Psalm 103.

All: **Bless the Lord, my soul;**
all my being, bless his holy name!

Leader: Bless the Lord, my soul;
do not forget all the gifts of God.

All: **Bless the Lord, my soul;**
all my being, bless his holy name!

Leader: Merciful and gracious is the LORD,
slow to anger, abounding in kindness.

All: **Bless the Lord, my soul;**
all my being, bless his holy name!

PSALM 103:1, 2, 8

Leader: Let us now pray together the prayer called the Act of Love.

All: **O my God, I love you above all things,**
with my whole heart and soul,
because you are all good and worthy of all my love.
I love my neighbor as myself for the love of you.
I forgive all who have injured me,
and ask pardon of all whom I have injured.
Amen.

With My Family

This Week . . .

In Chapter 21, "Love of God," your child learned:

▶ The First Commandment teaches us that we are to worship only God. We are to believe in, hope in, and love God above all else. God alone is and should always be at the center of our lives.

▶ The Second Commandment teaches us that we are to honor the name of God. We are to speak the name of God reverently and respectfully.

▶ The Third Commandment teaches us that we are to set aside one day each week as the Lord's Day. It is the most important holy day of obligation. On Sundays, Catholics have the obligation to take part in the Mass. We are to avoid all work that prevents us from keeping God as the center of our lives.

▶ Exercising the gift of piety is a way we can make God our top priority in life.

For more about related teachings of the Church, see the *Catechism of the Catholic Church*, 2083–2195, and the *United States Catholic Catechism for Adults*, pages 337–371.

■ Sharing God's Word

Read together Exodus 20:1–17. Emphasize that we give glory to God when we live the Ten Commandments.

■ We Live as Disciples

The Christian home and family is a school of discipleship. Choose one of the following activities to do as a family, or design a similar activity of your own:

▶ Choose one thing this week that your family can do together to show that God is the top priority in your lives.

▶ Visit or call someone who is important to the family so that you can honor God by loving others, especially if they were not present at Sunday Mass.

▶ Create table placemats proclaiming Sunday as the Lord's Day. Use these placemats at your Saturday evening and Sunday family meals.

■ Our Spiritual Journey

Fasting is a form of piety that Jesus emphasized (read Matthew 9:16–18). This is also an obligation for Catholics as a way to prepare ourselves to receive the Eucharist and to help us place God first in our lives. This week, as a family, pray together the Act of Love on page 291.

For more ideas on ways your family can live as disciples of Jesus, visit **BeMyDisciples.com**

Looking Ahead

In this chapter, the Holy Spirit invites you to ▶

EXPLORE how the Church calls us to stand up for a culture of life.

DISCOVER the joys and threats to life, love, and human relationships.

DECIDE how you can ask God in prayer to help you love responsibly.

CHAPTER
22

Commandments of Love

? You know when someone's "heart is in it?" What challenges do you face in expressing love to your family?

Learn about what Jesus said to the Pharisees, who said that the Law of Moses permitted divorce.

But Jesus told them [the Pharisees], "Because of the hardness of your hearts, he wrote you this commandment. But from the beginning of creation, 'God made them male and female . . . and the two shall become one flesh. Therefore what God has joined together, no human being must separate.'"

MARK 10:5–9

? What does Jesus mean when he speaks of "the hardness of your heart?"

Disciple Power

Temperance

One of the four Cardinal Virtues, temperance includes other virtuous acts and attitudes such as chastity, self-control, and responsible living according to God's plan for life and love. This virtue helps us to moderate our actions so that we do what is good and right.

Conflicting Cultures

In 1995, Saint John Paul II wrote an encyclical letter, the *Gospel of Life*, to the Church and the world. He called for all Christians to stand up for the culture of life rather than the culture of death. He asked them to adopt a "new heart," or to have a loving outlook toward life; to recognize that human life is sacred and a holy gift from God.

Thousands of miles away from Rome in a parish in the United States, some parishioners read the Pope's encyclical. These members of St. Luke's Parish studied the Pope's encyclical and took it to heart. They thought about what it meant to live recognizing that life is sacred. They listed all the ways that they were already supporting a culture of life: the parish committee that provided housing for the homeless, the food collection program, and the family events throughout the year. They wondered what more they could do and asked the children of the parish to assist them.

Many of the school's classes discussed the question. One class in particular thought of ways their families supported life by caring for one another and helping the poor and needy. One student, Lin Zhang, who is of Chinese descent, remarked that Chinese people have great respect for their elders, especially when they can no longer care for themselves. He said, "We respect their wisdom and all they have done for us."

 How would you explain to someone what the term "culture of life" means?

The Culture of Life

"So do the people of my culture," said Estella, who is of Mexican descent. "Our *abuelos* and *abuelas*, our grandparents, are the most respected members of our families. We ask their advice about everything. My *abuela* lives with us and takes good care of us."

Their teacher said, "I have an idea. Maybe we could make the elderly in our parish our special concern. Let's brainstorm some ideas about how we can respect and care for the elder members of our parish. Then we will present these to the parish staff."

Today, St. Luke's Parish is known throughout the community for its care for the elderly. They prepare meals and run errands for the senior citizens in the community. A transportation program helps elderly people get to their medical appointments. St. Luke's parishioners visit care centers for the elderly to read to them, entertain them with songs and skits, and listen to them while visiting. They send friendship and get-well cards to those they cannot visit. All the people of St. Luke's support a culture of life.

? In what ways does your school help others, especially the elderly?

Activity Text three ways you can show your respect for the older members of your family. Jot down your ideas first, then write your texts.

Ideas _____

_____

_____

Messages

Name _____

Text 1 _____

_____

Text 2 _____

_____

Text 3 _____

_____

FAITH FOCUS
What do the Fourth and Fifth Commandments teach us about living the Law of Love?

FAITH VOCABULARY
murder
The direct and intentional killing of an innocent person is murder.

Respect for Others

Strengthening the Family

Honor your father and your mother.

EXODUS 20:12

The Fourth Commandment is one way that God tells us to build a culture of life. He commands that each family member contribute to the family's well-being.

This means that family care for all members, especially the elderly and most vulnerable, is to be a top priority. After God, we are to honor our parents, even as adults. We are to respect and obey them and offer appropriate assistance when they are in need. We are to care for our parents later in their lives, in honor of their caring for us at the beginning of ours.

Families are to care for the physical and spiritual needs of their children. The Fourth Commandment also teaches, in a general way, about our responsibilities as citizens. As long as persons in authority follows God's Law, they should be obeyed for the common good for everyone. The Fourth Commandment strengthens the family so all its members can live as the domestic Church, or church of the home.

What are some examples of what it means to honor the adult members of your family?

Promoting the Culture of Life

You shall not kill.

ExODUS 20:13

The principle underlying the Fifth Commandment is that all life is sacred. This Commandment teaches that we must protect and nurture all human life, from conception to natural death. We are to respect and care for our own lives, health, and bodies, and those of others. We are to act safely and not put ourselves or others in unnecessary danger. We are to live as peacemakers.

The Fifth Commandment forbids abortion, **murder,** suicide, euthanasia, bullying, terrorism, unjust wars, and any act that violates the right to life or disrespects the dignity of the human person. This Commandment, however, does not prohibit defending human life if someone is attacked. All people, a nation or an individual, have the right to safety and security in life. However, the spread of nuclear weapons is an evil threatening human life that must be overcome for the good of all. The Fifth Commandment promotes the culture of life.

? How do you think the Fifth Commandment helps us live Jesus' Law of Love?

Activity Work with a group. Brainstorm ideas for a poster inviting families in your school to support a culture of life. Write your ideas here. Make the poster and display it in your classroom.

_____

_____

_____

_____

_____

_____

_____

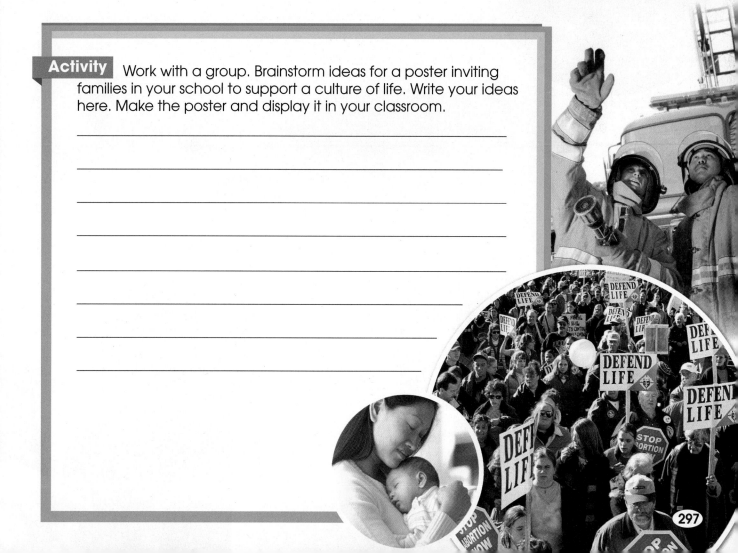

The Commandment of Faithfulness

You shall not commit adultery.

EXODUS 20:14

The Sixth Commandment teaches everyone to live a chaste life. This means that we behave in appropriate ways, showing respect for ourselves and others. **Chastity** is integrating the gift of human sexuality within the whole person. This involves self-control and modesty.

Self-control means being respectful and honest and to choose not to act or speak in inappropriate or selfish ways. Modest means being careful to make choices that show that we respect ourselves and others. For example, recognizing that we can send a message about who we are to other people by the way we dress, speak, and live Christian values. It takes practice to learn how to make wise choices! This Commandment guides Christians to follow Christ as our model in the way we express our love for our family, friends, and others.

 What are the ways a person can live a chaste life in words as well as actions?

The Commandment of Self-Respect

The Sixth Commandment also teaches about God's plan for marriage. In their marriage commitment, the husband and wife have promised to love, honor, and be faithful to each other until death. When a person has sexual relations with a person he or she is not married to, that person violates the Sixth Commandment. Marriage is broken or seriously weakened when this happens. The Sixth Commandment calls for faithfulness in which both spouses freely, fully, faithfully, and forever give the gift of self to the other.

Among sins gravely contrary to the Sixth Commandment are adultery, artificial, contraception, fornication, pornography, and sterilization. Everyone experiences temptations to misuse the gift of sexuality. To dwell on these thoughts and desires can easily lead people to disrespect themselves and others. God's grace is always there to help us deal with such temptations.

? In what ways can you practice the virtues of faithfulness, loyalty, and chastity now so that you will prepare yourself for the lasting commitments of adulthood?

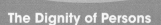

Catholics Believe

The Dignity of Persons

God created us to love and respect one another as persons, not to use each other as objects. In creating us male and female, God gives men and women equal personal dignity. Each of the two genders is an image of the power and tenderness of God, equal in dignity, distinct in sexual identity (see CCC 2333-2336).

Activity Give an example of one way you can practice the virtues of faithfulness, loyalty, and chastity. Then respond to the question.

Faithfulness _____

_____

Loyalty _____

_____

Chastity _____

_____

How will these practices prepare you for the commitments in your adult life?

_____

_____

_____

_____

FAITH FOCUS
What does the Ninth
Commandment teach us?

FAITH VOCABULARY
covet
To unjustly desire what
rightfully belongs to
someone else.

Practice Purity of Heart

You shall not covet your neighbor's wife.

EXODUS 20:17

The Ninth Commandment teaches that everyone is to respect and honor the promises a husband and wife make to one another in marriage. We are not to do anything, not even desire to do anything, that would break up a marriage.

This Commandment also guides us to train ourselves to be pure in mind and heart, and in our actions. To **covet** someone or something, which is one of the Capital Sins, is to have an unjust desire for someone or something that belongs to someone else. The Beatitudes and the commandments are similar to one another. The Ninth Commandment teaches us we are to practice purity of heart.

When we act according to purity of heart, we practice the Cardinal Virtue of temperance. We demonstrate modesty through patience, decency, and discretion. Not only do we honor and respect others, we protect the "intimate center" of ourselves. This means we are to love ourselves as God loves us.

? What do you think it means to respect yourself?

Activity

Marriage Today

Name a popular television show about people in a relationship. Are the people in that relationship living according to the Commandments? How might the show affect the people viewing it?

TV Show	My Analysis
_____	_____
_____	_____

I FOLLOW JESUS

The Ten Commandments are reminders of how to be in loving relationships. In order to act responsibly in our relationships, we often channel our desires to meet the needs of others first. Prayer is an effective way to refocus on our attention on what is most important in life.

THE CULTURE OF LIFE

Choose one of the Commandments addressed in this chapter. Create the outline of a story that supports a culture of life. Write or draw three scenes for the story in the boxes.

MY FAITH CHOICE

This week, I will think of the needs of older members of my family. I will respect them. I will

_____

_____

 Pray, "Jesus, you show us how to love. Help me to channel my desires so that I can see others with respect, as Jesus does. Amen."

1. The Fourth Commandment teaches that all family members are to contribute to the well-being of the family.

2. The Fifth Commandment teaches that we are to respect all human life as sacred and live as peacemakers.

3. The Sixth and Ninth Commandments teach us to live chaste lives in our thoughts and actions.

Chapter Review

Recall

Mark the true statements "T" and the false statements "F." Change the false statements into true statements.

F   T   1. Adult children who live away from home have more responsibility to honor their parents than do younger children who still live at home.

F   T   2. All human life is sacred from the first moment of conception to natural death.

F   T   3. Everyone is called to live a chaste life.

F   T   4. The virtues of temperance and modesty help us to live the Sixth and Ninth Commandments.

F   T   5. The Fifth Commandment is about promoting the culture of life.

Reflect

Sit quietly. Write a prayer telling God what it means for you to love and respect others. Thank God for the gift of life.

_____

_____

_____

_____

_____

_____

_____

_____

Share   With a partner, list ways we show that life is sacred. Discuss these ways with your class. Then write a class prayer thanking God for the gift of life.

Peace Prayer

This well-known prayer of Saint Francis of Assisi summarizes the attitude of the person who supports a culture of life in human relationships. Pray it often with your class and with your family.

Lord, make me an instrument of your peace:

where there is hatred, let me sow love;

where there is injury, pardon;

where there is doubt, faith;

where there is despair, hope;

where there is darkness, light;

and where there is sadness, joy.

O Divine Master, grant that I may not so much seek

to be consoled as to console;

to be understood as to understand;

to be loved as to love.

For it is in giving that we receive;

it is in pardoning that we are pardoned;

and it is in dying that we are born to eternal life.

Amen.

With My Family

This Week . . .

In Chapter 22, "Commandments of Love," your child learned:

▶ The Fourth Commandment teaches that all family members are to contribute to the well-being of the family.

▶ The Fifth Commandment teaches that we are to respect all human life as sacred and to live as peacemakers.

▶ The Sixth and Ninth Commandment teach us to live a chaste life like Jesus.

▶ The Cardinal Virtue of temperance helps us to moderate our actions so that we do what is good and right.

For more about related teachings of the Church, see the *Catechism of the Catholic Church,* 2196–2400, 2514–2533, and the *United States Catholic Catechism for Adults,* pages 373–416, 439–446.

■ Sharing God's Word

Read together Luke 1:46–55 (The Magnificat) and Luke 1:69–79 (The Canticle of Zechariah). Emphasize that prayer helps us to recognize God as the source of life and love. In prayer, we can turn to God for his loving kindness and tender mercies.

■ We Live as Disciples

The Christian home and family is a school of discipleship. Choose one of the following activities to do as a family, or design a similar activity of your own:

▶ Blessed Mother Teresa said, "Prayer enlarges the heart until it is capable of containing God's gift of himself." Invite family members to share how they invite God into their hearts.

▶ Use family prayer time to pray for the specific needs of others. Then form a family action plan to help meet those needs.

▶ Have each family member handwrite a "love letter" to one another.

■ Our Spiritual Journey

Prayer is way that helps us to preserve in love. Saint Paul calls for all Christians to pray without ceasing. This is possible if our wills are aligned with God's. The Church teaches us such tireless activity comes from love. Love opens our hearts to faith, making prayer possible. This week pray pray the Prayer of Saint Francis on page 303 with your family.

For more ideas on ways your family can live as disciples of Jesus, visit **BeMyDisciples.com**

Looking Ahead

In this chapter, the Holy Spirit invites you to ▶

EXPLORE a model of generosity in Venerable Henriette Delille.

DISCOVER how the Commandments teach us to live generously.

DECIDE how daily prayer can help you keep a generous heart.

CHAPTER
23

Love of Neighbor

❓ Who do you consider to be your neighbor? How do you show generosity to others?

Jesus points out for us a model to follow when it comes to practicing generosity. One day when Jesus was teaching in the Temple, he noticed a poor woman making an offering of two small coins.

> He said, "I tell you truly, this poor widow put in more than all the rest; for those others have all made offerings from their surplus wealth, but she, from her poverty, has offered her whole livelihood."
>
> LUKE 21:3–4

❓ According to Jesus, how is generosity measured? How difficult would it be for you to give like this poor widow in the Gospel?

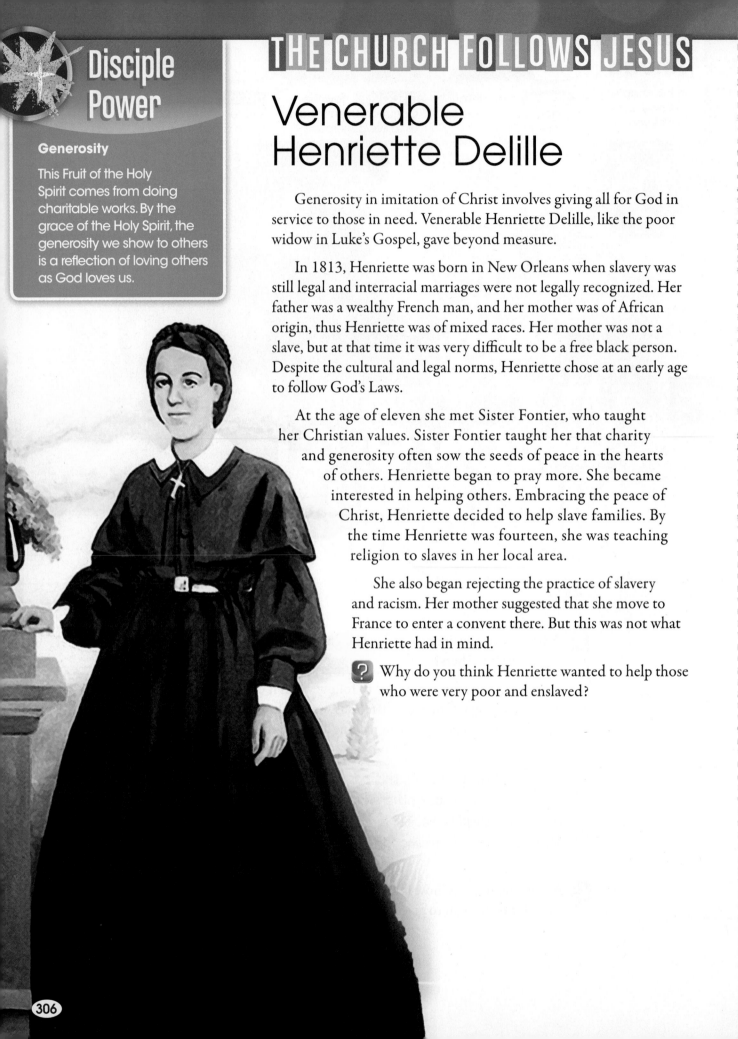

Disciple Power

Generosity

This Fruit of the Holy Spirit comes from doing charitable works. By the grace of the Holy Spirit, the generosity we show to others is a reflection of loving others as God loves us.

Venerable Henriette Delille

Generosity in imitation of Christ involves giving all for God in service to those in need. Venerable Henriette Delille, like the poor widow in Luke's Gospel, gave beyond measure.

In 1813, Henriette was born in New Orleans when slavery was still legal and interracial marriages were not legally recognized. Her father was a wealthy French man, and her mother was of African origin, thus Henriette was of mixed races. Her mother was not a slave, but at that time it was very difficult to be a free black person. Despite the cultural and legal norms, Henriette chose at an early age to follow God's Laws.

At the age of eleven she met Sister Fontier, who taught her Christian values. Sister Fontier taught her that charity and generosity often sow the seeds of peace in the hearts of others. Henriette began to pray more. She became interested in helping others. Embracing the peace of Christ, Henriette decided to help slave families. By the time Henriette was fourteen, she was teaching religion to slaves in her local area.

She also began rejecting the practice of slavery and racism. Her mother suggested that she move to France to enter a convent there. But this was not what Henriette had in mind.

? Why do you think Henriette wanted to help those who were very poor and enslaved?

Generosity Abounds

By 1836, after her mother's death, Henriette sold all of her property to start a religious community called the Sisters of the Holy Family. They were devoted to serving the needs of the poor, especially the enslaved.

Henriette's generosity was abundant, not only in giving up all her possessions to start a religious community, but also in devoting her own life to help those in most need. Through her acts of charity and service, she honored the dignity of every human being, including slaves who were not legally recognized as persons with rights.

Henriette Delille died in 1862, before slavery was abolished. She never saw a time when the people she worked so hard to help were free.

Her most notable prayer points to the source of her generosity and the reason why she did what she did: "I want to live and die for God." Today the Church recognizes her life of heroic virtue with the honor of Venerable.

? Venerable Henriette directed her efforts to those least protected by society. What group in society most needs to experience the love of the Christian community?

Activity Research one way the Church helps to honor the rights and dignity of others. Write a short article to tell others about how they can help. Be sure to include a headline!

_____

_____ _____

_____ _____

_____ _____

_____ _____

FAITH VOCABULARY

reparation
The process of righting a wrong; making amends.

almsgiving
Money, food, or material things given to the poor as an act of penance or charity.

Truth and Justice for All

The Seventh Commandment

You shall not steal.   EXODUS 20:15

The Seventh Commandment teaches that we live the virtues of justice and charity in our relationships with other people. We are to respect others by respecting their property.

The Commandment forbids stealing, cheating, human trafficking (slavery), misusing or damaging another's property, and paying unjust wages. If we break this Commandment, we have the obligation to make up for or repair whatever damage we have caused and to restore what we have unjustly done. This is called **reparation.**

We are to use the goods of the Earth responsibly and with generous hearts. How we treat the environment and use natural resources has an impact not only on our own but future generations. God consistently calls us to be good stewards of his creation. We are to use our resources without waste, yet out of generosity for those most in need.

❓ What are some ways you and your family are good stewards of God's creation?

Honesty and Charity

The Seventh Commandment also teaches us about the importance of good honest work. Our virtuous work is a participation in the work of God the Creator. Because we are joined to Christ in Baptism, our work is to be joined to his. We should do our work to the best of our ability and not avoid work we have agreed to do.

The idea of work also includes the responsibilities we have toward others. This Commandment guides us in living out the responsibilities we have toward others.

One important work of the Christian life is **almsgiving**. In this way, the work we do is an act of generosity and charity—loving our neighbor as God loves all of us. All of daily activity is to give honor and glory to God.

 How would you explain that good honest work is part of living the Seventh Commandment?

Activity The Church asks us to give of our time, talent, and treasure for the good of the community. In what ways might you have wasted all three at times, and what you would be willing to give for reparation?

	Waste	Give
Time		
Talent		
Treasure		

FAITH FOCUS
How does the Eighth
Commandment teach us to
imitate Jesus?

The Eighth Commandment

*You shall not bear false witness against
your neighbor.*   EXODUS 20:16

Our daily activity should also be about seeking and upholding the
truth. The Eighth Commandment is about truth. It commands that
we live honest and truthful lives. We are to respect the good name of
others. Jesus taught us in the Sermon on the Mount,

*"Let your 'Yes' mean 'Yes,' and your 'No' mean 'No.'
Anything more is from the evil one."*   MATTHEW 5:37

Jesus is challenging us to be truthful in all that we do and say. We are
not to be hypocrites, believing or doing one thing but saying another.
We must avoid all occasions to sin against truth. We need to respect
others and lead an honest life.

The Eighth Commandment guides us in being honest and
respecting others. Just like we do not want others telling lies about
us, we are not to lie about others. This Commandment helps us to
follow Jesus' teaching to love our neighbor as ourselves.

? What are some examples that show how to live the
Eighth Commandment?

A Good Name

Breaking the Eighth Commandment weakens our trust and respect for others. If we break this Commandment, we have the obligation to repair the damage that our misuse of the truth has caused. A person's good name is one of his or her most valued possessions. If we tell lies, spread false rumors, or promote damaging gossip, we bear false witness against a person and are required to make amends.

When we lie, we can receive forgiveness for this sin by participating in the Sacrament of Penance and Reconciliation. We are always obligated to tell the truth to those who have the right to know it.

 What are some effective ways to stop the spread of false rumors and gossip?

Activity What do we mean by the expression "Honesty is the best policy"?

_____

_____

_____

Write a letter to someone you know who lives by the motto, "Honesty is the best policy." Write the name of the person at the top and then write your letter. Find a way to share your letter with this person.

Dear _____

_____

_____

_____

_____

_____

FAITH FOCUS
How is the Tenth
Commandment about
generosity?

FAITH VOCABULARY
stewardship
The actions of responsibly
caring for what God has
given in service to others.

The Tenth Commandment

You shall not covet your neighbor's house.   EXODUS 20:17

We are to share the blessings that God has given to us with others. We are to avoid greed and envy, which are Capital Sins. The Tenth Commandment teaches us to treat others fairly and justly. We know that we are tempted to break the Tenth Commandment when we desire too much or are jealous of what others have. This kind of coveting can lead us to placing material possessions before personal relationships. For example, if someone feels resentful of a possession that a friend has, that may be a sign of greed and envy.

The Tenth Commandment also calls us to be thankful for what God has given us and to be generous with the gifts we have received. All blessings and gifts are from God. Many of the gifts given to us by God are to be used for the benefit and good of others. When we take care of what God has provided us, we exercise **stewardship**. And in our generosity, we live according to the Cardinal Virtue of justice.

How is stewardship a form of generosity?

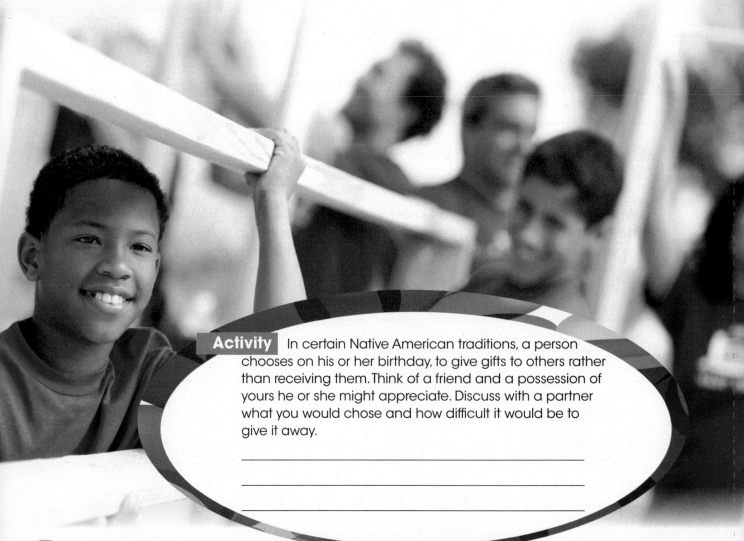

Activity   In certain Native American traditions, a person chooses on his or her birthday, to give gifts to others rather than receiving them. Think of a friend and a possession of yours he or she might appreciate. Discuss with a partner what you would chose and how difficult it would be to give it away.

_____

_____

_____

I FOLLOW JESUS

The Church teaches that the Holy Spirit guides and strengthens us in our ability to love our neighbor as God loves us. Works of charity come from a generous heart, and our generosity can sow the seeds of peace. The Holy Spirit invites you to pray often throughout the day, seeking a generous heart.

PRAYER AND ACTION

Take the time to fill out this daily planner. Set aside several different times during the day for praying. Choose reasonable time slots in which you can pray for something. In another slot, write something you will do that demonstrates a generous spirit. Write down what you plan to pray for in that slot.

MY FAITH CHOICE

This week, I will spend more time with God, the source of all love and generosity, in prayer. I will act with generosity. I will

_____

_____

 Pray, "Holy Spirit, guide my heart to love others as you love me. Amen."

Chapter Review

► TO HELP YOU
REMEMBER

1. The Seventh and Tenth Commandments teach us to treat others justly.

2. The Eighth Commandment is about speaking and living the truth.

3. We are to make amends with penance and reparation if we violate any of God's Commandments.

Recall

For each scenario, identify which Commandment is being violated. Then tell how the person could make reparation for his or her wrongdoing.

1. Jason's parents bought him his own tablet for his birthday. His older sister, Jane, became jealous because his tablet was newer than hers. Jane complained. Since she is older, she thinks she should have the new one and Jason should have hers.

_____

_____

_____

_____

2. Sam and Sophie were proud of their new tablets. So they went to school the next day and showed them off to everyone. Then they noticed George had an even better tablet than theirs. They took George's and left it where it would be damaged by water.

_____

_____

_____

_____

_____

Reflect

Which of the Seventh, Eighth, and Tenth Commandments do you think is the most difficult to keep? Why?

_____

_____

_____

Share Working with others, come up with a plan for keeping the Seventh, Eighth, and Tenth Commandments. Tell one thing you would do to keep each Commandment.

Prayer for Honesty

We are called to be honest with others in both word and deed. Pray this prayer to ask for help in being honest each day.

Leader : God created the world and filled our lives with blessings and gifts. Let us offer our prayers that we use these wisely and honestly.

All : **May the glory of the Lord last forever.**

Reader 1 : Blessed are you, O Lord, who gave us the command to work, so that we might devote ourselves to perfecting creation.

All : **May the glory of the Lord last forever.**

Reader 2 : Blessed are you, O Lord. Your Son Jesus knew how to work every day as a carpenter. Help us to imitate him.

All : **May the glory of the Lord last forever.**

Reader 3 : Blessed are you, O Lord, who guides us in always striving to do our best.

All : **May the glory of the Lord last forever.**

Reader 4 : Blessed are you, O Lord, who guides us to speak the truth and respect others by doing so.

All : **May the glory of the Lord last forever.**

Leader : Thank you, Lord, who have placed the Earth and its fruits under our care so that by our labor we may work to ensure that all share in the benefits of your creation.

All : **May the glory of the Lord last forever.**

BASED ON *THE BOOK OF BLESSINGS*

With My Family

This Week . . .

In Chapter 23, "Love of Neighbor," your child learned.

▶ The Seventh and Tenth Commandments teach us that we are to be just and generous. We are to use and care for all of God's creation wisely.

▶ The Eighth Commandment teaches us to live honest and truthful lives.

▶ If we violate any of God's Commandments, we are to make amends with penance and reparation, correcting the wrong we have done.

▶ Through almsgiving and stewardship, we can show our generosity and thanksgiving for all we have been given by God.

For more about related teachings of the Church, see the *Catechism of the Catholic Church*, 2401–2513, 2534–2557, and the *United States Catholic Catechism for Adults*, pages 417–438, 447–457.

■ Sharing God's Word

Read together John 14:15–21. Emphasize that faithfully living the Ten Commandments is a sign of a faithful disciple of Jesus. Find strength in knowing that Christ has given us the Holy Spirit as our Advocate to guide us in truth and justice.

■ We Live as Disciples

The Christian home and family is a school of discipleship. Choose one of the following activities to do as a family, or design a similar activity of your own:

▶ Talk about how your family lives as good stewards of God's creation. Focus on various "green initiatives" like gardening, conservation and recycling.

▶ During the holiday seasons, make an extra effort to meet the needs of those in need before purchasing extra gifts for the family.

▶ Give as a sacrifice—not from your excess but from what you value. Be intentional about using the family's talents and treasures for the good of others.

■ Our Spiritual Journey

Almsgiving is as much a spiritual activity as it is a material one. Giving of our money and material goods as an act of penance may be a foreign concept. Reflect on ways to take charity to the next level by making the act of giving one of sacrifice or penance. This week, pray together as a family the prayer for honesty on page 315.

For more ideas on ways your family can live as disciples of Jesus, visit **BeMyDisciples.com**

Looking Ahead

In this chapter, the Holy Spirit invites you to ▶

EXPLORE the prayer lives of Saints who inspire hope in God.

DISCOVER that the Lord's Prayer is the prayer of all Christians.

DECIDE how you can proclaim your faith, hope, and love for God.

CHAPTER

24

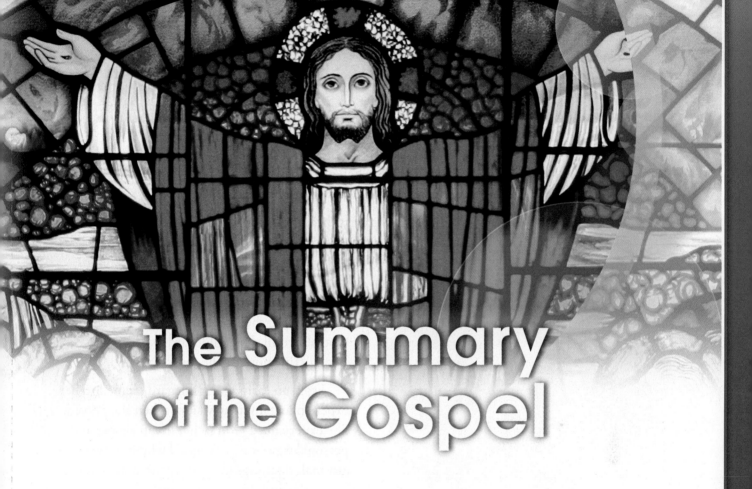

The Summary of the Gospel

❓ What do you anticipate for your future? What do you hope for?

Here is how the psalmist prayed with hope in his heart.

> Our soul waits for the LORD,
>   who is our help and shield.
> For in God our hearts rejoice;
>   in your holy name we trust.
> May your kindness, LORD, be upon us;
>   we have put our hope in you.
>
> PSALM 33:20–22

❓ What do you think the psalmist means by our souls wait for God? In what ways do you put your hope in God?

Disciple Power

Hope

This is one of the three Theological Virtues by which we desire and trust that God will fulfill all his promises, especially the promise of eternal happiness. Because of the Resurrection, Christianity is a religion of hope.

Saint Hildegard of Bingen

The history of the Church is filled with examples of people of hope. They turn to God in prayer. Some are called Saints, like Hildegard of Bingen, who exhibited the virtue of hope. Catholics pray for advice and direction from her and other Saints to keep hope alive in their hearts.

Hildegard of Bingen (1098–1179) was blessed with a sense of God's closeness to her, placing hope in her heart. She had a great love of creation as God's great gift to us.

Hildegard's parents brought her to a holy woman. This woman's name was Blessed Jutta and she was the leader of a group of women who lived together in a religious community. They had joined together to live their lives according to the Rule of Saint Benedict. They ordered their priorities in life by placing God above all else. Hildegard lived as a Benedictine nun for the rest of her life.

From an early age, Hildegard seemed to be experiencing mystical visions when she prayed. She experienced God in her life in a close and personal way. She questioned whether she was just making things up or trying to make herself seem very special and important.

? What can we learn from Saint Hildegard about the importance of prayer?

Prayer and Hope

Hildegard turned to a priest and told him what was happening to her when she prayed. He told her to write down what she was experiencing and he would read the writings. She wanted to be sure that her experiences were from God.

The priest read what Hildegard wrote and felt that her experiences were from God. He went to the bishop. The bishop also read what she had written and he also agreed with the priest that her visions were from God.

At the age of thirty-eight, she was elected abbess, or leader, of her religious community. People came to her for advice. She also prayed for them and encouraged them to pray. She gave them hope for their lives.

Hildegard kept prayer at the heart and center of her life. Through her example, she continues to inspire people today. She taught that through prayer, we deepen our friendship with God, in whom we trust and have hope. The Church honors Saint Hildegard of Bingen on her feast day, September 17.

❓ Why do you think prayer can bring hope?

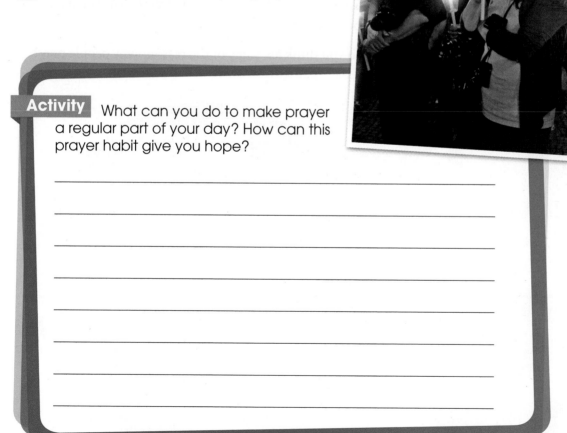

Activity What can you do to make prayer a regular part of your day? How can this prayer habit give you hope?

_____

_____

_____

_____

_____

_____

_____

FAITH VOCABULARY

adoration
A form of prayer that declares God is the source of all. We acknowledge God is Almighty Creator, on whom we depend for everything.

meditation
A form of silent prayer in which we listen to God through our thoughts and imagination, using Scripture, art, and music.

contemplation
A form of prayer without using words, in which we focus on minds and hearts on God alone.

Being with God

Prayer is a way we express the longing in our hearts for God. Prayer strengthens our faith, hope, and love for God. The Holy Spirit teaches us to pray through the Tradition of the Church. There is no secret to praying. Christians respond to the Holy Spirit by expressing our prayers in three basic ways. They are vocal prayer, meditation, and contemplation. They all share one thing in common—all prayer flows from our hearts.

Vocal Prayer

How natural it is for us to use words when we pray. Vocal prayer is prayer that uses words. Vocal prayers are prayed aloud or silently. They are prayed alone or with others. **Adoration** is a form of prayer in which our words praise God as the source of all.

Some vocal prayers are traditional prayers that have been prayed for centuries by Catholics. These prayers include the Our Father and the Hail Mary. Other times, we use our own words to say to God in prayer whatever is in our hearts.

The words we speak in our prayers express our thoughts and emotions. They enable us to share with God our joys and sorrow, our achievements and dreams. They give us the power to share with God everything about ourselves.

? What do you think are some of the reasons why people pray?

Meditation

God is a loving Father who is an active part of our lives at every moment. In a prayer of **meditation**, we connect our lives more closely with God. We use our imaginations, minds and desires to live the new life in Christ which we have received in Baptism.

We seek not only to know about Christ, but also to grow in our love and friendship with him. When we meditate, we often do not use words. We spend time with God the Father and give him all our attention. We listen as the Holy Spirit shows us how to live as children of God and disciples of Jesus.

Contemplation

Remember, words are not always necessary in prayer. God knows our innermost thoughts. He knows what we want to say before we put it into words. We can seek the presence of God without words.

Saint Teresa of Jesus (Saint Teresa of Avila, 1535–1582), Doctor of the Church and Spanish mystic, describes the prayer of **contemplation** as "nothing less than a close sharing between friends; it means taking time frequently to be alone with him who we know loves us." This is what we call communion with God the Father, in Christ, through the power of the Holy Spirit.

? Which form of prayer do you use the most? Which one would you like to try?

Activity Write a phrase to describe the different kinds of prayer.

Vocal _____

Meditation _____

Contemplation _____

Write a prayer of hope to help you in your life.

_____

_____

_____

The Lord's Prayer

The Lord's Prayer, or the Our Father, is the prayer of all Christians. It is truly a summary of the whole Gospel. In the Gospels, it has been handed on to the Church in two different forms. A shorter form is found in the Gospel of Luke (see Luke 11:2–4). The longer, more traditional form is found in the Gospel of Matthew. This version is the form the Church prays today. Both versions address God by name, honor God, and finally ask God to respond to our needs.

In Matthew's Gospel, the Lord's Prayer is part of the Sermon on the Mount. Jesus had just finished warning his disciples about doing good deeds so that everyone would know about them and praise the person who did them. Then while teaching his disciples about prayer, he said:

"This is how you are to pray:
Our Father in heaven,
    hallowed by your name,
        your kingdom come,
your will be done,
        on earth as in heaven.
    Give us today our daily bread;
    and forgive us our debts,
    as we forgive our debtors;
    and do not subject us to the final test,
    but deliver us from the evil one."

Matthew 6:9–13

If someone asked you what the Lord's Prayer was about, what would you tell them?

Living Life As A Prayer

Jesus lived his life as a prayer to the Father. His life gave praise to God the Father, and he placed total trust in the Father. This trust was especially clear as Jesus approached his Death on the Cross. Facing his Death, Jesus opened his heart to his Father, saying:

"I am troubled now. Yet what should I say? 'Father, save me from this hour'? But it was for this purpose that I came to his hour, Father, glorify your name."

JOHN 12:27–28

All that Jesus did gave glory and honor to the Father. The Lord's Prayer teaches us not only how to pray but also how to live so that we too give glory and honor to the Father as Jesus did.

? How might the words of the Lord's Prayer help you to live as a disciple of Jesus? What part of it has been the hardest for you to follow? Why?

Activity For centuries, artists have tried to depict the feelings they have when they hear and pray the Lord's Prayer. Create your own piece of art about how the Lord's Prayer makes you feel. Use words, symbols or your own art rendering.

The Meaning of the Lord's Prayer

The Lord's Prayer teaches us how to pray, but it also teaches us how to live a life in God the Father, as Jesus taught us.

Our Father. Through our Baptism, we are joined to Christ and become one with him and one another. The Holy Spirit is poured into our hearts, enabling us to call God, Abba (or Father), as Jesus did.

Who Art in Heaven. The word Heaven points to God's majesty and glory. The Church on Earth joins with the angels and Saints in Heaven in praising God.

Hallowed Be Thy Name. Glory and praise truly belong to God who creates, redeems, and sanctifies us.

Thy Kingdom Come. We pray that the Kingdom announced by Jesus will come to completion when he comes again in glory at the end of time. We promise to prepare a way for the coming that Kingdom by being his disciples now and doing all we can to proclaim the Kingdom.

Thy Will Be Done on Earth as It Is in Heaven. God's will is for all people to live in communion with him forever. When we pray, "thy will be done," we promise to live according to God's will and plan and to actively seek to do God's will in our lives.

Give Us This Day Our Daily Bread. Our daily bread is Christ himself, who said, "I am the living bread that came down from heaven" (John 6:51). We ask God to watch over our physical and spiritual needs and to keep us honest and attentive about what we really need in order to live a life in Christ.

And Forgive Us Our Trespasses as We Forgive Those Who Trespass Against Us. Forgiveness is a two-way street. Those who receive God's forgiveness and mercy must be willing to be as forgiving and merciful toward others as God is toward them.

And Lead Us Not into Temptation. Temptation tries to convince us that there is something better than God's will. We ask God for the courage to face temptation with strong faith, confident hope, and generous love.

But Deliver Us from Evil. Satan and forces of evil in the world try to lead us away from God's love. There is no one, no power, stronger than Jesus. We pray that God's victory in Jesus Christ will be our victory as well.

❓ What part of the Lord's Prayer is most meaningful to you? Why?

I FOLLOW JESUS

Jesus gave the Church the Lord's Prayer. That means he gave it to you! The Holy Spirit gives you the power to call God, Abba, Father. What a wonderful privilege! Stay in touch with God your Father each by sharing your faith, hope, and love for God with others.

THE LORD'S PRAYER ONLINE

You have been given the job of Web master of a new Web site. Design a Web page to tell the world all about the hope that comes from the Lord's Prayer.

MY FAITH CHOICE

Each morning this week, I will pray one petition of the Lord's Prayer. I will think about what it means that day. I will

_____

_____

 Pray, "Heavenly Father, your name is holy. I trust and hope in you and that your will be done. Amen."

1. The Lord's Prayer is the prayer of all Christians.

2. The Lord's Prayer teaches us to make our whole life a prayer.

3. The Lord's Prayer shows us how to live as people who place our faith, hope, and love of God above all else.

Chapter Review

Recall

Match the prayer terms in the word box with their descriptions.

vocal prayer	meditation	contemplation
	Lord's Prayer	adoration

1. _____ A prayer that uses words that we say aloud or quietly in our hearts.

2. _____ A prayer that is a close sharing between friends without words; being alone with God who we know loves us.

3. _____ A prayer that uses our imagination, mind, and desire to live as a faithful disciple of Christ.

4. _____ A prayer that Jesus himself gave to us.

5. _____ A form of prayer in which we praise God.

Reflect

Why do you think Christians should pray?

_____

_____

_____

_____

_____

_____

_____

_____

Share Share with a classmate the meaning of the Lord's Prayer in your life. Now go forth to live a life of prayer.

The Lord's Prayer

The Lord's Prayer is the prayer of all Christians. Take time every day to pray it with a sense of faith, hope, and love. Begin your prayer today in silence and a spirit of thanksgiving. Then pray together in the words that Jesus taught us.

Leader: Our Father, who art in heaven,
hallowed be thy name;

Group 1: thy kingdom come,
thy will be done
on earth as it is in heaven.

Group 2: Give us this day our daily bread,
and forgive us our trespasses,

Group 1: as we forgive those
who trespass against us;

Group 2: and lead us not into temptation
but deliver us from evil.

All: **Amen.**

With My Family

This Week . . .

In Chapter 24, "The Summary of the Gospel," your child learned:

▶ The Church describes three main expressions of prayer: vocal prayer, meditation, and contemplation.

▶ Jesus' teaching of the Lord's Prayer is part of the Sermon on the Mount.

▶ The Lord's Prayer is the prayer of all Christians and is an expression of our faith, hope and love in God.

▶ When we pray the Lord's Prayer, the Holy Spirit teaches us how to pray and to live the Gospel.

▶ Hope is one of the three Theological Virtues which we desire and trust that God will fulfill his promises.

For more about related teachings of the Church, see the *Catechism of the Catholic Church*, 2558–2865, and the United States *Catholic Catechism for Adults*, pages 461–495.

◼ Sharing God's Word

The Christian family is the first place for education in prayer. Read as a family Matthew 6:9–13. Emphasize that Jesus lived his life as a prayer. Discuss how each family member can do likewise.

◼ We Live as Disciples

The Christian home and family is a school of discipleship. Choose one of the following activities to do as a family, or design a similar activity of your own:

▶ Be sure every family member can recite from memory the Lord's Prayer. Emphasize that you pray from your heart.

▶ This week, use the Lord's Prayer for family prayer at least once a day.

▶ Purchase additional items to donate to your local food bank the next time you go grocery shopping for the family. Your parish or school can give you the location of the food bank.

◼ Our Spiritual Journey

Saint Thomas Aquinas called the Lord's Prayer the "most perfect of prayers." He said, "This prayer not only teaches us to ask for things, but also in what order we should desire them." Reflect in prayer on how you can align your will with the will of God the Father this week. As a family, pray the Lord's Prayer together.

For more ideas on ways your family can live as disciples of Jesus, visit **BeMyDisciples.com**

A Lesson About Rights

WE PROTECT THE RIGHTS OF OTHERS

Every person has certain rights. These include a right to life and other basic rights, such as freedom and justice.

"I want to try on a pair of handcuffs," Joel said to Officer Merino. Joel's scout troop was touring the police department in their town. All of the boys were excited about the tour. They met the police chief and several other police officers.

As they walked along, they badgered Officer Merino with questions. What was it like to arrest someone? Had he ever shot his gun in the line of duty? What was it like to drive a police car with the siren on?

Among other places, he took them to an empty prison cell. He unlocked the door and swung the door of bars wide.

"If I saw a robber, I would lock him up and throw away the key!" Nick exclaimed. Officer Merino smiled, "Well, it's not quite that simple."

"Right!" Joel declared. "The judge is the one that decides that." "Well, before someone even gets to the judge we read them their rights," Officer Merino said. "Their rights?" someone asked. "Yes, even people who are arrested have rights," one of the other boys said. "I don't think so," Nick shook his head. "If he did the crime, he does the time."

"Yes, if someone commits a crime, they will be punished," Officer Merino said. He went on to say, "But to make sure that people are treated fairly and justly, we tell them their rights. For example, they have a right to an attorney to help them understand the law."

The boys nodded in agreement. It was the correct thing to do so that everyone is treated fairly and justly.

MAKING CONNECTIONS

Sister Helen Prejean, CSJ

The Catholic Church teaches that criminals have rights and everyone deserves to be fairly treated under the law. Learn more about justice in the United States.

with CREATIVE ARTS

Research the story about Sister Helen Prejean and how she ministers to prisoners. Write and perform a skit about how Sister Helen helps the prisoners, families, victims and the justice system protect the rights and freedom of everyone.

with SOCIAL STUDIES

Research the correctional system in the United States to understand the rights of those who are in prison. Write a report on your findings. Include in your report, how many correctional facilities there are in the United States and how many men and women are held in these prisons. Also include the purpose for prisons and how they can be a way to help prisoners. Present your findings to the class.

with LANGUAGE ARTS

Write four paragraphs, explaining each sentence of the Miranda Rights. The Miranda Rights state:

"You have the right to remain silent. Anything you say can and will be used against you in a court of law. You have the right to speak to an attorney, and to have an attorney present during any questioning. If you cannot afford a lawyer, one will be provided for you at government expense."

Share your report with the class. Allow time to discuss the meaning of the Miranda Rights.

As the class talks about the Miranda Rights, include the following questions in your discussions. How are the Miranda Rights an example of living God's Laws? Which of the Ten Commandments are we following when the Miranda Rights are read to someone?

Faith Action

This week, reflect on the freedom and rights that are part of the legal system in the United States. Describe how the legal system recognizes that the public good must be balanced with fairness toward individuals.

_____

_____.

Unit 6 Review

A. Choose the Best Word

Fill in the blanks to complete each of the sentences of the paragraph. Use the words from the word bank.

adoration	communion	contemplation
meditation	prophets	petition

The Christian tradition of prayer has its roots in the Old

Testament. Abraham, King David, and the _____
are some of the Old Testament's models for Christians seeking
a prayer life. The Old Testament also reveals one of the five

basic forms of prayer that Christians use is _____ to
declare God as the source of all, We express our prayers

in three ways: vocal prayers, prayers of _____ and

prayers of _____.

B. Show What You Know

Read each question and circle the best answer.

1. Which of the Ten Commandments focuses on our
   relationship with God?

   A. First   B. First and Second

   C. First, Second, and Third   D. First, Second, Third, and Fourth

2. Which of the Ten Commandments teaches us not to
   cheat on a test?

   A. Fifth   B. Seventh

   C. Eighth   D. Tenth

3. Which of the Ten Commandments teaches us to live chaste lives?

   A. First   B. Fifth

   C. Seventh   D. Sixth

4. Which of the Ten Commandments teaches us to respect
   all human life as sacred?

   A. First   B. Fourth

   C. Fifth   D. Tenth

C. Connect with Scripture

*Reread the Scripture passage on the first Unit Opener page.
What connection do you see between this passage and
what you learned in this unit?*

_____

_____

_____

_____

_____

D. Be a Disciple

1. *Review the four pages in this unit titled, The Church Follows Jesus.
What person or ministry of the Church on these pages will inspire
you to be a better disciple of Jesus? Explain your answer.*

_____

_____

_____

_____

_____

2. *Work with a group. Review the four Disciple Power virtues, or gifts,
you have learned about in this unit. After jotting down your own
ideas, share with the group practical ways that you will live these
gifts day by day.*

_____

_____

_____

_____

_____

WE CELEBRATE THE CHURCH YEAR

The Year of Grace

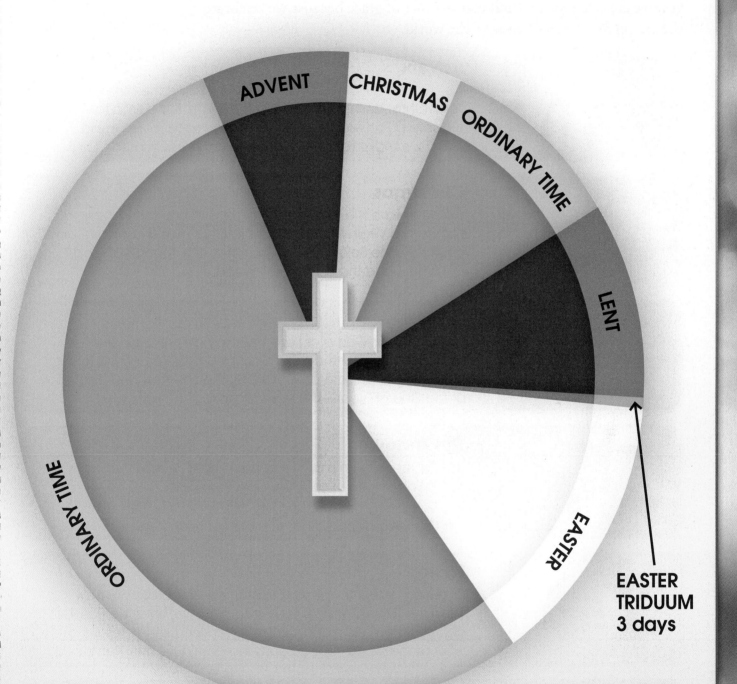

ADVENT

CHRISTMAS

ORDINARY TIME

LENT

ORDINARY TIME

EASTER

EASTER TRIDUUM 3 days

The Liturgical Year

While many things you see and hear at Mass are always the same, other things change. The readings change, as do the colors of banners and vestments. All of the changes help us know what part of the Church year we are celebrating. Each year is a year of grace because we celebrate the saving presence of Christ in the world.

Advent

We begin the liturgical year by anticipating the birth of Jesus Christ during the season of Advent. It is a time to prepare ourselves through prayer and sacrifice. In these ways, we make room in our hearts for the birth of the Lord.

Christmas

We celebrate the Incarnation of Jesus Christ through his birth to the Virgin Mary. During the Christmas season, we also celebrate the Solemnity of Mary, the Holy Mother of God, Epiphany, and the Baptism of the Lord.

Lent

During the forty days of Lent, we pray and make personal sacrifices so that we can turn our hearts more completely toward God. We are preparing for the greatest celebration of the Church year—the Resurrection of the Lord.

The Triduum

The Easter Triduum is at the center of our year of worship. Beginning on the evening of Holy Thursday and ending on Easter Sunday evening, the Triduum is our three-day solemn celebration of the Paschal Mystery.

Easter

On each of the fifty days of Easter, we celebrate our new life in the Risen Christ. At the Easter Vigil, we light the Paschal candle in the midst of darkness to remind us that Jesus is the Light of the world. Our celebration continues until Pentecost.

Ordinary Time

The rest of the Church year is called Ordinary Time. We celebrate many events in the life and ministry of Jesus. We also celebrate other great feasts and solemnities honoring Jesus, Mary, and the Saints.

Exaltation of the Holy Cross

FAITH FOCUS

What does the Feast of the Exaltation of the Holy Cross celebrate?

THE WORD OF THE LORD

Choose one of the readings for the Exaltation of the Holy Cross. Read and discuss it with your family.

First Reading
Numbers 21:4–9

Second Reading
Philippians 2:6–11

Gospel
John 3:13–17

Most of the time we do not consider a sign of pain and suffering to be a symbol of Good News. The Cross, though, is a sign of our Redemption. Whenever Catholics pray, we begin and end our prayer with the Sign of the Cross. We wear crosses as jewelry and may hang crosses on the walls of our homes. The cross is the primary symbol of the followers of Jesus. It is a symbol of hope.

Since the Cross is so much a part of our faith, the Church celebrates the Feast of the Exaltation of the Holy Cross every year on September 14. On this holy day we remember that because of the Cross, we have the promise of eternal life. Without Jesus' Death on the Cross, we would be without new life in Christ and without the hope of the coming of the Kingdom of God.

The Cross has always been important as a symbol of the faith for Christians that for centuries people sought the actual cross that

Jesus died on. The Feast of the Exaltation of the Holy Cross may have started as early as the seventh century to commemorate the finding of the Cross in Jerusalem. The Cross was this important to Christians more than fifteen hundred years ago.

Today we seek to deepen our understanding of the Paschal Mystery—Jesus' Passion, Death, Resurrection, and Ascension. We know that the real meaning for us is in the gift of eternal life. Jesus taught his disciples that his heavenly Father wants us to love our neighbors and to follow his Son. The Feast of the Exaltation of the Holy Cross helps us to do this by reminding us of what Jesus has done for us.

A Glorious Sign of Victory

Use some of the key words on page 335 to design a page for your school Web site. Help others to understand the gift of the Cross through Jesus Christ and ways to live as one of his disciples.

MY FAITH CHOICE

This week, I will follow Jesus by treating everyone as if they were my neighbor. I will

_____

_____

_____

 Pray, "Lord, whenever I see the Cross, help me to be ever inspired to follow you more completely. Amen."

All Saints

FAITH FOCUS
How are the Saints a source of hope for the Church?

THE WORD OF THE LORD
This is the Gospel for the Solemnity of All Saints. Read it and talk about the reading with your family.

Gospel
Matthew 5:1–12a

The Church is a communion of the holy people of God. When we say this, we express our belief that we are all united, or in communion, with Christ and all the members of the Church, the Body of Christ. We are all a part of the Communion of Saints. The Communion of Saints includes all the faithful members of the Church on Earth and those who have died. It includes both the Saints living with God in Heaven and those faithful in Purgatory who are being prepared to receive the gift of eternal life in Heaven.

The Church officially declares someone a Saint through a process called canonization. There are several steps involved in recognizing an individual as a Saint. Over the course of many years, the person's life and virtue is carefully examined by the Congregation for the Causes of Saints in Rome.

The holy person is first named Servant of God, then Venerable, then Blessed, and finally, in some cases, canonized by the Pope as a Saint. Each step requires investigation and evidence.

Although we know the names and life stories of many of the Saints and celebrate special feast days in their honor, there are many Saints in Heaven who are known only to God. The Church teaches that anyone in Heaven is a Saint. On the Solemnity of All Saints we honor all the Saints in Heaven, those we know and those we do not know.

We celebrate the Solemnity of All Saints on November 1. This special day is a holy day of obligation on which we honor the Saints as a source of hope and renewal for all members of the Church. They inspire us to put God first in our lives and to live as Jesus taught. All Saints day is a time to thank God for giving us so many examples of how to live our faith. We remember that the Saints pray for us and that we can pray to them, asking them to show us the way to holiness.

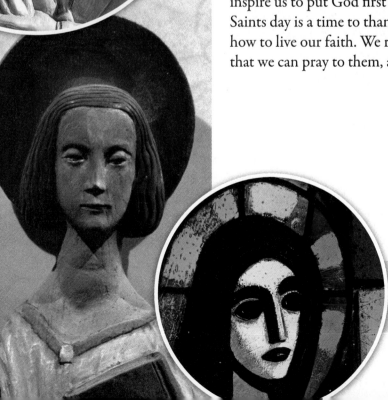

Blesseds Louis and Zélie Martin, Saint Lawrence, Mary Magdalene

The Little Way

Saint Thérèse of the Child Jesus, a Carmelite nun, known as "the Little Flower," is one of the Church's most well-loved Saints. She was only twenty-four years old when she died. She once wrote, "What matters in life is not great deeds, but great love." Saint Thérèse wanted everyone to know that love is the way to holiness.

On the page below, write down the little ways that you have shown love to others during the past week. Memorize Saint Thérèse's words and reflect on them often.

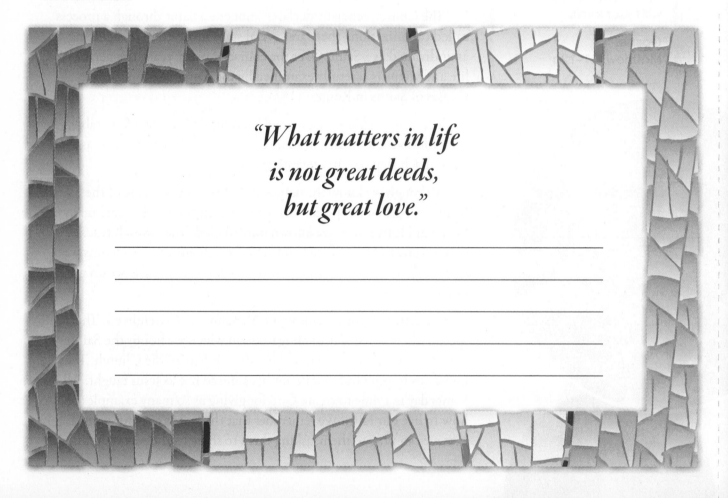

"What matters in life is not great deeds, but great love."

_____

_____

_____

_____

MY FAITH CHOICE

This week, I will follow Saint Thérèse's little way of doing small deeds with great love. I will

_____

_____

 Pray, "Dear Saint Thérèse, beloved friend of God and friend of mine, help me to love God with all my heart. Amen."

FAITH FOCUS
How does the
Jesse Tree help us
celebrate Advent?

**THE WORD
OF THE LORD**
These are the Gospel
readings for the First
Sunday of Advent.
Choose this year's
reading. Read and
discuss it with your
family.

Year A
Matthew 24:37–44

Year B
Mark 13:33–37

Year C
Luke 21:25–28, 34–36

Advent

All families have a history and a story to tell. All the people who are part of your family history make up your family tree—your parents, brothers and sisters, grandparents, aunts, uncles, and family members who lived generations ago.

Jesus has a family tree too. We Christians use it to help us celebrate Advent. We call it the Jesse Tree. The tree is named for Jesse, a shepherd from Bethlehem. He lived about one thousand years before Jesus. Jesse was the father of David, who grew up to be the greatest king of the people of Israel. David is an ancestor of Jesus.

During Advent, we remember the people—like Jesse and David—who are part of Jesus' family tree. We decorate the Jesse Tree with symbols of these Old and New Testament figures. The Jesse Tree is like our family tree. Each person on the Jesse Tree is part of the long story of God's loving plan of Salvation that is fulfilled in Jesus.

Remembering the faith stories of the people on the Jesse Tree helps us remember God's great love for us—and for all people.

The Tree of Jesse,
from "Heures a l'Usage
de Rome"
(16th century)

The Story of Salvation

Make your own Jesse Tree. You can use a small evergreen tree.
Make a symbol for each of these figures. Add others of your own.
Put the symbols on your Jesse Tree.

When **Adam and Eve** refused to obey, God promised a Savior would come some day.

Noah is a man to note; while others laughed, he built a boat.

Abraham and **Sarah** obeyed God's call. Their faith is an example for one and for all.

When **Isaac** was born, Sarah was old. Her laughter rang out, so we are told.

Isaac's son **Jacob** was rich and able; soon twelve healthy sons sat at his table.

Joseph saved his family from starvation. In Egypt they grew into a very strong nation.

Moses, leader and man of God, led Israel through the Red Sea dry-shod.

David, the Lord's shepherd and king, could rule, protect, play, and sing.

Isaiah was one who spoke for his Lord. The faithful listened to every word.

John the Baptist's announcement was clear: "Prepare the way! The Lord draws near!"

On **Mary**, God's blessings were abundantly poured. Yes was her response to the angel of the Lord.

Joseph cared for Mary as he promised he would, Joseph the mild, the patient, the good.

Angels came and shepherds adored, **Jesus** is born, our Savior and Lord!

MY FAITH CHOICE

The season of Advent is a time to prepare for the coming of Jesus. To prepare for Jesus' coming, I will

_____

_____.

Pray, "The Lord, our God, is in our midst. Amen"
Based on ZEPHANIAH 3:17

FAITH FOCUS
Why was Mary able always to say yes to God?

THE WORD OF THE LORD
These are the readings for the Solemnity of the Immaculate Conception of the Blessed Virgin Mary. Choose one and read it. Talk about the reading with your family.

First Reading:
Genesis 3:9–15, 20

Second Reading:
Ephesians 1:3–6, 11–12

Gospel:
Luke 1:26–38

Immaculate Conception

On December 8, 1854, Blessed Pope Pius IX declared the Church's belief in the Immaculate Conception an official dogma of the Church. A dogma is a teaching of the faith that is revealed by God and must be believed by all Catholics. The date the teaching was formally announced was also made the day of the liturgical feast of the Solemnity of the Immaculate Conception of the Blessed Virgin Mary. A solemnity is the highest ranking celebration in the liturgical calendar.

In the United States of America, the Solemnity of the Immaculate Conception of the Blessed Virgin Mary is a holy day of obligation. This means that Catholics in the United States of America have the responsibility to go to Mass on December 8th as they do on Sundays.

God chose Mary to have a unique role in the divine plan of Salvation. He chose Mary to be the mother of the Savior of the world, the Mother of the Son of God, who would become one of us in all things but sin.

Because of this unique role, Mary received the unique grace of being conceived without Original Sin and the graces to remain free from all sin her whole life on Earth. Mary glorified God by her whole life on Earth from her conception to her Assumption. She continues to glorify God in Heaven with all of the angels and Saints.

Patroness of the United States

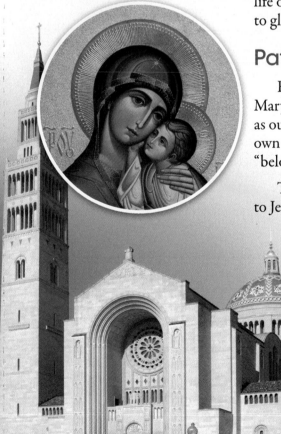

From her earliest days, the Church has expressed her faith in Mary to be the Mother of the Church. Jesus asked us to honor Mary as our Mother. He asked Mary to care for us as a mother cares for her own children. Read the words that Jesus spoke to Mary and to the "beloved disciple," Saint John the Apostle, in John 19:26–27.

The Catholic Church in the United States of America responded to Jesus' words. The bishops of the United States chose Mary, as the Immaculate Conception, to be the patron Saint of the United States. A basilica, or church, in Washington, D.C., was named the National Shrine of the Immaculate Conception. This shrine honors both God and Mary. Our devotion to Mary gives glory to God, our Father. It reminds us to honor him and thank him. With Mary we praise God,

"My soul proclaims the greatness of the Lord; my spirit rejoices in God, my savior."

LUKE 1:46–47

The Miraculous Medal

In 1830, Sister Catherine Labouré, a nun in Paris, had a vision of Mary as the Immaculate Conception. Mary gave Sister Catherine a mission—to have a special medal made for Catholics to wear. Our Blessed Mother described the medal she wanted. The front was to have an image of Mary on it, along with this prayer: "O Mary, conceived without sin, pray for us who have recourse to thee." Mary promised special graces to all those who wore the medal. With the approval of the bishop, the medals were made, and a new devotion to Mary was established. So many people who wore the medal received blessings, good health, peace, and other graces that people began to call it the Miraculous Medal. It is still worn today. It honors the Immaculate Conception and her special place in God's plan of Salvation.

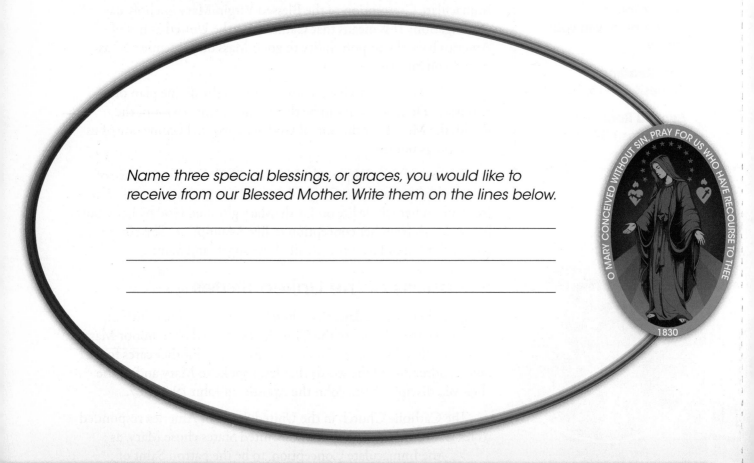

Name three special blessings, or graces, you would like to receive from our Blessed Mother. Write them on the lines below.

_____

_____

_____

MY FAITH CHOICE

This week, I will honor Mary. I will sing her praises by the way I live. I will

_____

_____.

_____.

Pray with Mary, your Mother and praise God saying, "My soul magnifies the Lord! Amen."

Our Lady of Guadalupe

FAITH FOCUS

Why do so many people visit the shrine of Our Lady of Guadalupe?

THE WORD OF THE LORD

These are the readings for the Feast of Our Lady of Guadalupe. Choose one of the readings and find it in a Bible. Read and discuss the reading with your family.

First Reading
Zechariah 2:14–17 or Revelation 11:19a; 12:1–6a, 10ab

Gospel
Luke 1:39–47 or Luke 1:26–38

On a cold morning in December, 1531, a peasant named Juan Diego was walking to Mass near the town of Tepeyac, Mexico. Suddenly, he heard music and saw a cloud surrounded by light. In the cloud was a beautiful lady dressed as an Aztec Indian princess. She spoke to Juan in his native language.

The Virgin Mary of Guadalupe asked Juan Diego to tell the bishop of Mexico that she wished a shrine to be built on that very spot to make her love known for all people. Because Juan did not speak Spanish, and the bishop did not understand the Aztec language, Nahuati, the bishop asked for a sign that the message was from the Virgin Mary.

Three days later, the Blessed Mother again appeared to Juan. She told Juan to gather roses and take them to the bishop. Because it was winter and roses were not growing, this certainly would be a sign the bishop would believe.

When Juan came to the bishop, he opened his cloak and the flowers fell out. To the astonishment of all, they saw an image of Mary dressed as an Aztec princess. The bishop built the shrine. Today that shrine is known as the Basilica of Our Lady of Guadalupe.

On the feast day of December 12, it is a custom in Mexico for young girls to dress up as Indian girls and young boys to dress up as Juan Diego. Many people carry roses.

Many of our Popes have honored Our Lady of Guadalupe. Saint John Paul II visited her shrine four times. Pope Benedict XVI called the Marian shrine the heart of Mexico and of all America. He entrusted all of the world's families to Our Lady of Guadalupe.

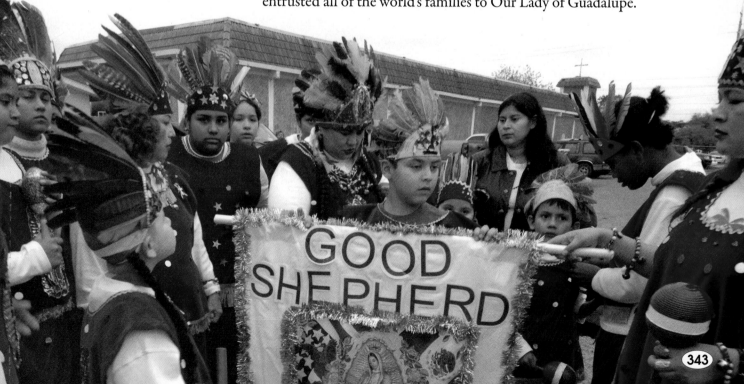

GOOD SHEPHERD

Blessed Are They

Our Lady of Guadalupe's message is that Jesus brings Salvation to all people, especially the weakest and most vulnerable members of our world. This is the message of the Beatitudes.

Read Matthew 5:3–10 in your Bible. Choose one of the Beatitudes and draw a picture of how you might live this Beatitude in your daily life.

_____

_____

MY FAITH CHOICE

This week, I will honor Our Lady of Guadalupe by working for peace and justice for all people. I will

_____

_____ .

Pray with Mary, "My soul procalims the greatness of the Lord; my spirit rejoices in God my savior! Amen." LUKE 1:46–47

Christmas

FAITH FOCUS
What do we learn from the Gospel story of the angel's announcement to the shepherds of the birth of Jesus?

THE WORD OF THE LORD
These are the Gospel readings for Mass on the Nativity of the Lord (Christmas). Choose one reading. Read and discuss it with your family.

Gospel
John 1:1–18 or
John 1:1–5, 9–14

Sometimes the people in our lives surprise us. They do something we do not expect. When that happens, we learn a new thing about them. What happened on the night Jesus was born tells us something new about him.

Luke's account of the Gospel includes the announcement of the birth of Jesus to the shepherds. They were the first to receive the Good News of Jesus' birth. As the shepherds watched their sheep, an angel appeared to them and said:

> "[T]oday in the city of David a savior has been born for you who is Messiah and Lord." LUKE 2:11

The shepherds hurried to Bethlehem. There they found Jesus and Mary and Joseph as the angel said they would.

Throughout the history of Israel, the writers of Sacred Scripture used the image of shepherds to speak about God. For the Israelites, God was a shepherd who watched over them, his sheep. They often prayed:

> "The Lord is my shepherd; there is nothing I lack." PSALM 23:1

However, at the time of Jesus' birth, many people thought that shepherds were of little worth. Their hard, dangerous work kept them in the fields day and night. This meant that they were unable to observe religious practices. Because of this, religious leaders thought shepherds were unfaithful, unimportant people. But it was to shepherds, Luke tells us, that God announced the birth of the Savior. Jesus is the Messiah and Lord of all.

The Lord Is Our Shepherd

For each letter of the word shepherd, write a word or phrase that tells us about who Jesus is. Then imagine that you are a newspaper reporter who has been asked to find out more about some amazing events that took place in a stable outside Bethlehem. Use your words and phrases to write a paragraph telling others about Jesus.

S _____

H _____

E _____

P _____

H _____

E _____

R _____

D _____

_____

_____

_____

MY FAITH CHOICE

This season of Christmas is a time of joy. I will rejoice in the birth of Jesus. I will

_____

_____

_____

Pray, "For today in the city of David a savior has been born for you who is Messiah and Lord. Amen."
LUKE 2:11

Mary, the Holy Mother of God

FAITH FOCUS
How does the Church honor Mary during the Christmas season?

THE WORD OF THE LORD
These are the readings for the Solemnity of Mary, the Holy Mother of God. Read and discuss them with your family.

First Reading
Numbers 6:22–27

Second Reading
Galatians 4:4–7

Gospel
Luke 2:16–21

Each year on Mother's Day we honor our mother. We thank her for taking us to the soccer game. We thank her for cooking our meals and for working to clothe us. We thank her for her love each day of the year. What are some other special times when you honor your mother?

The Church honors Mary, the Mother of God, many times during the year. During the Christmas season, we think about Mary in a special way.

While the celebration of the birth of Jesus is at the heart of our Christmas season, we also celebrate the Feast of the Holy Family between Christmas and January 1. At our celebration of Mass on that day, we pray that through Mary's prayers and the prayers of her husband, Joseph, that our families may live in peace and love.

The Church also sets aside the first day of the new year, January 1, as the Solemnity of Mary, the Holy Mother of God. On this holy day and holiday, we gather to celebrate Mass. We ask God to bless our new year. We ask that Mary's prayer and her motherly love bring us joy forever.

By remembering Mary as the Mother of God and our mother too, we begin the year with blessings. Mary reminds us of what the whole Church desires to do. We all want to say yes to God as she did. We all want to do God's will all our lives, just as Mary did.

Mary, Pray for Us

A litany is a prayer in which a series of petitions are followed by the same response. The litany to the Blessed Virgin Mary on this page is based on one that was composed in the Middle Ages.

Pray this litany with your class to honor Mary, the Mother of God.

Group 1:	Lord, have mercy.	**All:**	**Lord, have mercy.**
Group 2:	Christ, have mercy.	**All:**	**Christ, have mercy.**
Group 1:	Lord, have mercy.	**All:**	**Lord, have mercy.**
Group 1:	Holy Mother of God	**All:**	**pray for us.**
	Mother of the Church		**pray for us.**
	Most honored of virgins		**pray for us.**
	Mother most pure		**pray for us.**
	Mother of our Savior		**pray for us.**
Group 2:	Seat of Wisdom	**All:**	**pray for us.**
	Mystical Rose		**pray for us.**
	Morning Star		**pray for us.**
Group 1:	Refuge of sinners,	**All:**	**pray for us.**
	Comfort of the afflicted,		**pray for us.**
	Help of Christians,		**pray for us.**
Group 2:	Queen of Angels	**All:**	**pray for us.**
	Queen of all Saints		**pray for us.**
	Queen of Peace		**pray for us.**
Group 1:	Pray for us, O holy Mother of God.		
Group 2:	That we may become worthy of the promises of Christ.		

BASED ON THE LITANY OF LORETO

MY FAITH CHOICE

This week, I will honor Mary. I will follow her example of saying yes to the Lord's call. I will

_____

_____

Pray, "May it be done to me according to your word. Amen."
LUKE 1:38

Epiphany of the Lord

FAITH FOCUS
Whom did Jesus come to save?

THE WORD OF THE LORD
This is the Gospel reading for the Solemnity of the Epiphany of the Lord. Find it in the Bible and read and discuss it with your family.

Years A, B, and C
Matthew 2:1–12

The word *epiphany* means to make visible, manifest, or known. The Church celebrates the Solemnity of the Epiphany of the Lord during the season of Christmas. On Epiphany, we remember and celebrate that Jesus was revealed to be the Savior of the world. The Magi were wise men who came from the East searching for the newborn King of the Jews. They had seen a star rising in the sky and recognized it to be a sign that a great ruler had been born.

We do not know how far the Magi had to travel or where they actually lived. We do not know what obstacles they had to overcome. But we what we know from Scripture is that the wise men believed that the light of the star that went before them was leading them to a very special newly born ruler. When the star stopped over the place where Jesus was, the Gospel tells us that the Magi

"were overjoyed at seeing the star, and on entering the house they saw the child with Mary his mother." MATTHEW 2:11

The tradition of the Church names the wise men Caspar, Melchior and Balthasar. Tradition also identifies them to be kings from different lands and of different races. Though they were kings, when they found the Holy Family,

"they prostrated themselves and did him homage. Then they opened their treasures and offered him gifts of gold, frankincense, and myrrh." MATTHEW 2:11

The Epiphany story reveals that Jesus is the Savior of the whole world, of all people, in all lands, and of all times. The Magi remind us of the joy of our meeting Jesus both in events of our daily life and especially in the Eucharist and the other Sacraments. The Magi teach us the importance of spending time in adoration of Jesus. They help us remember and trust that we are guided by the light of our faith in Jesus. We will always have that light to find our way to God here on Earth, and it will lead us to Heaven when our earthly journey is ended.

Kings and Gifts

In the word search below, find the names of the three kings, the three gifts they offered to Jesus, and key words about the solemnity. The words may be found in any direction. Some words may be written backwards. Gifts don't always have to be wrapped in packages. What gifts do you think Jesus would want you to bring to him today? Discuss your thoughts with your class.

```
F  Z  D  F  N  E  O  F  B  H  P  I
G  I  V  R  R  G  M  G  R  C  Z  Y
S  R  U  A  R  O  H  R  O  G  W  N
F  O  S  N  A  O  Y  I  S  A  C  A
R  I  C  K  L  M  I  V  I  A  T  H
A  V  E  I  T  A  A  H  Y  W  N  P
P  A  W  N  Q  V  T  X  C  L  Y  I
S  S  X  C  I  G  A  M  M  L  D  P
A  U  J  E  S  U  S  P  Z  A  E  E
C  M  P  N  U  J  Z  E  Y  J  S  M
A  R  A  S  A  H  T  L  A  B  N  N
A  E  F  E  G  O  L  D  C  J  F  E
```

This week, I will adore Jesus in the Sacrament of Eucharist. I will

_____

_____

_____

Pray, "Most Holy Trinity, Father, Son, and Holy Spirit—I adore you with my whole heart. Amen."

FAITH FOCUS
How does the celebration of Ash Wednesday help us live as members of the Church?

THE WORD OF THE LORD
This is the First Reading for Ash Wednesday. Read and discuss it with your family.

First Reading
2 Corinthians 5:20–6:2

Ash Wednesday

On Ash Wednesday, some people may wonder why there are people with ashes on their foreheads in the shape of a cross. But Catholics from all over the world can tell you that each of those people with the smudge on his or her forehead is a disciple of Jesus Christ. They are all members of the Body of Christ, the Church.

Ash Wednesday marks the beginning of Lent and reminds us of our Baptism and our need to live as disciples of Jesus. It reminds us that we need to become more like Christ. This is what we call *conversions* to becoming more like Christ.

On Ash Wednesday, when the sign of the cross is traced in ashes on our foreheads, we remember that we are children of God. Like our first parents, Adam and Eve, we were created out of dust. Like them, we also sin. Beginning on Ash Wednesday and during the season of Lent, we will focus our attention on ways we can live our lives more in line with God's will. We will remember that Jesus began his ministry by spending forty days in the desert, fasting and praying. We remember that Jesus rejected the temptations of the Devil and that he was strengthened by the Holy Spirit and by God the Father.

From her earliest days, the Church has used ashes as a public sign that a person has sinned and needs to turn away from sin and back to God. When our foreheads are marked with ashes in the form of a cross, it symbolizes that we acknowledge that we have sinned. We promise that we will cooperate with God's grace. We will work on changing our attitudes and actions. On Ash Wednesday, we pray for a change of heart. We join with the whole Church and proclaim:

"Rend your hearts, not your garments, and return to the Lord, your God. For gracious and merciful is he, slow to anger, rich in kindness, and relenting in punishment."

JOEL 2:13

Faithful to the Gospel

When the priest traces a cross on our foreheads, he may say, "Repent, and believe in the Gospel" (*ROMAN MISSAL*).

On the journal page below, write a Lenten pledge on how you can be faithful to the Gospel during Lent.

Repent, and believe in the Gospel

_____

_____

_____

_____

_____

_____

_____

_____

_____

_____

_____

_____

MY FAITH CHOICE

This week, I will try to live out my Lenten pledge. I will

_____

_____

_____

Pray, "Come, Holy Spirit, help me to resist temptation. Teach me to become more like Jesus. Amen."

Lent

FAITH FOCUS
What are we called
to do during Lent?

**THE WORD OF
THE LORD**
Choose this year's
Gospel reading for the
First Sunday of Lent.
Read and discuss it
with your family.

Year A
Matthew 4:1–11

Year B
Mark 1:12–15

Year C
Luke 4:1–13

WHAT YOU SEE
In our churches,
we see signs that
Lent is a season of
discipline. The color
of Lent is purple, the
color of penitence.
No flowers or brightly
colored decorations
greet us. We sing no
joyous Alleluia.

For many of us, the winter landscape seems bare. Leaves fall from trees, flowers die, and grass turns brown. But we trust that after winter, spring will come and bring new life. Each year during Lent, we renew the new life of Christ we received in Baptism.

Lent begins on Ash Wednesday. On Ash Wednesday, the Church gathers to begin its Lenten journey. As ashes are placed on our foreheads, we hear the words:

"Repent, and believe in the Gospel."

ROMAN MISSAL

During Lent, the Church calls us to enter more fully into Jesus' Death and Resurrection. We make sacrifices to do this. We may decide to share more of our time and talents with others. We may give up something that we enjoy. We want habits of goodness to live in us. We support one another in our decisions during Lent. Together we look forward to celebrating the joy of Easter.

Take Up Your Cross

Choose two small twigs or pieces of wood and tie them with twine to form a simple cross. Place your cross on the prayer table as you gather for prayer. Then pray the prayer together.

Leader: During Lent we walk with Jesus. We hope to share in his Resurrection at Easter.

Reader: *(Proclaim Mark 10:35–45.)*

Leader: Jesus looked ahead at the Cross he would bear. Are you willing to take up your cross this Lent?

All: **We are.**

Leader: Let us pause and decide on one thing we know we need to do to be more like Jesus. *(Pause.)* As I call your name, please come forward. *(Name)*, will you strive to take up your Lenten cross and follow Jesus?

Student: I will.

(Choose a wooden cross from the prayer table.)

Leader: May the Cross of Christ remind us to open our minds and hearts to God.

All: **Amen!**

Leader: May we all walk with Jesus and enter into the joy of Easter.

All: **Amen!**

Leader: May we pray for one another. May we support one another as we take up our cross as a sign of our love of Jesus, who carried his Cross because of his love for us.

All: **Amen!**

MY FAITH CHOICE

This season of Lent, I will turn away from sin. I will

_____

_____.

 Pray, "I have sinned against you. Have mercy on me, O Lord. Amen."

FAITH FOCUS
Why do we celebrate Palm Sunday of the Passion of the Lord?

THE WORD OF THE LORD
Choose this year's Gospel reading for Palm Sunday of the Passion of the Lord. Read and discuss it with your family.

Year A
Matthew 26:14–27: 66 or Matthew 27:11–54

Year B
Mark 14:1–15:47 or Mark 15:1–39

Year C
Luke 22:14–23:56 or Luke 23:1–49

Palm Sunday of the Passion of the Lord

When a well-known person comes to your school or town, you welcome them with a marching band and banners and balloons. When Jesus entered the city of Jerusalem, the people gave him a special welcome.

On that day, the people of Jerusalem welcomed Jesus the Messiah. He did not ride on a mighty horse or in a gilded chariot as a great soldier or a conquering hero. Jesus entered Jerusalem riding a donkey. But as he entered, the people cheered him as they would a great king:

> "Hosanna to the Son of David;
> blessed is he who comes in the name of the Lord;
> hosanna in the highest."   MATTHEW 21:9

The people proclaimed "Hosanna," a greeting of joy, praise, or adoration. The people spread cloaks on the road to make the path smooth and less dusty for Jesus. They waved branches taken from palm trees. This welcome of Jesus, as the Messiah riding on a donkey, reminds us that Jesus is the King of everyone, even the lowly. Jesus is a king filled with compassion and care.

The celebration of Palm Sunday of the Passion of the Lord begins Holy Week. We begin our celebration with a procession. Everyone walks into church carrying palm branches. This recalls the day Jesus rode into Jerusalem.

HOSANNA!   Laura James

Hosanna! A Meditation

- *Sit quietly.*

- *Close your eyes and breathe slowly.*

- *Remember the story of Jesus' entry into Jerusalem.*

- *Compare the meaning of this story to your own life and share your thoughts with Jesus. Take the time to praise him for the gifts he has brought to your life.*

- *After a few quiet moments, write down any key words or phrases that will help you remember this prayer experience.*

_____

_____

_____

_____

_____

_____

- *To close your meditation, pray aloud with your class the words with which the people welcomed Jesus to Jerusalem:*

> Hosanna to the Son of David;
>> blessed is he who comes in the name of the Lord;
>> hosanna in the highest." MATTHEW 21:9

MY FAITH CHOICE

This day, Jesus is welcomed as the Messiah. I will honor Jesus on Palm Sunday. I will

_____

_____

_____.

Pray, "Jesus, you are the Messiah and I give you praise. Welcome Jesus into my heart. Amen."

Triduum/Holy Thursday

FAITH FOCUS
What do we remember as the Church celebrates Holy Thursday evening?

THE WORD OF THE LORD
Choose one of the Scripture readings for Holy Thursday evening. Read and discuss it with your family.

Reading I
Exodus 12:1–8, 11–14

Reading II
1 Corinthians 11:23–26

Gospel
John 13:1–15

Do you remember eating a special meal with your family or your friends? What made it special to you? Did you eat special food? Did someone say something that made you feel good about yourself? The Church remembers a special meal that Jesus ate with his disciples.

On the evening of Holy Thursday, we remember the last time before his Death and Resurrection that Jesus gathered the disciples and shared a meal with them. This meal celebrated the Passover. On this special day, the Jewish people celebrate their passage from slavery in Egypt to freedom. They remember the Covenant with God.

All his life, Jesus celebrated this greatest of Jewish feasts with his family and friends. Now he shared the foods of the Passover for the last time. But at this Last Supper, Jesus did something special. Jesus changed the bread and wine he shared with his disciples into his own Body and Blood. He took the bread and broke it and said,

"This is my body, which will be given for you; do this in memory of me."
LUKE 22:19

After the meal, he passed the cup of wine for them to drink. He said,

"This cup is the new covenant in my blood, which will be shed for you."
LUKE 22:20

Later that night, one of the disciples betrayed Jesus, and he was arrested.

Traditional food for a Jewish Seder.

The Lord's Supper

Tonight, at the celebration of the Eucharist, the Church continues to do what Jesus asked his disciples to do. On Holy Thursday evening, we especially remember his last Passover with his disciples. We call our evening celebration the Mass of the Lord's Supper.

Create an announcement inviting your family to join in celebrating the Evening Mass of the Lord's Supper. Point out to them the importance of sharing the celebration. Display your announcement in your home.

_____

_____

_____

_____

_____

MY FAITH CHOICE

On Holy Thursday, I will honor Jesus' command to remember the special meal he shared with the disciples. I will

_____

_____

_____.

 Pray, "Help me remember the depth of your love for me. Amen."

Triduum/Good Friday

FAITH FOCUS
How does the Church remember the Death of Jesus?

THE WORD OF THE LORD
Choose one of the Scripture readings for Good Friday of the Passion of the Lord. Read and discuss it with your family.

Reading I
Isaiah 52:13–53:12

Reading II
Hebrews 4:14–16; 5:7–9

Gospel
John 18:1–19:42

At some time in your life, someone you love will die. This may have already happened to you. You know that when this happens, everyone in your house is sad. People tell stories about the one who has died. The Church does this too, as it remembers the Death of Jesus.

On Good Friday, our churches have no decorations. The tabernacle is empty; its door is open. There is no altar cloth covering the altar. The Church gathers to reflect on the Passion and Death of Jesus.

Our liturgy on Good Friday is called the Celebration of the Passion of the Lord. Good Friday is the only day of the year on which Mass is not celebrated. The Celebration of the Passion of the Lord is made up of three parts:

- The first part is the Liturgy of the Word. The Gospel reading is a proclamation of the Passion and Death of Jesus according to John. After the Gospel proclamation, the Church invites us to pray for the needs of the world (Solemn Intercessions).

- The second part of the Celebration of the Passion of the Lord is the Adoration of the Holy Cross. In this part of the liturgy, we show reverence and respect for the Cross because Jesus died for us on a cross. We might do this by walking in procession, bowing before the Cross, and kissing it.

- The third part of the Celebration of the Passion of the Lord is Holy Communion. The Church invites us to receive the Body of Christ, which was consecrated at Mass on Holy Thursday and reserved in a tabernacle as a place of repose, meaning pause or rest.

The Celebration of the Passion of the Lord ends as it began. The altar cloth is removed from the altar and the tabernacle is empty. In deep silence, we leave to begin the long sabbath rest until the celebration of the Easter Vigil.

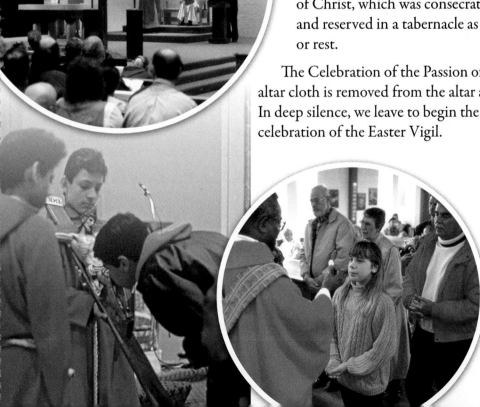

Jesus Asks, You Respond

Each day, you do many things to show your love for God and others as Jesus did. You make sacrifices. You give your time. You share your gifts. You take up your cross and follow Jesus as he asked you to do.

On one of the beams of this cross, describe something you did for someone during Lent. On the other cross beam, describe how it helped the person.

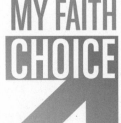

MY FAITH CHOICE

On Good Friday, Jesus died on the Cross for my Salvation. I will honor his sacrifice of love. I will

_____

_____

_____.

 Pray, "Jesus, you saved all people from sin and death. All glory and praise to you! Amen."

Triduum/Easter Sunday

FAITH FOCUS
Why is the Easter season a time of rejoicing?

THE WORD OF THE LORD
Choose the Gospel readings for Easter Sunday this year. Read and discuss them with your family.

Year A
John 20:1–9
or Matthew 28:1–10
or Luke 24:13–35

Year B
John 20:1–9
or Mark 16:1–7
or Luke 24:13–35

Year C
John 20:1–9
or Luke 24:1–12
or Luke 24:13–35

On our best days, we feel great joy just to be alive. We can do many wonderful things. Easter Sunday of the Resurrection of the Lord is a wonderful day in the Church—a day when we rejoice because God has raised Jesus to new life.

Saint Augustine reminds us that we are Easter people and Alleluia is our song. *Alleluia* is a Hebrew word that means "Praise the Lord." At the Easter Vigil, the presider solemnly intones the Alleluia, which we have not heard all during Lent. The Church sings "Alleluia!" repeatedly during the Easter season. We continuously thank and praise God for the new life of Easter. We praise God because we have passed from death to life through our Baptism.

Throughout Lent, we focused on turning away from sin to become followers of Jesus. During the Easter season, we rejoice in our new life in Christ. We sing "Alleluia!" and proclaim,

*"This is the day the Lord has made;
let us rejoice in it and be glad."* Psalm 118:24

Celebrating Easter

Write a cinquain to celebrate Easter. Share the Good News of the Resurrection with a classmate and with your family.

_____
Title

_____ _____
Write two words
that describe the title.

_____ _____ _____
Write three action words
that describe the title.

_____ _____ _____ _____
Write four words that tell
a feeling about the title.

_____
Write another word for the title.

MY FAITH CHOICE

Easter marks new life in Christ. I will live my new life in Christ. I will

_____

_____

_____.

Pray, "Alleluia, Alleluia! Jesus Christ has risen! Alleluia, Alleluia! Amen."

FAITH FOCUS
How is the Ascension part of the Paschal Mystery?

THE WORD OF THE LORD
These are the Gospel readings for the Ascension of the Lord. Choose the reading for this year and read it. Talk about the reading with your family.

Year A
Matthew 28:16–20

Year B
Mark 16:15–20

Year C
Luke 24:46–53

Ascension of the Lord

For forty days after the Resurrection, the Risen Jesus appeared to his disciples and continued to teach them about the Kingdom of God. At their last meeting, he gathered them together on a hill near Jerusalem and reminded them that they must wait for the promise of the Father, the Holy Spirit.

Jesus knew he would soon be home in Heaven with his Father. The power of the Holy Spirit would fill the disciples with wisdom and courage to continue the mission of Jesus on Earth.

Jesus said to the disciples, "All power in heaven and on earth has been given to me. Go, therefore, and make disciples of all nations, . . ." (Matthew 28:18). Then, as the disciples looked on, Jesus was taken up into Heaven.

The Ascension of the Lord completes Jesus' Paschal Mystery, the passing over of Jesus from life on Earth through his Passion, Death, Resurrection, and Ascension into a new and glorified life with God, the Father in Heaven.

The Church celebrates the Solemnity of the Ascension of the Lord forty days after Easter (or on the Seventh Sunday of Easter). This holy day of obligation expresses our belief that Jesus has returned to his Father in glory and majesty to reign with him in Heaven. We believe Jesus has prepared a place for those who love him. We believe that, like the disciples, we must continue the mission of Jesus on Earth.

Continuing Christ's Mission

Before he ascended to the Father, Jesus gave his disciples a mission. He asked them to continue his work in the world. Your school and parish respond to Jesus' command in many different ways.

Look through your school newsletter, a parish bulletin, or on the school or parish Web sites. Find four ministries that serve your community. Write the names of these ministries on the church steps. Choose a ministry you would like to participate in and explain your reasons on the steps below.

MY FAITH CHOICE

This week, I will celebrate the Ascension of the Lord by continuing Jesus' mission on Earth. I will

_____

_____

_____

 Pray, "Jesus, your Passion, Death, Resurrection, and Ascension are the source of our glory and hope. Alleluia! Amen."

Pentecost Sunday

FAITH FOCUS
How did the gift of the Holy Spirit on Pentecost strengthen the disciples?

THE WORD OF THE LORD
Choose this year's Gospel reading for Pentecost Sunday. Read and discuss it with your family.

Year A
John 20:19–23

Year B
John 20:19–23 or John 15:26–27; 16:12–15

Year C
John 20:19–23 or John 14:15–16, 23b–26

Can you think of a day when you felt as if you could do anything you set your mind to? What happened to make you feel that way? Did someone say something to you or give you a gift?

The disciples knew a day like that. They received a great gift that made them strong in their belief in the Risen Lord. That day was Pentecost.

Pentecost is a Jewish harvest festival. On this holy day, the Jewish people offer the first fruits of the new harvest to God. At the time of Jesus, Jews traveled to Jerusalem for this great feast.

The disciples gathered in Jerusalem too. As they prayed together in an upper room, they heard the noise of a great wind. Flames gently settled over their heads.

They were filled with the Holy Spirit. They felt new and strong. They went out and boldly proclaimed the Risen Lord. As they spoke, all the people in the crowd heard the message in their own languages. People who could not understand one another before suddenly did! People who were separated drew together. The Holy Spirit came upon the disciples as Jesus promised. The Church was born. The work of the Church, filled with the Holy Spirit, had begun.

My Proclamation

What do you wish all people could know about Jesus? Write here the Good News you would like to proclaim. Then pray to the Holy Spirit to help you tell others.

_____

_____

_____

Come, Holy Spirit,

fill the hearts of your faithful.

And kindle in them

the fire of your love.

Send forth your Spirit and

they shall be created.

And you will renew the
face of the earth.

MY FAITH CHOICE

On Pentecost, I will honor the gift of the Holy Spirit. I will

_____

_____

_____.

 Pray, "Holy Spirit, fill us with the grace and strength to tell others the Good News about Jesus. Amen."

Catholic Prayers and Practices

Sign of the Cross

In the name of the Father,
and of the Son,
and of the Holy Spirit. Amen.

Signum Crucis

In nómine Patris,
et Fílii,
et Spíritus Sancti. Amen.

Our Father

Our Father, who art in heaven,
hallowed be thy name;
thy kingdom come,
thy will be done
on earth as it is in heaven.
Give us this day our daily bread,
and forgive us our trespasses,
as we forgive those who trespass
    against us;
and lead us not into temptation
    but deliver us from evil.
Amen.

Pater Noster

Pater noster, qui es in cælis:
sanctificétur nomen tuum;
advéniat regnum tuum;
fiat volúntas tua, sicut in cælo,
    et in terra.
Panem nostrum cotidiánum da
nobis hódie;
et dimítte nobis débita nostra,
sicut et nos dimíttimus debitóribus
    nostris;
et ne nos indúcas in tentatiónem;
sed líbera nos a malo. Amen.

Glory Be (Doxology)

Glory be to the Father
and to the Son
and to the Holy Spirit,
as it was in the beginning
is now, and ever shall be
world without end. Amen.

Gloria Patri

Glória Patri
et Fílio
et Spirítui Sancto.
Sicut erat in princípio,
et nunc et semper
et in sæcula sæculórum. Amen.

The Hail Mary

Hail, Mary, full of grace,
the Lord is with thee.
Blessed art thou among women
and blessed is the fruit
    of thy womb, Jesus.
Holy Mary, Mother of God,
pray for us sinners,
now and at the hour of our death.
Amen.

Ave, Maria

Ave, María, grátia plena,
Dóminus tecum.
Benedícta tu in muliéribus,
et benedíctus fructus ventris tui, Iesus.
Sancta María, Mater Dei,
ora pro nobis peccatóribus,
nunc et in hora mortis nostræ.
Amen.

Apostles' Creed

(from the *Roman Missal*)

I believe in God,
the Father almighty,
Creator of heaven and earth,
and in Jesus Christ, his only Son,
    our Lord,

*(At the words that follow, up to and
including the Virgin Mary, all bow.)*

who was conceived by the Holy Spirit,
born of the Virgin Mary,
suffered under Pontius Pilate,
was crucified, died and was buried;
he descended into hell;
on the third day he rose again
    from the dead;
he ascended into heaven,
and is seated at the right hand of God
    the Father almighty;
from there he will come to judge
    the living and the dead.

I believe in the Holy Spirit,
the holy catholic Church,
the communion of saints,
the forgiveness of sins,
the resurrection of the body,
and life everlasting. Amen.

Nicene Creed

(from the *Roman Missal*)

I believe in one God,
the Father almighty,
maker of heaven and earth,
of all things visible and invisible.

I believe in one Lord Jesus Christ,
the Only Begotten Son of God,
born of the Father before all ages.

God from God, Light from Light,
true God from true God,
begotten, not made, consubstantial
    with the Father;
through him all things were made.
For us men and for our salvation
he came down from heaven,

*(At the words that follow up to and
including and became man, all bow.)*

and by the Holy Spirit was incarnate
    of the Virgin Mary,
and became man.

For our sake he was crucified under
    Pontius Pilate,
he suffered death and was buried,
and rose again on the third day
in accordance with the Scriptures.
He ascended into heaven
and is seated at the right hand
    of the Father.

He will come again in glory
to judge the living and the dead
and his kingdom will have no end.

I believe in the Holy Spirit, the Lord,
    the giver of life,
who proceeds from the Father and
    the Son,
who with the Father and the Son is
    adored and glorified,
who has spoken through the prophets.

I believe in one, holy, catholic and
    apostolic Church.
I confess one Baptism for the forgiveness
    of sins
and I look forward to the resurrection
    of the dead
and the live for the world to come. Amen.

Morning Prayer

Dear God,
as I begin this day,
keep me in your love and care.
Help me to live as your child today.
Bless me, my family, and my friends
    in all we do.
Keep us all close to you. Amen.

Evening Prayer

Dear God,
I thank you for today.
Keep me safe throughout the night.
Thank you for all the good I did today.
I am sorry for what I have chosen
    to do wrong.
Bless my family and friends.
Amen.

Grace Before Meals

Bless us, O Lord,
    and these thy gifts,
which we are about to receive
    from thy bounty,
        through Christ our Lord.
Amen.

Grace After Meals

We give thee thanks,
    for all thy benefits, almighty God,
who lives and reigns forever.
Amen.

A Vocation Prayer

God, I know you will call me
for special work in my life.
Help me follow Jesus each day
and be ready to answer your call. Amen.

Prayer to the Holy Spirit

Come, Holy Spirit, fill the hearts
    of your faithful.
And kindle in them the
    fire of your love.
Send forth your Spirit and
    they shall be created.
And you will renew the
    face of the earth. Amen.

Act of Contrition

My God,
I am sorry for my sins
    with all my heart.
In choosing to do wrong
and failing to do good,
I have sinned against you,
whom I should love above all things.
I firmly intend, with your help,
to do penance,
to sin no more,
and to avoid whatever leads me to sin.
Our Savior Jesus Christ
suffered and died for us.
In his name, my God, have mercy. Amen.

The Beatitudes

"Blessed are the poor in spirit,
  for theirs is the kingdom of heaven.
Blessed are they who mourn,
  for they will be comforted.
Blessed are the meek,
  for they will inherit the land.
Blessed are they who hunger
    and thirst for righteousness,
  for they will be satisfied.
Blessed are the merciful,
  for they will be shown mercy.
Blessed are the clean of heart,
  for they will see God.
Blessed are the peacemakers,
  for they will be called children of God.
Blessed are they who are persecuted for
    the sake of righteousness,
  for theirs is the kingdom of heaven."

MATTHEW 5:3–10

The Angelus

Leader: The Angel of the Lord declared unto Mary,

Response: And she conceived of the Holy Spirit.

All: Hail, Mary . . .

Leader: Behold the handmaid of the Lord,

Response: Be it done unto me according to your Word.

All: Hail, Mary . . .

Leader: And the Word was made flesh,

Response: And dwelt among us.

All: Hail, Mary . . .

Leader: Pray for us, O Holy Mother of God,

Response: That we may be made worthy of the promises of Christ.

Leader: Let us pray.

All: Pour forth, we beseech you, O Lord, your grace into our hearts; that we, to whom the Incarnation of Christ your Son was made known by the message of an Angel, may by his Passion and Cross be brought to the glory of his Resurrection. Through the same Christ our Lord. Amen.

The Ten Commandments

1. I am the LORD your God: you shall not have strange gods before me.
2. You shall not take the name of the LORD your God in vain.
3. Remember to keep holy the LORD's Day.
4. Honor your father and your mother.
5. You shall not kill.
6. You shall not commit adultery.
7. You shall not steal.
8. You shall not lie.
9. You shall not covet your neighbor's wife.
10. You shall not covet your neighbor's goods.

BASED ON EXODUS 20:2–3, 7–17

Precepts of the Church

1. Participate in Mass on Sundays and holy days of obligation, and rest from unnecessary work.
2. Confess sins at least once a year.
3. Receive Holy Communion at least during the Easter season.
4. Observe the prescribed days of fasting and abstinence.
5. Provide for the material needs of the Church, according to one's abilities.

The Great Commandment

"You shall love the Lord, your God, with all your heart, with all your soul, and with all your mind. . . . You shall love your neighbor as yourself."

MATTHEW 22:37, 39

The Law of Love

"This is my commandment: love one another as I love you."

JOHN 15:12

Corporal Works of Mercy

Feed people who are hungry.
Give drink to people who are thirsty.
Clothe people who need clothes.
Visit people who are in prison.
Shelter people who are homeless.
Visit people who are sick.
Bury people who have died.

Spiritual Works of Mercy

Help people who sin.
Teach people who are ignorant.
Give advice to people who have doubts.
Comfort people who suffer.
Be patient with other people.
Forgive people who hurt you.
Pray for people who are alive and for those who have died.

The Rosary

Catholics pray the Rosary to honor Mary and remember the important events in the lives of Jesus and Mary. There are twenty mysteries of the Rosary. Follow the steps from 1 to 5.

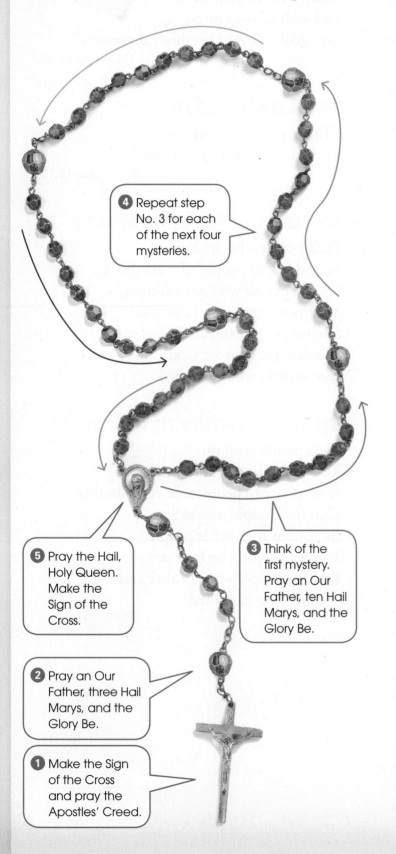

4 Repeat step No. 3 for each of the next four mysteries.

5 Pray the Hail, Holy Queen. Make the Sign of the Cross.

3 Think of the first mystery. Pray an Our Father, ten Hail Marys, and the Glory Be.

2 Pray an Our Father, three Hail Marys, and the Glory Be.

1 Make the Sign of the Cross and pray the Apostles' Creed.

Joyful Mysteries

1 The Annunciation
2 The Visitation
3 The Nativity
4 The Presentation in the Temple
5 The Finding of the Child Jesus After Three Days in the Temple

Luminous Mysteries

1 The Baptism at the Jordan
2 The Miracle at Cana
3 The Proclamation of the Kingdom and the Call to Conversion
4 The Transfiguration
5 The Institution of the Eucharist

Sorrowful Mysteries

1 The Agony in the Garden
2 The Scourging at the Pillar
3 The Crowning with Thorns
4 The Carrying of the Cross
5 The Crucifixion and Death

Glorious Mysteries

1 The Resurrection
2 The Ascension
3 The Descent of the Holy Spirit at Pentecost
4 The Assumption of Mary
5 The Crowning of the Blessed Virgin as Queen of Heaven and Earth

Hail, Holy Queen

Hail, holy Queen, Mother of mercy:
Hail, our life, our sweetness,
   and our hope.
To you do we cry, poor banished
   children of Eve.
To you do we send up our sighs,
mourning and weeping
   in this valley of tears.
Turn then, most gracious advocate,
your eyes of mercy toward us;
and after this our exile
show unto us the blessed fruit
   of your womb, Jesus.
O clement, O loving, O sweet
   Virgin Mary.

Stations of the Cross

1. Jesus is condemned to death.

2. Jesus accepts his cross.

3. Jesus falls the first time.

4. Jesus meets his mother.

5. Simon helps Jesus carry the cross.

6. Veronica wipes the face of Jesus.

7. Jesus falls the second time.

8. Jesus meets the women of Jerusalem.

9. Jesus falls the third time.

10. Jesus is stripped of his clothes.

11. Jesus is nailed to the cross.

12. Jesus dies on the cross.

13. Jesus is taken down from the cross.

14. Jesus is buried in the tomb.

(Some parishes conclude the Stations by reflecting on the Resurrection of Jesus.)

The Seven Sacraments

Jesus gave the Church the Seven Sacraments. The Sacraments are the main liturgical signs of the Church. They make the Paschal Mystery of Jesus, who is always the main celebrant of each Sacrament, present to us. They make us sharers in the saving work of Christ and in the life of the Holy Trinity.

Sacraments of Christian Initiation

Baptism

Through Baptism, we are joined to Christ and become members of the Body of Christ, the Church. We are reborn as adopted children of God and receive the gift of the Holy Spirit. Original Sin and all personal sins are forgiven.

Confirmation

Confirmation completes Baptism. In this Sacrament, the gift of the Holy Spirit strengthens us to live our Baptism.

Eucharist

Sharing in the Eucharist joins us most fully to Christ and to the Church. We share in the one sacrifice of Christ. The bread and wine become the Body and Blood of Christ through the power of the Holy Spirit and the words of the priest. We receive the Body and Blood of Christ.

Sacraments of Healing

Penance and Reconciliation

Through the ministry of the priest, we receive forgiveness of sins committed after our Baptism. We need to confess all mortal sins.

Anointing of the Sick

Anointing of the Sick strengthens our faith and trust in God when we are seriously ill, dying, or weak because of old age.

Sacraments at the Service of Communion

Holy Orders

Through Holy Orders, a baptized man is consecrated to serve the whole Church as a bishop, priest, or deacon in the name of Christ. Bishops, who are the successors of the Apostles, receive this Sacrament most fully. They are consecrated to teach the Gospel, to lead the Church in the worship of God, and to guide the Church to live holy lives. Bishops are helped in their work by priests, their coworkers, and by deacons.

Matrimony

Matrimony unites a baptized man and a baptized woman in a lifelong bond of faithful love to honor each other always and to accept the gift of children from God. In this Sacrament, the married couple is consecrated to be a sign of God's love for the Church.

We Celebrate the Mass

The Introductory Rites

We remember that we are the community of the Church.
We prepare to listen to the Word of God and to celebrate the Eucharist.

The Entrance

We stand as the priest, deacon, and other ministers enter the assembly. We sing a gathering song. The priest and deacon kiss the altar. The priest then goes to the chair where he presides over the celebration.

Sign of the Cross and Greeting

The priest leads us in praying the Sign of the Cross. The priest greets us, and we say,

"And with your spirit."

The Penitential Act

We admit our wrongdoings.
We bless God for his mercy.

The Gloria

We praise God for all the good that he has done for us.

The Collect

The priest leads us in praying the Collect. We respond, "Amen."

The Liturgy of the Word

God speaks to us today.
We listen and respond to God's Word.

The First Reading

We sit and listen as the reader reads from the Old Testament or from the Acts of the Apostles. The reader concludes, "The word of the Lord." We respond,

"Thanks be to God."

The Responsorial Psalm

The song leader or cantor leads us in singing a psalm.

The Second Reading

The reader reads from the New Testament, but not from the four Gospels. The reader concludes, "The word of the Lord." We respond,

"Thanks be to God."

The Acclamation

We stand to honor Christ, present with us in the Gospel. The song leader leads us in singing **"Alleluia, Alleluia, Alleluia"** or another chant during Lent.

The Gospel

The deacon or priest proclaims,
"A reading from the holy Gospel according to (name of Gospel writer)." We respond,
> **"Glory to you, O Lord."**

He proclaims the Gospel. At the end he says, "The Gospel of the Lord."
We respond,
> **"Praise to you, Lord Jesus Christ."**

The Homily

We sit. The priest or deacon preaches the Homily. He helps the people gathered to understand the Word of God spoken to us in the readings.

The Profession of Faith

We stand and profess our faith.
We pray the Nicene Creed together.

The Prayer of the Faithful

The priest leads us in praying for our Church and her leaders, for our country and its leaders, for ourselves and others, for those who are sick and those who have died. We can respond to each prayer in several ways. One way that we respond is
> **"Lord, hear our prayer."**

The Liturgy of the Eucharist

We join with Jesus and the Holy Spirit
to give thanks and praise to God the Father.

The Preparation of the Altar and Gifts

We sit as the altar is prepared and the collection is taken up. We share our blessings with the community of the Church and especially with those in need. The song leader may lead us in singing a song. The gifts of bread and wine are brought to the altar.

The priest lifts up the bread and blesses God for all our gifts. He prays, "Blessed are you, Lord God of all creation. . . ."
We respond,
"Blessed be God for ever."

The priest lifts up the chalice of wine and prays, "Blessed are you, Lord God of all creation. . . . "
We respond,
"Blessed be God for ever."

The priest invites us,
"Pray, brethren (brothers and sisters), that my sacrifice and yours may be acceptable to God, the almighty Father."
We stand and respond,
"May the Lord accept the sacrifice at your hands for the praise and glory of his name, for our good and the good of all his holy Church."

The Prayer over the Offerings

The priest leads us in praying the Prayer over the Offerings.
We respond, **"Amen."**

Preface

The priest invites us to join in praying the Church's great prayer of praise and thanksgiving to God the Father.

Priest: "The Lord be with you."

Assembly: **"And with your spirit."**

Priest: "Lift up your hearts."

Assembly: **"We lift them up to the Lord."**

Priest: "Let us give thanks to the Lord our God."

Assembly: **"It is right and just."**

After the priest sings or prays aloud the Preface, we join in acclaiming,

**"Holy, Holy, Holy Lord God of hosts.
Heaven and earth are full of your glory.
Hosanna in the highest.
Blessed is he who comes in the name of the Lord.
Hosanna in the highest."**

The Eucharistic Prayer

The priest leads the assembly in praying the Eucharistic Prayer. We call on the Holy Spirit to make our gifts of bread and wine holy so that they become the Body and Blood of Jesus. We recall what happened at the Last Supper. The bread and wine become the Body and Blood of the Lord. Jesus is truly and really present under the appearances of bread and wine.

The priest sings or says aloud, "The mystery of faith." We respond using this or another acclamation used by the Church,

"We proclaim your Death, O Lord, and profess your Resurrection until you come again."

The priest then prays for the Church. He prays for the living and the dead.

Doxology

The priest concludes the praying of the Eucharistic Prayer. He sings or prays aloud,

"Through him, and with him,
and in him,
O God, almighty Father,
in the unity of the Holy Spirit,
all glory and honor is yours,
for ever and ever."

We respond by singing **"Amen."**

The Communion Rite

The Lord's Prayer
We pray the Lord's Prayer together.

The Sign of Peace
The priest invites us to share a sign of peace, saying, "The peace of the Lord be with you always." We respond,
   "And with your spirit."
We share a sign of peace.

The Fraction, or the Breaking of the Bread
The priest breaks the host, the consecrated bread. We sing or pray aloud,
   **"Lamb of God, you take away
   the sins of the world,
      have mercy on us.
   Lamb of God, you take away
   the sins of the world,
      have mercy on us.
   Lamb of God, you take away
   the sins of the world,
      grant us peace."**

Communion
The priest raises the host and says aloud,
   "Behold the Lamb of God,
     behold him who takes away the sins
      of the world.
     Blessed are those called to the supper
      of the Lamb."

We join with him and say,
   **"Lord, I am not worthy
   that you should enter under my roof,
   but only say the word
   and my soul shall be healed."**
The priest receives Communion. Next, the deacon, the extraordinary ministers of Holy Communion, and the members of the assembly receive Communion.

The priest, deacon, or extraordinary minister of Holy Communion holds up the host. We bow, and the priest, deacon, or extraordinary minister of Holy Communion says, "The Body of Christ." We respond, **"Amen."** We then receive the consecrated host in our hands or on our tongues.

If we are to receive the Blood of Christ, the priest, deacon, or extraordinary minister of Holy Communion holds up the cup containing the consecrated wine. We bow, and the priest, deacon, or extraordinary minister of Holy Communion says, "The Blood of Christ." We respond, **"Amen."** We take the cup in our hands and drink from it.

The Prayer After Communion
We stand as the priest invites us to pray, saying, "Let us pray." He prays the Prayer After Communion. We respond, **"Amen."**

The Concluding Rites

We are sent forth to do good works, praising and blessing the Lord.

Greeting

We stand. The priest greets us as we prepare to leave. He says, "The Lord be with you." We respond,

"And with your spirit."

Final Blessing

The priest or deacon may invite us,
"Bow for the blessing."
The priest blesses us, saying,
"May almighty God bless you,
the Father, and the Son,
and the Holy Spirit."
We respond, **"Amen."**

Dismissal of the People

The priest or deacon sends us forth, using these or similar words,
"Go in peace, glorifying the Lord
by your life."
We respond,
"Thanks be to God."
We sing a hymn. The priest and the deacon kiss the altar. The priest, deacon, and other ministers bow to the altar and leave in procession.

The Sacrament of Penance and Reconciliation

Individual Rite

Greeting

"When the penitent comes to confess [his or her] sins, the priest welcomes [him or her] warmly and greets [the penitent] with kindness" (*Rite of Penance* 41).

Scripture Reading

"[T]hrough the word of God Christians receive light to recognize their sins and are called to conversion and to confidence in God's mercy" (*Rite of Penance* 17).

Confession of Sins and Acceptance of Penance

"[The priest] urges [the penitent] to be sorry for [his or her] faults, reminding [him or her] that through the sacrament of penance the Christian dies and rises with Christ and is renewed in the paschal mystery" (*Rite of Penance* 44).

Act of Contrition

"The most important act of the penitent is contrition . . . The genuineness of penance depends on . . . heartfelt contrition" (*Rite of Penance* 6a).

Absolution

"The form of absolution indicates that the reconciliation of the penitent comes from the mercy of the Father" (*Rite of Penance* 19).

Closing Prayer

"After receiving pardon for sin, the penitent praises the mercy of God and gives him thanks . . . Then the priest bids the penitent to go in peace" (*Rite of Penance* 20).

Communal Rite

Greeting

"When the faithful have assembled, they may sing a psalm, antiphon, or other appropriate song while the priest is entering the church" (*Rite of Penance* 48).

Scripture Reading

"[T]hrough his word God calls his people to repentance and leads them to a true conversion of heart" (*Rite of Penance* 24).

Homily

"The homily . . . should lead the penitents to examine their consciences and renew their lives" (*Rite of Penance* 52).

Examination of Conscience

"A period of time may be spent in making an examination of conscience and in arousing true sorrow for sins" (*Rite of Penance* 53).

Litany of Contrition, and the Lord's Prayer

"The deacon or another minister invites all to kneel or bow, and to join in saying a general formula for confession" (*Rite of Penance* 54).

Individual Confession and Absolution

"[T]he penitents go to the priests designated for individual confession, and confess their sins. Each one receives and accepts a fitting act of satisfaction and is absolved" (*Rite of Penance* 55).

Closing Prayer

"After the song of praise or the litany [for God's mercy], the priest concludes the common prayer" (*Rite of Penance* 57).

Key Teachings of the Catholic Church

The Mystery of God

Divine Revelation

Who am I?

Every human person has been created by God to live in friendship with him both here on Earth and forever in Heaven.

How do we know this about ourselves?

We know this because every human person desires to know and love God and wants God to know and love them. We also know this because God told us this about ourselves and about him.

How did God tell us?

First of all, God tells us this through creation, which is the work of God; creation reflects the goodness and beauty of the Creator and tells us about God the Creator. Secondly, God came to us and told us, or revealed this about himself. He revealed this most fully by sending his Son, Jesus Christ, who became one of us and lived among us.

What is faith?

Faith is a supernatural gift from God that enables us to know God and all that he has revealed, and to respond to God with our whole heart and mind.

What is a mystery of faith?

The word *mystery* describes the fact that we can never fully comprehend or fully grasp God and his loving plan for us. We only know who God is and his plan for us through Divine Revelation.

What is Divine Revelation?

Divine Revelation is God's free gift of making himself known to us and giving himself to us by gradually communicating in deeds and words his own mystery and his divine plan for humanity. God reveals himself so that we can live in communion with him and with one another forever.

What is Sacred Tradition?

The word *tradition* comes from a Latin word meaning "to pass on." Sacred Tradition is the passing on of Divine Revelation by the Church through the power and guidance of the Holy Spirit.

What is the deposit of faith?

The deposit of faith is the source of faith that we draw from in order to pass on God's Revelation. The deposit of faith is the unity of Sacred Scripture and Sacred Tradition handed on by the Church from the time of the Apostles.

What is the Magisterium?

The Magisterium is the teaching authority of the Church. Guided by the Holy Spirit, the Church has the responsibility to authentically and accurately interpret the Word of God, both in Sacred Scripture and in Sacred Tradition. She does this to assure that her understanding of Revelation is faithful to the teaching of the Apostles.

What is a dogma of faith?

A dogma of faith is a truth taught by the Church as revealed by God and to which we are called to give our assent of mind and heart in faith.

Sacred Scripture

What is Sacred Scripture?

The words *sacred scripture* come from two Latin words meaning "holy writings." Sacred Scripture is the collection of all the writings God has inspired authors to write in his name.

What is the Bible?

The word *bible* comes from a Greek word meaning "book." The Bible is the collection of the forty-six books of the Old Testament and the twenty-seven books of the New Testament named by the Church as all the writings God has inspired human authors to write in his name.

What is the canon of Scripture?

The word *canon* comes from a Greek word meaning "measuring rod," or standard by which something is judged. The canon of Scripture is the list of books that the Church has identified and teaches to be the inspired Word of God.

What is biblical inspiration?

Biblical inspiration is a term that describes the Holy Spirit guiding the human authors of Sacred Scripture so that they faithfully and accurately communicate the Word of God.

What is the Old Testament?

The Old Testament is the first main part of the Bible. It is the forty-six books inspired by the Holy Spirit, written before the birth of Jesus and centered on the Covenant between God and his people, Israel, and the promise of the Messiah or Savior. The Old Testament is divided into the Torah/Pentateuch, historical books, wisdom literature, and writings of the prophets.

What is the Torah?

The Torah is the Law of God that was revealed to Moses. The written Torah is found in the first five books of the Old Testament, which are called the "Torah" or the "Pentateuch."

What is the Pentateuch?

The word *pentateuch* means "five containers." The Pentateuch is the first five books of the Old Testament, namely Genesis, Exodus, Leviticus, Numbers, and Deuteronomy.

What is the Covenant?

The Covenant is the solemn agreement of fidelity that God and his people freely entered into. It was renewed and fulfilled in Jesus Christ, the new and everlasting Covenant.

What are the historical books of the Old Testament?

The historical books tell about the fidelity and infidelity of God's people to the Covenant and about the consequences of those choices.

What are the Wisdom writings of the Old Testament?

The Wisdom writings are the seven books of the Old Testament that contain inspired practical advice and common-sense guidelines for living the Covenant and the Law of God. They are the Book of Job, Book of Psalms, Book of Ecclesiastes, Book of Wisdom, Book of Proverbs, Book of Sirach (Ecclesiasticus), and Song of Songs.

What are the writings of the prophets in the Old Testament?

The word *prophet* comes from a Greek word meaning "those who speak before others." The biblical prophets were those people God had chosen to speak in his name. The writings of the prophets are the eighteen books of the Old Testament that contain the message of the prophets to God's people. They remind God's people of his unending fidelity to them and of their responsibility to be faithful to the Covenant.

What is the New Testament?

The New Testament is the second main part of the Bible. It is the twenty-seven books inspired by the Holy Spirit and written in apostolic times that center on Jesus Christ and his saving work among us. The main parts are the four Gospels, the Acts of the Apostles, the twenty-one letters, and the Book of Revelation.

What are the Gospels?

The word *gospel* comes from a Greek word meaning "good news." The Gospel is the Good News of God's loving plan of Salvation, revealed in the Passion, Death, Resurrection, and Ascension of Jesus Christ.

The Gospels are the four written accounts of Matthew, Mark, Luke, and John. The four Gospels occupy a central place in Sacred Scripture because Jesus Christ is their center.

What is an epistle?

The word *epistle* comes from a Greek word meaning "message or letter." An epistle is a formal type of letter. Some of the letters in the New Testament are epistles.

What are the Pauline epistles and letters?

The Pauline epistles and letters are the fourteen letters in the New Testament traditionally attributed to Saint Paul the Apostle.

What are the Catholic Letters?

The Catholic Letters are the seven New Testament letters that bear the names of the Apostles John, Peter, Jude, and James, and which were written to the universal Church rather than to a particular Church community.

The Holy Trinity

Who is the Mystery of the Holy Trinity?

The Holy Trinity is the mystery of One God in Three Divine Persons—God the Father, God the Son, God the Holy Spirit. It is the central mystery of the Christian faith.

Who is God the Father?

God the Father is the First Person of the Holy Trinity.

Who is God the Son?

God the Son is Jesus Christ, the Second Person of the Holy Trinity. He is the Only-Begotten Son of the Father who took on flesh and became one of us without giving up his divinity.

Who is God the Holy Spirit?

God the Holy Spirit is the Third Person of the Holy Trinity, who proceeds from the Father and Son. He is the Advocate, or Paraclete, sent to us by the Father in the name of his Son, Jesus.

What are the divine missions, or the works of God?

The entire work of God is common to all Three Divine Persons of the Trinity. The work of creation is the work of the Trinity, though attributed to the Father. Likewise, the work of Salvation is attributed to the Son and the work of sanctification is attributed to the Holy Spirit.

Divine Work of Creation

What is the divine work of creation?

Creation is the work of God bringing into existence everything and everyone, seen and unseen, out of love and without any help.

Who are angels?

Angels are spiritual creatures who do not have bodies as humans do. Angels give glory to God without ceasing and sometimes serve God by bringing his message to people.

Who is the human person?

The human person is uniquely created in the image and likeness of God. Human dignity is fulfilled in the vocation to a life of happiness with God.

What is the soul?

The soul is the spiritual part of a person. It is immortal; it never dies. The soul is the innermost being, that which bears the imprint of the image of God.

What is the intellect?

The intellect is an essential power of the soul. It is the power to know God, yourself, and others; it is the power to understand the order of things established by God.

What is free will?

Free will is an essential quality of the soul. It is the God-given ability and power to recognize him as part of our lives and to choose to center our lives around him as well as to choose between good and evil. By free will, the human person is capable of directing oneself toward the truth, beauty and good, namely, life in communion with God.

What is Original Sin?

Original Sin is the sin of Adam and Eve by which they chose evil over obedience to God. By doing so, they lost the state of original holiness for themselves and for all their descendants. As a result of Original Sin, death, sin, and suffering entered into the world.

Jesus Christ, the Incarnate Son of God

What is the Annunciation?

The Annunciation is the announcement by the angel Gabriel to Mary that God chose her to be the Mother of Jesus, the Son of God, by the power of the Holy Spirit.

What is the Incarnation?

The word *incarnation* comes from a Latin word meaning "take on flesh." The term *Incarnation* is the event in which the Son of God, the Second Person of the Holy Trinity, truly became human while remaining truly God. Jesus Christ is true God and true man.

What does it mean that Jesus is Lord?

The word *lord* means "master, ruler, a person of authority" and is used in the Old Testament to name God. The designation, or title, "Jesus, the Lord" expresses that Jesus is truly God.

What is the Paschal Mystery?

The Paschal Mystery is the saving events of the Passion, Death, Resurrection, and glorious Ascension of Jesus Christ; the passing over of Jesus from death into a new and glorious life; the name we give to God's plan of Salvation in Jesus Christ.

What is Salvation?

The word *salvation* comes from a Latin word meaning "to save." Salvation is the saving, or deliverance, of humanity from the power of sin and death through Jesus Christ. All Salvation comes from Christ through the Church.

What is the Resurrection?

The Resurrection is the historical event of Jesus being raised from the dead to a new glorified life after his Death on the Cross and burial in the tomb.

What is the Ascension?

The Ascension is the return of the Risen Christ in glory to his Father, to the world of the divine.

What is the Second Coming of Christ?

The Second Coming of Christ is the return of Christ in glory at the end of time to judge the living and the dead; the fulfillment of God's plan in Christ.

What does it mean that Jesus is the Messiah?

The word *messiah* is a Hebrew term meaning "anointed one." Jesus Christ is the Anointed One, the Messiah, who God promised to send to save people. Jesus is the Savior of the world.

The Mystery of the Church

What is the Church?

The word *church* means "convocation," those called together. The Church is the Sacrament of Salvation— the sign and instrument of our reconciliation and communion with God the Holy Trinity and with one another. The Church is the Body of Christ, the people God the Father has called together in Jesus Christ through the power of the Holy Spirit.

What is the central work of the Church?

The central work of the Church is to proclaim the Gospel of Jesus Christ and to invite all people to come to know and believe in him and to live in communion with him. We call this work of the Church "evangelization," a word that comes from a Greek word that means "to tell good news."

What is the Body of Christ?

The Body of Christ is an image for the Church used by Saint Paul the Apostle that teaches that all the members of the Church are one in Christ, who is the Head of the Church, and that all members have a unique and vital work in the Church.

Who are the People of God?

The People of God are those the Father has chosen and gathered in Christ, the Incarnate Son of God, the Church. All people are invited to belong to the People of God and to live as one family of God.

What is the Temple of the Holy Spirit?

The Temple of the Holy Spirit is a New Testament image used to describe the indwelling of the Holy Spirit in the Church and within the hearts of the faithful.

What is the Communion of Saints?

The Communion of Saints is the communion of holy things and holy people that make up the Church. It is the communion, or unity, of all the faithful, those living on Earth, those being purified after death, and those enjoying life everlasting and eternal happiness with God, the angels, Mary and all the Saints.

What are the Marks of the Church?

The Marks of the Church are the four attributes and essential characteristics of the Church and her mission, namely, one, holy, catholic, and apostolic.

Who are the Apostles?

The word *apostle* comes from a Greek word meaning "to send away." The Apostles were those twelve men chosen and sent by Jesus to preach the Gospel and to make disciples of all people.

Who are the Twelve?

The Twelve is the term that identifies the Apostles chosen by Jesus before his Death and Resurrection. "The names of the twelve apostles are these: first, Simon called Peter, and his brother Andrew; James, the son of Zebedee, and his brother John; Philip and Bartholomew, Thomas and Matthew the tax collector; James the son of Alphaeus, and Thaddaeus; Simon the Cananean, and Judas Iscariot who betrayed him" (Matthew 10:2–4). The Apostle Matthias was chosen after Jesus' Ascension.

What is Pentecost?

Pentecost is the coming of the Holy Spirit upon the Church as promised by Jesus; it marks the beginning of the work of the Church.

Who are the ordained ministers of the Church?

The ordained ministers of the Church are those baptized men who are consecrated in the Sacrament of Holy Orders to serve the whole Church. Bishops, priests, and deacons are the ordained ministers of the Church and make up the clergy.

How do the Pope and other bishops guide the Church in her work?

Christ, the Head of the Church, governs the Church through the Pope and the college of bishops in communion with him. The Pope is the bishop of Rome and the successor of Saint Peter the Apostle. The Pope, the Vicar of Christ, is the visible foundation of the unity of the whole Church. The other bishops are the successors of the other Apostles and are the visible foundation of their own particular Churches. The Holy Spirit guides the Pope and the college of bishops working together with the Pope, to teach the faith and moral doctrine without error. This grace of the Holy Spirit is called *infallibility*.

What is the consecrated life?

The consecrated life is a state of life for those baptized who promise or vow to live the Gospel by means of professing the evangelical counsels of poverty, chastity, and obedience, in a way of life approved by the Church. The consecrated life is also known as the "religious life."

Who are the laity?

The laity (or laypeople) are all the baptized who have not received the Sacrament of Holy Orders nor have promised or vowed to live the consecrated life. They are called to be witnesses to Christ at the very heart of the human community.

The Blessed Virgin Mary

What is Mary's role in God's loving plan for humanity?

Mary has a unique role in God's plan of Salvation for humanity. For this reason she is full of grace from the first moment of her conception, or existence. God chose Mary to be the Mother of the Incarnate Son of God, Jesus Christ, who is truly God and truly man. Mary is the Mother of God, the Mother of Christ, and the Mother of the Church. She is the greatest Saint of the Church.

What is the Immaculate Conception?

The Immaculate Conception is the unique grace given to Mary that totally preserved her from the stain of all sin from the very first moment of her existence, or conception, in her mother's womb and throughout her life.

What is the perpetual virginity of Mary?

The *perpetual virginity of Mary* is a term that describes the fact that Mary remained always a virgin. She was a virgin before the conception of Jesus, during his birth, and remained a virgin after the birth of Jesus her whole life.

What is the Assumption of Mary?

At the end of her life on Earth, the Blessed Virgin Mary was taken body and soul into Heaven, where she shares in the glory of her Son's Resurrection. Mary, the Mother of the Church, hears our prayers and intercedes for us with her Son. She is an image of the heavenly glory in which we all hope to share when Christ, her Son, comes again in glory.

Life Everlasting

What is eternal life?
Eternal life is life after death. At death, the soul is separated from the body. In the Apostles' Creed, we profess faith in "life everlasting." In the Nicene Creed we profess faith in "the life of the world to come."

What is the particular judgment?
The particular judgment is the assignment given to our souls at the moment of our death to our final destiny based on what we have done in our lives.

What is the Last Judgment?
The Last Judgment is the judgment at which every human being will appear in their own bodies and give an account of their deeds. At the Last Judgment, Christ will show his identity with the least of his brothers and sisters.

What is the beatific vision?
The beatific vision is seeing God "face-to-face" in heavenly glory.

What is Heaven?
Heaven is eternal life and communion with the Holy Trinity. It is the supreme state of happiness—living with God forever for which he created us.

What is the Kingdom of God?
The Kingdom of God, or Kingdom of Heaven, is the image used by Jesus to describe all people and creation living in communion with God. The Kingdom of God will be fully realized when Christ comes again in glory at the end of time.

What is Purgatory?
Purgatory is the opportunity after death to purify and strengthen our love for God before we enter Heaven.

What is Hell?
Hell is the immediate and everlasting separation from God.

Celebration of the Christian Life and Mystery

Liturgy and Worship

What is worship?
Worship is the adoration and honor given to God. The Church worships God publicly in the celebration of the liturgy. The liturgy is the Church's worship of God. It is the work of the whole Church. In the liturgy the mystery of Salvation in Christ is made present by the power of the Holy Spirit.

What is the liturgical year?
The liturgical year is the cycle of seasons and great feasts that make up the Church's year of worship. The main seasons and times of the Church year are Advent, Christmas, Lent, Easter Triduum, Easter, and Ordinary Time.

The Sacraments

What are the Sacraments?
The Sacraments are seven signs of God's love and the main liturgical actions of the Church through which the faithful are made sharers in the Paschal Mystery of Christ. They are effective signs of grace, instituted by Christ and entrusted to the Church, by which divine life is shared with us.

What are the Sacraments of Christian Initiation?
The Sacraments of Christian Initiation are Baptism, Confirmation, and the Eucharist. These three Sacraments are the foundation of every Christian life. "Baptism is the beginning of new life in Christ; Confirmation is its strengthening; the Eucharist nourishes the faithful for their transformation into Christ."

What is the Sacrament of Baptism?
Through Baptism, we are reborn into new life in Christ. We are joined to Jesus Christ, become members of the Church, and are reborn as God's children. We receive the gift of the Holy Spirit; and Original Sin and our personal sins are forgiven. Baptism marks us indelibly and forever as belonging to Christ. Because of this, Baptism can be received only once.

What is the Sacrament of Confirmation?
Confirmation strengthens the graces of Baptism and celebrates the special gift of the Holy Spirit. Confirmation also imprints a spiritual or indelible character on the soul and can be received only once.

What is the Sacrament of the Eucharist?
The Eucharist is the source and summit of the Christian life. In the Eucharist the faithful join with Christ to give thanksgiving, honor, and glory to the Father through the power of the Holy Spirit. Through the power of the Holy Spirit and the words of the priest, the bread and wine become the Body and Blood of Christ.

What is the obligation of the faithful to participate in the Eucharist?
The faithful have the obligation to participate in the Eucharist on Sundays and holy days of obligation. Sunday is the Lord's Day. Sunday, the day of the Lord's Resurrection, is "the foundation and kernel of the whole liturgical year." Regular participation in the Eucharist and receiving Holy Communion is vital to the Christian life. In the Eucharist we receive the Body and Blood of Christ.

What is the Blessed Sacrament?

The Blessed Sacrament is another name for the Eucharist. The term is often used to identify the Eucharist reserved in the tabernacle.

What is the Mass?

The Mass is the main celebration of the Church at which we gather to listen to the Word of God (Liturgy of the Word) and through which we are made sharers in the saving Death and Resurrection of Christ and give praise and glory to the Father (Liturgy of the Eucharist).

What are the Sacraments of Healing?

Penance and Reconciliation and Anointing of the Sick are the two Sacraments of Healing. Through the power of the Holy Spirit, Christ's work of Salvation and healing of the members of the Church is continued.

What is the Sacrament of Penance and Reconciliation?

The Sacrament of Penance and Reconciliation is one of the two Sacraments of Healing through which we receive God's forgiveness for the sins we have committed after Baptism.

What is confession?

Confession is the telling of sins to a priest in the Sacrament of Penance and Reconciliation. This act of the penitent is an essential element of the Sacrament. Penance and Confession are other names for the Sacrament.

What is the seal of confession?

The seal of confession is the obligation of the priest to never reveal to anyone what a penitent has confessed to him.

What is contrition?

Contrition is sorrow for sins that includes the desire and commitment to make reparation for the harm caused by one's sin and the purpose of amendment not to sin again. Contrition is an essential element of the Sacrament of Penance and Reconciliation.

What is a penance?

A penance is a prayer or act of kindness that shows we are truly sorry for our sins and that helps us repair the damage caused by our sin. Accepting and doing our penance is an essential part of the Sacrament of Penance and Reconciliation.

What is absolution?

Absolution is the forgiveness of sins by God through the ministry of the priest.

What is the Sacrament of the Anointing of the Sick?

The Sacrament of the Anointing of the Sick is one of the two Sacraments of Healing. The grace of this

Sacrament strengthens our faith and trust in God when we are seriously ill, weakened by old age, or dying. The faithful may receive this Sacrament each time they are seriously ill or when an illness gets worse.

What is Viaticum?

Viaticum is the Eucharist, or Holy Communion, received as food and strength for a dying person's journey from life on Earth through death to eternal life.

What are the Sacraments at the Service of Communion?

Holy Orders and Matrimony are the two Sacraments at the Service of Communion. These Sacraments bestow a particular work, or mission, on certain members of the Church to serve in building up the People of God.

What is the Sacrament of Holy Orders?

The Sacrament of Holy Orders is one of the two Sacraments at the Service of Communion. It is the Sacrament in which baptized men are consecrated as bishops, priests, or deacons to serve the whole Church in the name and person of Christ.

Who is a bishop?

A bishop is a priest who receives the fullness of the Sacrament of Holy Orders. He is a successor of the Apostles and shepherds a particular Church entrusted to him by means of teaching, leading divine worship, and governing the Church as Jesus did.

Who is a priest?

A priest is a baptized man who has received the Sacrament of Holy Orders. Priests are coworkers with their bishops, who have the ministry of "authentically teaching the faith, celebrating divine worship, above all the Eucharist, and guiding their Churches as true pastors."

Who is a deacon?

A deacon is ordained to assist bishops and priests. He is not ordained to the priesthood but to a ministry of service to the Church.

What is the Sacrament of Matrimony?

The Sacrament of Matrimony is one of the two Sacraments at the Service of Communion. In the Sacrament of Matrimony a baptized man and a baptized woman dedicate their lives to the Church and to one another in a lifelong bond of faithful life-giving love. In this Sacrament they receive the grace to be a living sign of Christ's love for the Church.

What are the sacramentals of the Church?

Sacramentals are sacred signs instituted by the Church. They include blessings, prayers, and certain objects that prepare us to participate in the sacraments. Sacramentals make us aware of and help us respond to God's loving presence in our lives.

Life in the Spirit

The Moral Life

Why was the human person created?

The human person was created to give honor and glory to God and to live a life of beatitude with God here on Earth and forever in Heaven.

What is the Christian moral life?

The baptized have new life in Christ in the Holy Spirit. They respond to the "desire for happiness that God has placed in every human heart" by cooperating with the grace of the Holy Spirit and living the Gospel. "The moral life is a spiritual worship that finds its nourishment in the liturgy and celebration of the Sacraments."

What is the way to happiness revealed by Jesus Christ?

Jesus taught that the Great Commandment of loving God above all else and our neighbor as ourselves is the path to happiness. It is the summary and heart of the Commandments and all of God's Law.

What are the Ten Commandments?

The Ten Commandments are the laws of the Covenant that God revealed to Moses and the Israelites on Mount Sinai. The Ten Commandments are also known as the Decalogue, or "Ten Words." They are the "privileged expression of the natural law," which is written on the hearts of all people.

What are the Beatitudes?

The Beatitudes are the teachings of Jesus that summarize the path to true happiness, the Kingdom of God, which is living in communion and friendship with God, and with Mary and all the Saints. The Beatitudes guide us in living as disciples of Christ by keeping our life focused and centered on God.

What is the New Commandment?

The New Commandment is the commandment of love that Jesus gave his disciples. Jesus said, "I give you a new commandment: love one another. As I have loved you, so you should also love one another" (John 13:34).

What are the Works of Mercy?

The word *mercy* comes from a Hebrew word pointing to God's unconditional love and kindness at work in the world. Human Works of Mercy are acts of loving kindness by which we reach out to people in their corporal and spiritual needs.

What are the precepts of the Church?

Precepts of the Church are specific responsibilities that concern the moral Christian life united with the liturgy and nourished by it.

Holiness of Life and Grace

What is holiness?

Holiness is the state of living in communion with God. It designates both the presence of God, the Holy One, with us and our faithfulness to him. It is the characteristic of a person who is in right relationship with God, with people, and with creation.

What is grace?

Grace is the gift of God sharing his life and love with us. Categories of grace are sanctifying grace, actual grace, charisms, and sacramental graces.

What is sanctifying grace?

The word *sanctifying* comes from a Latin word meaning "to make holy." Sanctifying grace is a gratuitous gift of God, given by the Holy Spirit, as a remedy for sin and the source of holiness.

What is actual grace?

Actual graces are the God-given divine helps empowering us to live as his adopted daughters and sons.

What are charisms?

Charisms are gifts or graces freely given to individual Christians by the Holy Spirit for the benefit of building up the Church.

What are sacramental graces?

Sacramental graces are the graces of each of the Sacraments that help us live out our Christian vocation.

What are the Gifts of the Holy Spirit?

The seven Gifts of the Holy Spirit are graces that strengthen us to live our Baptism, our new life in Christ. They are wisdom, understanding, right judgment (or counsel), courage (or fortitude), knowledge, reverence (or piety), and wonder and awe (or fear of the Lord).

What are the Fruits of the Holy Spirit?

The twelve Fruits of the Holy Spirit are visible signs and effects of the Holy Spirit at work in our life. They are charity (love), joy, peace, patience, kindness, goodness, generosity, gentleness, faithfulness, modesty, self-control, and chastity.

The Virtues

What are virtues?

The virtues are spiritual powers, habits, or behaviors that help us do what is good. The Catholic Church speaks of Theological Virtues, Moral Virtues, and Cardinal Virtues.

What are the Theological Virtues?

The Theological Virtues are the three virtues of faith, hope, and charity (love). These virtues are "gifts from God infused into the souls of the faithful to make them capable of acting as his children and of attaining eternal life" (CCC 1813).

What are the Moral Virtues?

The Moral Virtues are "firm attitudes, stable dispositions, habitual perfections of intellect and will that govern our actions, order our passions, and guide our conduct according to reason and faith. They make possible ease, self-mastery, and joy in leading a morally good life" (CCC 1804).

What are the Cardinal Virtues?

The Cardinal Virtues are the four Moral Virtues of prudence, justice, fortitude, and temperance. They are called the Cardinal Virtues because all of the Moral Virtues are related to and grouped around them.

What is conscience?

The word *conscience* comes from a Latin word meaning "to be conscious of guilt." Conscience is that part of every human person that helps us judge whether a moral act is in accordance or not in accordance with God's Law; our conscience moves us to do good and avoid evil.

Moral Evil and Sin

What is moral evil?

Moral evil is the harm we willingly inflict on one another and on God's good creation.

What is temptation?

Temptation is everything, either within us or outside us, that tries to move us from doing something good that we know we can and should do to instead do or say something we know is contrary to the will of God. Temptation is whatever tries to move us away from living a holy life.

What is sin?

Sin is freely and knowingly doing or saying that which is against the will of God and the Law of God. Sin sets itself against God's love and turns our hearts away from his love. The Church speaks of mortal sin, venial sin, and Capital Sins.

What is mortal sin?

A mortal sin is a serious, deliberate failure in our love and respect for God, our neighbor, creation, and ourselves. It is knowingly and willingly choosing to do something that is gravely contrary to the Law of God. The effect of mortal sin is the loss of sanctifying grace and, if unrepented, brings eternal death.

What are venial sins?

Venial sins are sins that are less serious than a mortal sin. They weaken our relationship with God and for one another and diminish our holiness.

What are Capital Sins?

Capital Sins are sins that are at the root of other sins. The seven Capital Sins are false pride, avarice, envy, anger, gluttony, lust, and sloth.

Christian Prayer

What is prayer?

Prayer is conversation with God. It is talking and listening to him, raising our minds and hearts to God the Father, Son, and Holy Spirit.

What is the prayer of all Christians?

The Lord's Prayer, or Our Father, is the prayer of all Christians. It is the prayer Jesus taught his disciples and gave to the Church. The Lord's Prayer is "a summary of the whole Gospel." Praying the Lord's Prayer "brings us into communion with the Father and his Son, Jesus Christ" and develops "in us the will to become like [Jesus] and to place our trust in the Father as he did" (CCC 2763).

What are the traditional expressions of prayer?

The traditional expressions of prayer are vocal prayer, the prayer of meditation, and the prayer of contemplation.

What is vocal prayer?

Vocal prayer is spoken prayer; prayer using words said aloud.

What is the prayer of meditation?

Meditation is a form of prayer in which we use our minds, hearts, imaginations, emotions, and desires to understand and follow what the Lord is asking us to do.

What is the prayer of contemplation?

Contemplation is a form of prayer that is simply being with God.

What are the traditional forms of prayer?

The traditional forms of prayer are the prayers of adoration and blessing, the prayer of thanksgiving, the prayer of praise, the prayer of petition, and the prayer of intercession.

What are devotions?

Devotions are part of the prayer life of the Church and of the baptized. They are acts of communal or individual prayer that surround and arise out of the celebration of the liturgy.

Glossary

A–B

adoration *page 320*

Adoration is a form of prayer that declares God is the source of all. We acknowledge God is Almighty Creator, in whom we depend upon for everything.

almsgiving *page 308*

Money, food, or material given to the poor as an act of penance or charity is almsgiving.

Anointing of the Sick *page 188*

The Anointing of the Sick is the Sacrament of Healing that strengthens our faith, hope, and love for God when we are seriously ill, weakened by old age, or dying.

Baptism *page 134*

Baptism is the Sacrament of Christian Initiation in which we are joined to Jesus Christ, become members of his Church, and are reborn as God's adopted children. We receive the gift of the Holy Spirit, and Original Sin and personal sins are forgiven.

Beatitudes *page 266*

The Beatitudes are the teachings of Jesus from his Sermon on the Mount that describe the attitudes and actions of people blessed by God; a word meaning "ways of happiness."

biblical inspiration *page 28*

This is the Holy Spirit guiding the human writers of Sacred Scripture so that they would faithfully and accurately communicate what God intended to reveal.

C–D

canon *page 28*

The word in general means "standard" or "official list." Thus, the canon of Scripture is the official list of books included in the Bible.

canonization *page 270*

The process by which the Pope declares that a deceased member of the faithful lived a life of heroic virtue and is to be honored as a Saint is canonization.

charism *page 96*

A charism is a grace of the Holy Spirit given to build up the Church and to help the Church fulfill her work in the world.

charity *page 252*

To love as God loves is what we call charity, or *caritas* in Latin. This is the standard by which all of us are to live by, and as Saint Paul says, charity is the greatest of the three Theological Virtues (read 1 Corinthians 13:13).

chastity *page 210*

When we exercise self-control with God's grace in our relationships, the Holy Spirit forms the virtue of chastity in us. This means that we can appropriately integrate the gift of our human sexuality according to God's calling for us. In other words, we respect each other as persons, and not as objects to be used.

Christ *page 70*

This title of Jesus identifies him as the Messiah, the Anointed One, whom God sent to save all of humanity.

Christian initiation *page 134*

Christian initiation is the liturgical process by which a person becomes a full member of the Church.

Church *page 104*

The Church is the new People of God, the Body of Christ, the Temple of the Holy Spirit, and the Bride of Christ, called together in Jesus Christ by the power of the Holy Spirit.

communion *page 200*

Communion is the unity in Christ of all the members of the Church, the Body of Christ; the word is from two Latin words meaning "sharing with." Full communion refers to full initiation into the Church.

complementarity *page 214*

Complementarity is living with and for each other as equal in dignity and unique in gender, helping each other according to God's plan for both genders.

Confirmation *page 146*

Confirmation is the Sacrament of Christian Initiation that strengthens the grace of Baptism and in which our life in Christ is sealed by the gift of the Holy Spirit.

conjugal love *page 212*

Conjugal love is the unique expression of sexual love between a husband and a wife, who freely give their whole selves to each other.

conscience *page 246*

Conscience is the gift of God that is part of every person that guides us to know and judge what is right and wrong.

consecrate *page 148*

To consecrate is to set aside and dedicate for a holy purpose.

contemplation *page 320*

Contemplation is a form of prayer without using words, in which we focus our minds and hearts on God alone.

counsel *page 90*

Counsel, or right judgment, is one of the seven Gifts of the Holy Spirit. This gift, or grace, helps a person sense the moral truth about how to live. The gift of counsel is the ability to judge correctly the daily activity of our lives according to God's will. The source of this gift is the Holy Spirit, who empowers us to form our consciences properly.

Covenant *page 26*

This is the solemn commitment of fidelity that God and the People of God made with one another, which was renewed in Christ, the new and everlasting Covenant.

covet *page 300*

To covet is to unjustly desire what rightfully belongs to someone else.

creed *page 18*

A creed is a statement of beliefs, a profession of faith, a summary of the principal beliefs of the Church.

diligence *page 120*

Diligence is the persistent ability to combat laziness. Diligence is related to the Cardinal Virtue of fortitude. Saint Peter gives advice to a Christian community, to be diligent, or vigilant and steadfast in faith (read 1 Peter 5:5-11). Full participation at Mass requires diligence.

Divine Revelation *page 26*

Divine Revelation is God making himself and his divine plan of creation and Salvation known over time.

Eucharist *page 160*

The Eucharist is the Sacrament of the Body and Blood of Christ; the Sacrament of Christian Initiation in which we receive the Real Presence of Christ and are most fully joined to Christ and to the Church.

faith *page 16*

Faith is one of the three Theological Virtues. It is the gift of God's invitation to us that enables us to know and believe in him, and the power God gives us to respond freely to his invitation.

faithfulness *page 156*

This Fruit of the Holy Spirit is the steadfast commitment a Christian demonstrates as an act of his or her faith in Jesus Christ as the Son of God, Lord, and Savior. Often faithfulness to God involves a struggle, but Jesus shows us the way to remain faithful to God, especially when it involves sacrifice.

fortitude *page 144*

Fortitude is one of the four Cardinal Virtues. It is the strength of mind and will to do what is good in the face of adversity or difficulty. It enables a person to be a steadfast witness for Christ.

generosity *page 306*

This Fruit of the Holy Spirit comes from doing charitable works. By the grace of the Holy Spirit, the generosity we show to others is a reflection of loving others as God loves us.

gentleness *page 186*

When we exercise the virtue of temperance, the Holy Spirit provides us with this fruit, which is related to self-control. A gentle person is one who pardons injury and is free from harshness, even in the face of injury or illness. A sense of gentleness is a sense of calming peace and care in the way we treat others and ourselves.

Golden Rule *page 256*

This is the rule to live by that is knowable by human reason. It is to do unto others as you would have them do unto you.

Gospels *page 92*

The Gospels are the first four books of the New Testament, which pass on the faith of the Church in Jesus Christ and in the saving events of the Paschal Mystery.

holiness *page 230*

The quality, or condition, of a person who is living in communion and in right relationship with God, with others, and with all of creation; being in the state of grace is holiness.

hope *page 318*

Hope is one of the three Theological Virtues by which we desire and trust that God will fulfill his promises, especially the promise of eternal happiness. Because of the Resurrection, Christianity is a religion of hope.

hospice care *page 186*

Hospice care is a ministry of caring for the terminally ill by offering them gentle end-of-life care that respects the dignity of the human person, according to Church teachings.

humility *page 66*

Humility helps us see and accept the truth about God and ourselves. A humble person acknowledges that God is the source of life and author of all that is good. Humility is often described as "poverty in spirit" when the humble person completely trusts in God.

I-J-K-L

idolatry *page 284*

Idolatry is the substitution of someone or worshiping a creature or thing (money, pleasure, power, etc.) instead of God the Creator.

Incarnation *page 68*

The Incarnation is the belief of the Church that the Son of God became fully human in all ways except sin, while remaining fully divine.

joy *page 264*

One of the Fruits of the Holy Spirit, joy demonstrates that we live according to the Spirit (see Galatians 5:22-23). Joy results from moral living and believing in the hope of eternal life.

justice *page 48*

Justice is one of the four Cardinal Virtues. Justice is the habit of consistently giving what is due to God and to our neighbor. We give God what is due to him when we worship him alone. Our worship of God includes loving our neighbor and respecting the dignity of every human person. Through Christian justice, we participate in preparing the way for the coming of the Kingdom of God.

Kingdom of God *page 106*

The Kingdom of God is the fulfillment of God's plan for all Creation in Christ at the end of time when Christ will come again in glory.

knowledge *page 24*

Part of the gift of faith is the desire to know God better. By accepting God's gift of faith, the Holy Spirit perfects our faith with gifts, such as wisdom, knowledge, and understanding. In other words, part of our response in faith is to know God more fully. The light of reason aids us in our journey to love, serve, and know God.

liturgy *page 122*

Liturgy is the work by the Church of worshiping God. Liturgy includes words, signs, symbols, and actions used to give praise and thanks, and honor and glory to God the Father.

Lord *page 71*

This title of Jesus indicates his divine sovereignty, or power.

M-N-O

Mass *page 160*

Mass is the main sacramental celebration of the Church at which we gather to listen to God's Word and through which we share in the saving Death of Christ, and give praise and glory to God the Father.

Matrimony *page 212*

The Sacrament of the Church that unites a baptized man and a baptized woman in a lifelong bond of faithful love as a sign of Christ's love for the Church is Matrimony.

meditation *page 320*

Meditation is a form of silent prayer in which we listen to God through our thoughts and imagination, using Scripture, art and music.

mercy *page 78*

This fruit of charity is the loving kindness and compassion shown to one who offends us. Even though our sins damage our relationship with God, he still loves us. Throughout his life, Jesus taught how the love of God is one of mercy. Jesus, the Son of God, suffered and died for our sake. Truly the Paschal Mystery reveals the depths of God's mercy for us.

modesty *page 132*

Modesty is one of the Fruits of the Holy Spirit. These are signs that a person is cooperating with the grace of the Holy Spirit. A modest person protects his or her inner self. Modesty encourages a person to respect the dignity of every human person including oneself.

morality *page 242*

Morality refers to the goodness or evil of human acts. The morality of human acts depends on the object, intention, and circumstances of the action.

mortal sin *page 176*

A mortal sin is a serious failure in our love and respect for God, our neighbor, and ourselves. For a sin to be mortal, it must be gravely wrong, we must know it to be gravely wrong, and we must freely choose it.

murder *page 296*

The direct and intentional killing of an innocent person is murder.

natural law *page 254*

It is the foundation of moral life for everyone. It enables us by human reason to know what is good and what is evil.

Ordination *page 202*

Ordination is the Sacrament of Holy Orders in which a baptized man is consecrated to serve the Church as a bishop, priest, or deacon.

original holiness *page 40*

Original holiness is that first state of grace in which Adam and Eve shared in God's divine life. They were therefore in a perfect state of grace before the Fall.

original justice *page 40*

Original justice is that first state of grace before the Fall, when Adam and Eve and all of creation were in harmony.

Original Sin *page 52*

Original Sin is the sin of Adam and Eve by which they lost the state of original holiness, and by which death, sin, and suffering entered into the world.

Paschal Mystery *page 80*

The Paschal Mystery is Jesus' passing over from life on Earth through his Passion, Death, Resurrection, and Ascension to a new and glorified life with the Father.

Passion *page 80*

The Passion is the suffering of Jesus on his way to the Cross and his Death on the Cross.

patience *page 198*

One of the Fruits of the Holy Spirit is patience, which is the result of virtuous living. Being patient does not mean doing nothing. Patience involves the wisdom of knowing how to wait for truth while actively seeking grace.

peace *page 102*

Peace is one of the twelve Fruits of the Holy Spirit. Peace on Earth is a reflection of the peace of Christ. Christ has reconciled humanity with God, and made the Church the sacrament of unity and peace. Disciples of Jesus are called to be peacemakers.

Pentecost *page 92*

Pentecost is the liturgical feast and holy day when the Church celebrates the coming of the Holy Spirit on the disciples and the birth of the Church.

perseverance in faith *page 12*

This gift is the ability to remain steadfast in one's beliefs because of the strength and Gifts of the Holy Spirit working within us. This gift is also helpful when someone is struggling with difficulties and doubts.

piety *page 282*

When we worship God, we exercise the gift of piety. It is one of the seven Gifts of the Holy Spirit, which helps us give devotion to God. The attitudes of reverence and respect accompany piety and pious activity.

prudence *page 240*

This Cardinal Virtue is also referred to as wisdom. Saint Thomas Aquinas defined prudence as "right reason in action." With experience comes wisdom, and prudence is often the guide for growing in wisdom.

reparation *page 308*

The process of righting a wrong or making amends is reparation.

Sacraments *page 122*

Sacraments are the seven sacred signs and causes of grace given to the Church by Christ to continue his saving action among us through the power of the Holy Spirit.

Salvation *page 80*

Salvation is the deliverance of humanity from the power of sin and death by God through Jesus Christ, who died for our sins in accordance with the Scriptures.

sanctify *page 40*

To sanctify is to put one in that state of grace in which sin is removed and we are made holy.

sanctifying grace *page 138*

Sanctifying grace is the grace that heals our human nature wounded by sin, by giving us a share in the divine life of the Holy Trinity.

self-control *page 174*

Self-control is a Fruit of the Holy Spirit that comes from a steadfast commitment to God. A person with self-control demonstrates that God's will comes first in life. Self-control helps us do what is good and just. When others see self-control in us, we become witnesses for Christ by placing the needs of others before our own and following the will of God the Father, in whom we place our trust.

Shema *page 256*

The Shema is a prayerful rule revealed by God in the Covenant that there is only one God, and the Lord is God.

sin *page 52*

Sin is freely choosing to do what we know is against God's will or freely choosing not to do something that we know God wants us to do.

stewardship *page 310*

Stewardship is the action of responsibly caring for what God has given in service to others.

temperance *page 300*

One of the four Cardinal Virtues, temperance includes other virtuous acts and attitudes such as chastity, self-control, and responsible living according to God's plan for life and love. This virtue helps us to moderate our actions so that we do what is good and right.

temptation *page 52*

Temptation is anything that tries to move us to do or say something that we know is wrong, or prevents us from doing something that we know is good and that we ought to do.

Theological Virtues *page 230*

The virtues of faith, hope, and charity; gifts of God that enable us to live a life of holiness, or a life in communion with the Holy Trinity are the Theological Virtues.

understanding *page 228*

This Gift of the Holy Spirit helps us to know ourselves better as we grow in our relationship with God. Saint Augustine said of this gift, "That I may know You, may I know myself." Ruth in the Old Testament understood the needs of others, and her actions showed it (read Ruth 1:11-18).

venial sin *page 176*

A venial sin is less serious than a mortal sin; it is a sin that does not have all three things necessary for a sin to be mortal.

wonder and awe *page 36*

Often this gift of the Holy Spirit is referred to as "fear of the Lord." This gift of awe before God enables us to be aware of God's mystery and majesty. We are humbled by his almighty power, perfect goodness, and unconditional love. Most sacred art reflects this kind of reverence to God and aids us in the worship due to God.

Works of Mercy *page 234*

Virtuous actions that we do to help others in need are the Works of Mercy. They are grouped as Corporal (bodily needs) and Spiritual (spiritual needs).

worship *page 284*

Worship is the honor and respect we give to God above all else; faith in, hope in, and love for God above all else.

Index

Credits

Cover Illustration: Marcia Adams Ho

Frontmatter: Page 6, © Jose Luis Pelaez Inc/Getty Images; 7, © Kushch Dmitry/Shutterstock.
Chapter 1: Page 11, © Ilia Shalamaev Wwwfocuswildlifecom/Getty Image; 12, © opa european pressphoto agency b.v./Alamy, ©EVELSON DE FREITAS/picture–alliance/dpa/AP Images; 16, © Bill Wittman; 18, © Digital Vision/Getty Images; 21, © Jeffrey Van Daele/Shutterstock; 22, © Jupiterimages/Getty Images.
Chapter 2: Page 23, © Bill Wittman; 26, © Radiant Light/The Bridgeman Art Library; 28, © JIM MONE/AP Images; 30, © Jane McIlroy/Shutterstock; 33, © Myrleen Pearson/PhotoEdit; 34, © Design Pics/SW Productions/Jupiterimages.
Chapter 3: Page 35, © Robert Simon/iStockphoto; 36, © The Crosiers/Gene Plaisted, OSC; 38, © MEHAU KULYK/SPL/Jupiterimages; 40, ©The Bridgeman Art Library Ltd./Alamy; 41, © Peter Barritt/Alamy; 42, © Larry Landolfi/Getty Images; 45, © moodboard/Jupiterimages; 46, © Paul Burns/Getty Images.
Chapter 4: Page 47, © Jack Hollingsworth/Getty Images; 48, © Hemera/Thinkstock; 48, © The Crosiers/Gene Plaisted, OSC; 49, © Hemera/Thinkstock; 50, © Andrew Penner/Getty Images; 53, © James Shaffer/PhotoEdit; 53, © Myrleen Pearson/PhotoEdit; 53, © KidStock/Blend Images/Corbis; 54, © ACE STOCK LIMITED/Alamy; 55, © Stockbroker/Alamy; 57, © Bill Wittman; 58, © IMAGEMORE Co; Ltd./Getty Images; 59, © Dr. Morley Read/Shutterstock; 59, © Jeremy Horner/Corbis; 60, © Elena Kalistratova/Getty Images.
Chapter 5: Page 65, © The Crosiers/Gene Plaisted, OSC; 66, © Look and Learn/The Bridgeman Art Library; 68, © Zvonimir Atleti_/Alamy; 70, © The Crosiers/Gene Plaisted, OSC; 72, © Bill Wittman; 75, © Vibrant Image Studio/Shutterstock; 76, © James Shaffer/PhotoEdit.
Chapter 6: Page 77, © SUCHETA DAS/Reuters/Corbis; 78, © The Crosiers/Gene Plaisted, OSC; 78, © Mary Wiltenburg/The Christian Science Monitor/Getty Images; 80, © The Crosiers/Gene Plaisted, OSC; 84, © SuperStock/Getty Images; 85, © James, Laura/The Bridgeman Art Library; 87, © The Crosiers/Gene Plaisted, OSC; 88, © Michael Newman/PhotoEdit.
Chapter 7: Page 89, © Comstock/Jupiterimages; 90, © Pietro Perugino/Getty Images; 90, © The Crosiers/Gene Plaisted, OSC; 92, © The Crosiers/Gene Plaisted, OSC; 93, © The Crosiers/Gene Plaisted, OSC; 96, © The Crosiers/Gene Plaisted, OSC; 97, © Laurence Mouton/Getty Images; 99, © Bill Wittman; 100, © Tetra Images/Alamy.
Chapter 8: Page 101, © John Elk III/Getty Images; 102, © The Crosiers/Gene Plaisted, OSC; 102, © Jeff Greenberg/PhotoEdit; 103, © Jeff Greenberg/PhotoEdit; 104, © Painet Inc./Alamy; 104, © Giorgio Cosulich/Getty Images; 105, © The Crosiers/Gene Plaisted, OSC; 106, © EVARISTO SA/AFP/Getty Images; 108, © Jeff Greenberg/Alamy; 111, © Tetra Images/Alamy; 112, © Myrleen Pearson/PhotoEdit; 113, © Patrick AVENTURIER/Gamma-Rapho/Getty Images; 114, © Chris McGrath/Getty Images.
Chapter 9: Page 119, © HIROI/a.collection/Jupiterimages; 120, © David Young-Wolff/PhotoEdit; 121, © Tarker/The Bridgeman Art Library; 121, © Al Riccio/Corbis; 122, © The Crosiers/Gene Plaisted, OSC; 124, © The Crosiers/Gene Plaisted, OSC; 124, © The Crosiers/Gene Plaisted, OSC; 125, © The Crosiers/Gene Plaisted, OSC; 129, © Godong/Robert Harding World Imagery/Corbis; 130, © Bill Wittman.
Chapter 10: Page 131, © Shay Levy/Alamy; 132, © David Lees/Time & Life Pictures/Getty Images; 132, © Mike Baldwin/Shutterstock; 134, © Bill Wittman; 136, © Bill Wittman; 136, © Bill Wittman; 138, © The Crosiers/Gene Plaisted, OSC; 138, © The Crosiers/Gene Plaisted, OSC; 138, © The Crosiers/Gene Plaisted, OSC; 141, © Bill Wittman; 142, © Bill Wittman.
Chapter 11: Page 143, © Patrick Orton/Aurora Open RF/Aurora Photos/Alamy; 144, © Archives Charmet/Bridgeman Art Library; 145, © Courtesy of the Holy Transfiguration Monastery; 146, © Larissa Leahy/

cultura/Corbis; 148, © Bill Wittman; 149, © Bill Wittman; 150, © Jeff Greenberg/Alamy; 153, © Bill Wittman; 154, © Inmagine/Alamy.
Chapter 12: Page 155, © Anneka/Shutterstock; 156, © Dennis Cox/Alamy; 157, © Alain Keler/Sygma/Corbis; 157, © Leif Skoogfors/CORBIS; 159, © Fuse/Jupiterimages; 159, © iStockphoto/Thinkstock; 159, © Fuse/Jupiterimages; 160, © The Crosiers/Gene Plaisted, OSC; 161, © Bill Wittman; 161, © Bill Wittman; 162, © Bill Wittman; 165, © The Crosiers/Gene Plaisted, OSC; 166, © Angela Coppola/Getty Images; 167, © George Olivar/AP Images; 167, © Hanan Isachar/Corbis; 168, © Bill Wittman.
Chapter 13: Page 173, © Bonnie Kamin/PhotoEdit; 174, © The Crosiers/Gene Plaisted, OSC; 174, © Kean Collection/Archive Photos/Getty Images; 175, © Christine Mariner/Vibe Images/Alamy; 176, © Bill Wittman; 176, © The Crosiers/Gene Plaisted, OSC; 176, © Bill Wittman; 178, © Bill Wittman; 180, © Fuse/Getty Images; 183, © Tetra Images/Getty Images; 184, © Blend Images/Jupiterimages.
Chapter 14: Page 185, © Bill Wittman; 186, © MBI/Alamy; 187, © Anna Peisl/Corbis; 187, © Blend Images/SuperStock; 189, © Spencer Grant/PhotoEdit; 190, © Bill Wittman; 191, © Bill Wittman; 192, © Camille Tokerud/Getty Images; 195, © Fuse/Getty Images; 196, © Con Tanasiuk/Jupiterimages.
Chapter 15: Page 197, © Robert Harding Picture Library Ltd/Alamy; 198, © Hulton-Deutsch Collection/Corbis; 199, © David Jones/AP Images; 200, © Bill Wittman; 201, © Bill Wittman; 202, © Robin Nelson/PhotoEdit; 203, © M.T.M. Images/Alamy; 204, © ALEXANDER NATRUSKIN/Reuters/Corbis; 204, © AFP/Getty Images; 207, © Ferguson Cate/PhotoEdit; 208, © Bill Wittman.
Chapter 16: Page 209, © Stockbyte/Getty Images; 210, © Ariel Skelley/Getty Images; 212, © Ariel Skelley/Getty Images; 212, © Drew Myers/Corbis/Jupiterimages; 214, © Nic Cleave Photography/Alamy; 216, © Rubberball/Mike Kemp/Jupiterimages; 219, © Daniel Sheehan Photographers/Getty Images; 220, © Radius Images/Jupiterimages; 221, © David Young-Wolff/PhotoEdit; 221, © Art-Siberia-/Getty Images; 221, © Brand X Pictures/Getty Images; 222, © David Young-Wolff/PhotoEdit.
Chapter 17: Page 227, © Игорь Гончаренко/iStockphoto; 228, © Jim West/Alamy; 229, © Big Cheese Photo/Corbis; 230, © Peter Beck/Corbis; 231, © Stockbyte/Jupiterimages; 232, © The Crosiers/Gene Plaisted, OSC; 232, © ULTRA.F/Jupiterimages; 232, © Adrian Britton/Alamy; 233, © Photosani/Shutterstock; 234, © Bill Wittman; 234, © Ted Foxx/Alamy; 237, © UpperCut Images/Alamy; 238, © Design Pics Inc./Alamy.
Chapter 18: Page 239, © Stockbyte/Jupiterimages; 240, © Steve Skjold/Alamy; 240, © Odilon Dimier/Jupiterimages; 241, © R. Lentz, courtesy of TrinityStores.com; 242, © Steven Puetzer/Getty Images; 242, © SW Productions/Getty Images; 243, © RubberBall/Alamy; 245, © Myrleen Pearson/PhotoEdit; 246, © Jose Luis Pelaez Inc/Getty Images; 246, © Michael Miller/iStockphoto; 249, © Corbis Super RF/Alamy; 250, © Comstock/Jupiterimages.
Chapter 19: Page 251, © Jetta Productions/Getty Images; 252, © OSSERVATORE ROMANO/Reuters/Corbis; 253, © William H. McNichols, www.fatherbill.org; 255, © Getty Images; 256, © Viktar Malyshchyts/Shutterstock; 257, © iStockphoto/Thinkstock; 258, © Founders Society Purchase/Bridgeman Art Library; 261, © Somos Images/Alamy; 262, © Bill Wittman.
Chapter 20: Page 263, © Hola Images/Alamy; 264, © Hank Walker/Time & Life Pictures/Getty Images; 264, © Luigi Felici/AP Images; 265, © SuperStock/Alamy; 266, © Bubbles Photolibrary/Alamy; 268, © Creatas Images/Thinkstock; 268, © iStockphoto/Thinkstock; 269, © Buslik/Shutterstock; 269, © Brownstock/Alamy; 274, © Corbis Bridge/Alamy; 275, © NOVASTOCK/PhotoEdit; 275, © Spencer Grant/PhotoEdit; 276, © Spencer Grant/Photo Edit.
Chapter 21: Page 281, © Shutterstock; 282, © Franco Origlia/Sygma/Corbis; 283, © Courtesy of Knights of Columbus Supreme Council; 284, © Superstock/Superstock; 285, © ilker canikligil/Shutterstock; 285, © Fedorov Oleksiy/Shutterstock; 285, © rzymuR/Shutterstock; 285, © Jani Bryson/iStockphoto; 286, © Myrleen Pearson/Alamy; 288,

© Bill Wittman; 291, © Fancy/Alamy; 292, © Design Pics/Don Hammond/Getty Images.
Chapter 22: Page 293, © Cultura/Nick Daly; 294, © RedChopsticks Batch 14/Glow Asia RF/Alamy; 294, © IS660/Alamy; 295, © Hill Street Studios/Crystal Cartier/Getty Images; 296, © moodboard/Corbis; 296, © Jose Luis Pelaez; Inc./Blend Images/Corbis; 296, © Tetra Images/SuperStock; 297, © Ariel Skelley/Jupiterimages; 297, © PBNJ Productions/Jupiterimages; 297, © SHAWN THEW/AFP/Getty Images; 298, © Bill Wittman; 298, © Digital Vision/Getty Images; 300, © Joshua Hodge Photography/Getty Images; 303, © Design Pics Inc./Alamy; 304, © Brand X Pictures/Jupiterimages.
Chapter 23: Page 305, © VIKTOR DRACHEV/AFP/Getty Images; 307, © Steve Debenport/iStockphoto; 307, © James Shaffer/PhotoEdit; 308, © Chris Cooper-Smith/Alamy; 308, © MIXA/Getty Images; 309, © Tim Graham/Corbis; 310, © Odilon Dimier/Getty Images; 310, © Stockbyte/Jupiterimages; 312, © Tim Pannell/Corbis; 315, Arrasmith; 316, © Tony Anderson/Getty Images.
Chapter 24: Page 317, © The Crosiers/Gene Plaisted, OSC; 318, © Waldhaeusl Franz/Alamy; 319, © Bill Wittman; 319, © Bill Wittman; 320, © Bill Wittman; 320, © Ted Foxx/Alamy; 324, © djgis/Shutterstock; 327, © Bill Wittman; 328, © The Washington Post/Getty Images; 329, © Jeff Greenberg/Alamy; 329, © spirit of america/Shutterstock; 330, © JULIE SMITH/AP Photo.
Liturgical Seasons: Page 334, © Dan Porges/Getty Images; 334, © Fameleaf Photos/Getty Images; 334, © The Crosiers/Gene Plaisted, OSC; 334, © Bill Wittman; 334, © Tony Freeman/PhotoEdit; 334, © Giraudon/The Bridgeman Art Library; 335, © AA World Travel Library/Alamy; 337, © Fameleaf Photos/Getty Images; 337, © The Crosiers/Gene Plaisted, OSC; 337, © The Crosiers/Gene Plaisted, OSC; 339, © Giraudon/The Bridgeman Art Library; 341, © Philip Scalia/Alamy; 341, © Backyard Productions/Alamy; 343, © Bob Daemmrich/PhotoEdit; 345, © Dan Porges/Getty Images; 347, © Crook, P.J./Private Collection/The Bridgeman Art Library; 349, © Baxter, Cathy/ Private Collection/The Bridgeman Art Library; 351, © Fameleaf Photos/Getty Images; 353, © Jim West/PhotoEdit; 355, © James, Laura/Private Collection/The Bridgeman Art Library; 357, © VYACHESLAV OSELEDKO/AFP/Getty Images; 359, © The Crosiers/Gene Plaisted, OSC; 359, © The Crosiers/Gene Plaisted, OSC; 359, © The Crosiers/Gene Plaisted, OSC; 361, © Bill Wittman; 365, © PhotoStock-Israel/Alamy.
Back Matter: Page 367, © Fuse/Getty Images; 369, © Andersen Ross/Blend Images/Corbis; 370, © The Crosiers/Gene Plaisted, OSC; 373, © The Crosiers/Gene Plaisted, OSC; 375, © Bill Wittman; 376, © Bill Wittman; 377, © James Shaffer/Photo Edit; 378, © Bill Wittman; 379, © Bill Wittman; 380, © Bill Wittman; 381, © Bill Wittman; 382, © Bill Wittman.

Illustration Credits
Unit 1 Opener: Page 9, Gustavo Mazali
Chapter 2: Page 24, Gustavo Mazali
Chapter 4: Page 52, Gustavo Mazali
Unit 2 Opener: Page 63, Gustavo Mazali
Chapter 5: Page 67, Gustavo Mazali
Chapter 6: Page 82, Gustavo Mazali; 83, Peter Francis
Chapter 7: Page 91, Carlos Aon; 94, Gustavo Mazali
Unit 3 Opener: Page 117, Gustavo Mazali
Chapter 10: Page 137, Peter Francis
Chapter 11: Page 145, and 147, Carlos Aon
Chapter 12: Page 158, Gustavo Mazali
Chapter 13: Page 179, Peter Francis
Unit 4 Opener: Page 171, Gustavo Mazali
Chapter 14: Page 188 Gustavo Mazali; 189, Peter Francis
Chapter 16: Page 211, Estudio Haus
Unit 5 Opener: Page 225: Gustavo Mazali
Chapter 18: Page 244, Gustavo Mazali
Chapter 19: Page 253; Peter Francis; 254, Gustavo Mazali
Chapter 20: Page 267, Estudio Haus; 270, Gustavo Mazali
Unit 6 Opener: Page 279, Gustavo Mazali
Chapter 24: Page 321, Carlos Aon; 323, Peter Francis; 324, Gustavo Mazali
Liturgical Seasons: Page 350, Rachel Clowes; 363, Doris Ettlinger